Praise for *Uncom...*
The Rise and Fall of...

'[A] colourful, richly marinated surv... rock star . . . After almost an adult lifet... ...witnessing the music industry at close quarters, Hepworth is, in many ways, a dream author' *Guardian*

'A celebratory but multifaceted look at this strangest of occupations' **** *Mojo*

'In a lifetime's devotion to the music and several decades as a journalist and TV presenter, Hepworth has acquired deep reservoirs of knowledge and a towering stack of anecdotes. He deploys his weaponry wisely and writes in an easy, fluid style' *New Statesman*

'*Uncommon People* attempts to preserve this vanishing breed in a kind of rock star bestiary . . . A composite biography of an almost folkloric figure, one made of bits of Bob Marley and Madonna, Prince and Ian Dury' *Sunday Times*

'This book is a kind of elegy for a glorious but passing phase in entertainment history . . . brim[s] with insight, humour and a certain genial astringency . . . terrific' Stuart Maconie, *Mail on Sunday*

'[A] wonderful portrait of rock stardom . . . Hepworth's writing is sublime' *Daily Mail*

'The effect is that of faded, evocative, partisan Polaroids scattered from the memory of one obsessive music fan . . . *Uncommon People* emerges as part of the drive to capture, analyse and archive key moments in musical history that might otherwise vanish from popular memory before we know it' *Observer*

'David Hepworth is such a clever writer . . . *Uncommon People* is a gorgeous read, celebratory and bittersweet, both pep rally and memorial, throbbing with insight and incident' Julie Burchill, *Spectator*

'Marvellous . . . wonderful . . . The age of the rock star is over, and Hepworth's never-less-than fascinating book is a more than fitting farewell' Dylan Jones, *GQ*

'Packed with pub-friendly facts and peppered with Hepworth's own memories from 30 years on the frontline, it celebrates rock while also mourning its demise' *Classic Rock*

'Hepworth's celebration of the golden age of rock 'n' roll will strike an emotive chord with those of us whose best times have been spent in the company of black vinyl or a live band, minus people filming on a mobile phone . . . The best compliment I can give it is that it feels like one of those evenings when you sit with your friends and talk about the music you love. *Uncommon People* leaves you with the same companionable glow' *Daily Express*

Praise for *1971: Never a Dull Moment*

'David Hepworth's forensic sweep of this astonishing twelve months is thoroughly absorbing and appropriately rollicking, expertly guiding us through one miraculous year in all its breathless tumble of creation' Danny Baker

'Soon every post-war year will have its own tombstone book, but this is already one of the best' *GQ*, Editor's Hit List

'David Hepworth's argument is simple: 1971 was "the most febrile and creative time in the entire history of popular music". It's an enormous assertion but he makes his point with infectious enthusiasm . . . Whether you agree is beside the point. This is a compelling love letter to a year of timeless music' *Q*

'An engaging and thought-provoking read. It's a dry-eyed but deeply felt love note to the date when rock was still busy inventing itself. Hepworth points out more than once that at the time he had no idea how lucky he was. He knows now – and so do we' *Mail on Sunday*

'Engaging . . . Hepworth, who wears his nostalgia on his sleeve, concedes that the music of one's youth inevitably rings most potently. Yet he is surely right that '71 marked a step change in pop history . . . *Never a Dull Moment* lives up to its title' *Observer*

'Action-packed . . . A good mix of entertainment, insight and odd facts. Hepworth's thesis is largely convincing' *Mojo*

'So much music, so many players. Hepworth recreates 1971, convincingly, as an ensemble play in which characters are constantly bumping into one another and having life-changing encounters . . . [he] has a sharp appreciation for the rich detail' *Washington Post*

'A slice of pop culture history from one of the best writers on the subject' *Sunday Post*

'The book is like listening to Hepworth himself: highbrow detail and context is intersected with personal reminisces, and all threaded together with an infectious enthusiasm' *Record Collector*

'Fond, funny, beautifully written and fizzing with sharp and sweeping theories that instantly feel like facts' Mark Ellen

'Whether you agree will depend on your age. But this book shows 1971 was definitely a GREAT rock year' *Sun*

'Laced with a wisdom gathered over many years as a journalist and industry insider and with an endless enthusiasm for the music . . . a highly readable assessment and a convincing argument for the importance of a year in which the culture of rock began to be aware that it was living out its good old days' *New Statesman*

'A clever and entertaining book . . . Hepworth proves a refreshingly independent thinker. His style is pithy and his eye for anecdotal detail sharp . . . Hepworth's guide to 1971 proves a thoroughly provoking delight' *Daily Telegraph*

'A mighty fine and convincing read' *Classic Rock*

'Near the beginning, Hepworth argues that 1971 saw the pop era giving way to rock. Even so, his own approach is much more like the best pop: never taking itself too seriously, essentially out to entertain – but also an awful lot smarter than its absence of solemnity might lead you to think' *Spectator*

'Entertaining and clever . . . [Hepworth's] writing might best be described as dapper, which is to say it's sharp, whip-smart, quick-witted, deeply knowledgeable beneath an occasionally knockabout veneer. Hepworth also knows how to work a room for laughs, of which there are plenty here, making *Never a Dull Moment* that welcome thing: a serious book about rock that doesn't take itself too seriously to be taken seriously' *Uncut*

UNCOMMON PEOPLE

THE RISE AND FALL OF THE ROCK STARS

BLACK SWAN

TRANSWORLD PUBLISHERS
61–63 Uxbridge Road, London W5 5SA
www.penguin.co.uk

Transworld is part of the Penguin Random House group of companies
whose addresses can be found at global.penguinrandomhouse.com

First published in Great Britain in 2017 by Bantam Press
an imprint of Transworld Publishers
Black Swan edition published 2018

A CIP catalogue record for this book
is available from the British Library.

ISBN
9781784162078

Typeset in 11/14pt Minion by Falcon Oast Graphic Art Ltd.
Printed and bound by Clays Ltd, Bungay, Suffolk.

Penguin Random House is committed to a sustainable
future for our business, our readers and our planet. This book is made from
Forest Stewardship Council® certified paper.

1 3 5 7 9 10 8 6 4 2

For Clare, Henry and Imogen

CONTENTS

FOREWORD

The age of the rock star, like the age of the cowboy, has passed.

The idea of the rock star, like the idea of the cowboy, lives on.

There are still people who dress like rock stars and do their best to act as they think rock stars would have acted in an earlier time, much as there are people who strap on replica holsters and re-enact the gunfight at the O.K. Corral. It's increasingly difficult to act like one or the other and keep a straight face.

The true rock stars rose and fell with the fortunes of the post-war record industry. They came along in the mid-fifties and they passed away in the last decade of the century just gone. We came to know them as rock stars but at first they had no generic name. In the early days, when Elvis Presley, Fats Domino and the like were coming out of nowhere, they might as easily have been called hillbilly cats, rhythm and blues shouters, specialists in western bop, plain pop singers or promoters of dance crazes.

The term 'rock star' really came into widespread use in the seventies and eighties when the music business was looking to sustain the careers of its biggest names. The business was no longer happy to hop from fad to fad. It was beginning to realize the value of brands. There was no better brand than a rock star. A rock star was supposed to be somebody you could rely on, somebody whose next record you had to have, often regardless of its merits. After that it was increasingly applied to everyone from Elvis Presley to David Bowie, from Morrissey to Madonna, from Ozzy Osbourne to Björk. By the twenty-first century, the term had been spread so thin as to be meaningless.

In the twenty-first century it seems rather inappropriate, to use a popular twenty-first-century term, to describe Kanye West, Adele or Justin Bieber as rock stars. These people are cut from a different cloth. The age of the rock star ended with the passing of physical product, the rise of automated percussion, the domination of the committee approach to hit-making, the widespread adoption of choreography and above all the advent of the mystique-destroying internet. The age of the rock star was coterminous with rock and roll, which in spite of all the promises made in some memorable songs proved to be as finite as the era of ragtime or big bands. The rock era is over. We now live in a hip hop world.

The game has changed. Rock stars were the product of an age when music was hard to access and was treasured accordingly. The stars of music no longer have a right to public attention simply by virtue of existing. Their products now compete on a level playing field with everything from virtual reality games to streaming movies. What was once hard to find is now impossible to escape. Music no longer belongs in a category of otherness. It's just another branch of the distraction business, owned by the same multinational conglomerates as the theme parks and the multiplexes.

This kind of change has happened before – when talkies

replaced silents, and then when TV stole the thunder of the movies. When record shops were replaced by online streams, twelve-inch records were exchanged for a ribbon of noughts and ones, and your favourite stars took to publishing pictures of their diurnal round on social media, everything changed. You simply can't live the life of a rock star any longer. The mobile phone alone saw to that. The rock star's mystique is at an end.

I may be wrong. I am of a certain age. I have prejudices, as do we all. It could be that the chart botherers of today, the people picking up their awards at the end of the year and headlining at the burgeoning number of rock festivals, the people getting those slightly trying-too-hard reviews in the posh papers – well, it could be that they will still be around in forty or fifty years' time, the same way that Keith Richards and Bruce Springsteen have been; it could be that with time they will prove every bit as mythic as their predecessors of the sixties and seventies. If they are I won't be around to tell you how surprised I am.

What interests me is this. If we no longer have a breed that qualifies for the description 'rock star', how can it be that the idea of the rock star as a social type remains so strong? This didn't happen yesterday. Back in 1973, just two years after the death of Jim Morrison, just as a new generation was beginning to warm to David Bowie's tongue-in-cheek rock-star figure Ziggy Stardust – a rock star in inverted commas for people who were beginning to find the unvarnished article just too corny – a magazine called *Texas Monthly* published what was the first recorded example of the term 'rock star' being applied to describe somebody who wasn't a rock star. In that case they were actually writing about a ballet in which one character was much adored by the others. 'He's a

Christ, a Buddha,' they said, and then, stretching for a parallel a young readership might relate to, 'a rock star'. In the years since 1973 we have grown increasingly used to 'rock star' being employed as a descriptor. Bill Clinton was supposed to be the first rock-star President. Russell Brand is a rock-star comedian. Marco Pierre White is a rock-star chef, Andre Agassi a rock-star tennis player. These days you can even be a rock-star fund manager.

In characterizing people as rock stars we are superimposing on them qualities we associated with actual rock stars in the past. It's only when we describe people who aren't rock stars as being like rock stars that we get an inkling of the qualities we came to associate with rock stars as a tribe.

What kind of qualities? Swagger. Impudence. Sexual charisma. Utter self-reliance. Damn-the-torpedoes self-belief. A tendency to act on instinct. A particular way of carrying themselves. Good hair. Interesting shoes.

Similarly there are qualities rock-star types do not have. A rock-star chef will not refer too closely to the recipe. A rock-star politician will not be overly in thrall to the focus group. A rock-star athlete will not go to bed at the time specified by the coach. A rock-star fund manager will make a huge call based on a gut feeling rather than indulge in a prolonged period of desk research and make a sober examination of the evidence.

Recklessness, thy name is rock. In fact a deficiency in reck is the defining characteristic we ascribe to rock stars as a social group. We believe in this recklessness so strongly we even ignore any evidence to the contrary, of which there is plenty. Keith Moon never did run a Rolls-Royce into a swimming pool, the Beatles never did smoke grass at Buckingham Palace, the police never did drop in to find guests at Keith

Richards' home munching a Mars bar between Marianne Faithfull's legs; but such is our need to believe that generations of followers of rock myths and legends have laid their heads on their pillows and screwed their eyes tight shut, hoping against hope they might wake to find out such things had been the case.

Rock stars didn't just live their own lives. They also lived a life on our behalf. They lived in our heads. If you were born in one of the decades immediately following the 1950s, a pantheon of rock stars provided you with a cast of fantasy friends who lived out their lives in a parallel universe of which you could only dream. They did things you wouldn't dare do with people you would never meet in places you could never afford to go to. Yet you felt, because you had in a sense both started at the same point – them as musician, you as fan – that you shared a certain kinship for ever. You checked in with them when the time came for them to release their latest album or visit your town on tour, tried to detect what might be going on in their personal lives from the remarks they made in interviews, looked at the state of their hairline or waistline and silently measured your vital signs against theirs. Sometimes in the middle of dull days you even found yourself wondering what they might be doing at that precise moment. That's one definition of a rock star.

The worship of rock heroes has some of the characteristics of religion. We believe rock stars know something we don't. Grown men who have long ago ceased believing in comic-book heroes have no trouble convincing themselves that the people who are their heroes because they once played a memorable tune on the electric guitar can offer them wise counsel in middle age. In the 2000 movie *High Fidelity*, Bruce Springsteen appeared to the hero to advise him on his unsuccessful love life. This is interesting because the one thing we know about Springsteen is that for much of his young adult life his love life was a disaster area, albeit one palliated by the ready availability of sex with beautiful women. The principal reason why his love life was so unsatisfactory was connected with the fact that he had, by dint of talent and superhuman dedication, turned himself into the rock star he had always wanted to be. In fact he was so busy becoming that rock star that he had no time for the things that being that rock star was supposed to give him mastery of.

We didn't see it that way. We thought of rock stars as living a life far removed from our daily cares. In doing that we saddled them with the often impossible requirements of our fantasies about what that larger life was. We liked to think of rock stars as being as rich as Croesus while not giving a fig for material possessions. We liked to think they had struggled to the very peak of one of the most competitive professions on earth without exhibiting any unseemly glimmer of ambition. We wanted them to become ever more famous and success-ful but reserved the right to complain if the popularity that we wished on them made it harder or more expensive for us to see them. Furthermore it was a condition of rock star-dom that our favourites were either underrated or rated for the wrong things. We liked to think we could discriminate between the common herd and 'the real fans'. We liked to feel that these rock stars were broadcasting on a particular wavelength which could only be picked up by true initiates like us – or, to be more precise, me. And most tragically and inevitably of all, we demanded that they remain unchanged, forever young on our behalf.

There was a greater premium on these rock stars remain-ing young as we got older; the need for them to embody what we saw as rock and roll values became more intense as our lives changed. The more the majority of the people who had grown up with rock and roll spent their days tethered to a work cubicle, earning their livings tapping at a computer keyboard, the company's badge on a lanyard round their necks, their every move tracked by an all-seeing corporation, and the more they found that in public life they were compelled to curb their tongues and bite back on whatever they were just about to say, the more they looked to rock stars to be the people they were no longer permitted to be.

We wanted rock stars to be glamorous but also authentic. We needed to feel that they were forced to beat off willing sexual partners with a stick while also living a fulfilled family life. We saw them as staying up too late, sleeping through the morning, never quite giving any one thing their full attention and yet still, by dint of some special rock-star magic, operating to their full potential.

If they were still performing in their fifties and sixties, that wasn't simply because they wanted to. It's because we demanded it. Being a rock star, as Bruce Springsteen said to me thirty years ago, retards adulthood and prolongs adolescence. This is precisely what we found so attractive about it. We imagined these rock stars, as somebody once said about Keith Richards, not so much burning the candle at both ends as applying a blowtorch to the middle. *That's* a rock star.

Ultimately, as another rock star observed, all things must pass. Now, like the cowboy, the cavalier, the wandering minstrel, the chorus girl, the burglar in the striped sweater, the top-hatted banker, the painter with his beret and the writer in his smoking jacket, the rock star must finally be consigned to the wardrobe of anachronistic stereotypes. In real life he has been overshadowed by hip hop stars who are brazen enough to make the most shameless rock star blush, and overtaken by talent-school munchkins who are far more manipulative than he would have dared be. His power base has been destroyed by the disappearance of the record industry, his magic fleeing in the twenty-four-hour daylight of social media.

Whether you think this is the end of that particular road or just a pause for breath, now is as good a time as any for an account of the rise and fall of this tribe of rock stars, who came to the fore in the years following the Second World War, waxed in the seventies, and waned with the twentieth century. They were a product of the rise of post-war prosperity and the end of an age of actual warriors, of a time when a new generation looked around for a new race of people to idolize, this time for different reasons. They rose on the back of the record business, which fancied it was going to be around for ever but lasted not much longer than the people who made 'What the Butler Saw' machines. Along with that business they have now departed the stage.

While they were on the stage they captured our imagination and our trust in a way no movie star or sports star or writer managed. They changed the way we looked, the way we talked, the way we walked, and what we considered an acceptable way to behave. We considered them more worthy of our trust than politicians, spiritual leaders or captains of industry. This is particularly amazing since, as most of the people who have been responsible for managing rock stars will tell you, many of them had difficulty finding their way from their hotel room to reception in time for the bus, let alone organizing a workable energy policy.

This is of course a cliché. But then it's a cliché that has been built up over fifty years. It's an interesting cliché because we've all had a hand in developing it. If being a rock star has been the ruination of some people then we should all accept part of the blame, because in a sense we helped do that to them. This book is about the people the rock stars were before being hit in the small of the back by rock fame, it's about the fantasy figures that rock fame transformed them into, and it's about the personal price they paid for playing a starring role in our dreams. It's about the people who found themselves becoming rock stars, about their abrupt social elevation, the changes that affected them and the people around them, and the consequences for their nearest and dearest.

There was never such a thing as an original pure rock-star archetype. Our mental picture of what a rock star is supposed to amount to has been imperceptibly built up over half a century as each successive tide of music has come in and gone out and left its mark on the shore. If there is a rock-star stereotype it has to encompass Little Richard and also Bob Dylan, Paul McCartney as well as Janis Joplin, Bruce Springsteen alongside Sid Vicious, The Edge with Bob Marley and both Kurt Cobain and Keith Moon, and on into infinity. The idea of a rock star contains, if not exactly multitudes, then certainly a number of facets all of which speak to our depths.

There is a good theory that musical eras tend to have a life span of around forty years. You can certainly say that for the era of the rock stars. In the pages that follow I've profiled one rock star per year over each of the forty years from 1955 to 1994, and listed ten records, either singles or albums, that were made, released or were hits that year in order to give a flavour of the time. I've done this to construct a big picture of all the many layers that went into building our idea of what a rock star is. Careers are surprisingly long in popular music. Inspiration, on the other hand, tends to be fleeting. What I've tried to do is focus on one day in these people's lives. These were the days when, for good or ill, their life changed in some respect. Something happened: it might have been the day they made one of those records which they then carried around on their backs for the rest of their lives; it might have been a day when they felt their old life slipping away; it might have been a day of great happiness or great sadness; it might have been the end of one phase or the beginning of another; it might have taken place on the concert stage in front of thousands or in a tiny rehearsal hall with barely any witnesses; it might have been a day when the tide of circumstance picked them up and delivered them to high ground, or a day when that same tide deposited them back on the beach. What all these stories have in common is that they form part of the biography of not just these particular rock stars but also The Rock Star. Each story, I hope, is not only interesting and illuminating in itself but also contributes something to the bigger story.

Why the title? Rock stars were uncommon people. They came from the masses and got to the top without the help of education, training, family ties, money or other conventional ladders. They came from ordinary lives and had no reason to expect that they would ever be special. At the same time they refused to accept that they would ever be anything but exceptional. Most surprising of all, many of them had careers that lasted far longer than they had any right to expect, because long after the hits stopped coming, their legends continued to endure. They endured because, like the stars of the great cowboy films of that earlier age, they were playing themselves and, at the same time, they were playing us.

David Hepworth
London, 2017

14 SEPTEMBER 1955
RAMPART STREET, NEW ORLEANS

The first rock star

Little Richard was unusual. He had always been unusual. He was one of the ten children of Leva Mae Penniman. She said he was more trouble than the rest put together.

According to Richard, who began burnishing his legend from an early age, he was born deformed. One eye was clearly bigger than the other. One leg was certainly shorter than the other. Hence Richard walked with short steps, which gave him a mincing gait. In the Pleasant Hill section of Macon, Georgia during the Second World War, at a time when sympathy for differences was in short supply, he came in for rough treatment. They called him faggot, sissy, punk and freak. And those were his friends.

Among his classmates he had a reputation for being happy to do the thing they were too sensible to do. At the age of twelve he placed one of his bowel movements in a shoebox, presented it to an elderly woman in the neighbourhood as a birthday present and then hid to witness her reaction as she opened it.

He had his first homosexual experience with a local man known as Madame Oop. Madame Oop was a friend of the family. Sometimes white men would pick Richard up in their cars and take him out to the woods.

His father, Bud, would beat him, say he wasn't a real boy. Bud ran moonshine whisky and was eventually shot and killed in front of Macon's Tip-In Inn.

The young Richard was excited by the gospel acts that came through Macon. Because they worked on the Lord's behalf these people seemed to be licensed to act crazy. Sometimes it wasn't possible to tell whether they were singing about heavenly or earthly reward. They were clearly moved by the spirit of free enterprise. Richard ingratiated himself with Sister Rosetta Tharpe when she played Macon. She allowed him to open her show and then crumpled $30 into his hand. This was a life-changing moment.

In 1949, at the age of seventeen, Richard went on the road with a snake oil salesman. Like many features of Little Richard's early life, this is not a metaphor. This is the reality in which he was raised. He performed with Doctor Nobilio, who carried with him 'the devil's child', allegedly a dead baby with the feet of a bird. He joined the minstrel show of Sugarfoot Sam from Alabam, who introduced him as Princess Lavonne. He performed in a dress.

As a teenager Richard had a job washing dishes in the diner in Macon's Greyhound bus station. Interesting trade would pass through, particularly in the night-time hours. This is how he met a fifteen-year-old from South Carolina called Eskew Reeder, who styled himself Esquerita, sported a pompadour so high there was snow on the top and was camp enough to make Richard seem like a longshoreman.

Richard took him home, and copied the hair-do and his hammering right hand on the piano. In fact Richard, who was to spend the rest of his life complaining that other people had stolen his style, picked up something from almost everybody he encountered. He played in the band of Billy Wright, who piled his hair up high and impressed upon him the value of a make-up range called Pancake 31. He observed a mountainous woman called Clara Hudmon who performed in shimmering raiment and went by the name of the Georgia Peach.

In the same week in September 1955 that Richard arrived in New Orleans for his recording date, two men went on trial in Money, Mississippi for having brutally beaten and murdered Emmett Till, a fourteen-year-old boy from Chicago who had been visiting relatives down south and made the mistake of addressing a white woman in a way she took to be fresh. The only reason there was a trial was because his mother had insisted his appallingly damaged body be flown back north and displayed in an open coffin. The killers were acquitted, as was the custom of the South, but the trial pricked the national conscience.

Even in the rest of the country, which didn't have the same history of slavery, the best that black people could hope for was indifference. It wasn't until 1950 that *Life* magazine considered it acceptable to put a black face on its cover, and even then it was Jackie Robinson, whose entry into the big leagues of baseball had taken place against a background of abuse. In January 1955 the white disc jockey Alan Freed had opened the doors to his 'Rock'n'roll Jubilee Ball' at St Nicholas Arena in New York and been amazed to see seven thousand kids flocking in. He was even more amazed to see they were white as well as black. It had never occurred to him that white kids might be listening to the rhythm and blues records he played on the radio.

Radio was the one medium that could afford to be colour blind. A year earlier, in the summer of 1954, the boy Elvis Presley had made his first broadcast appearance on the Memphis radio show of Dewey Phillips. Dewey made sure that the listeners knew he went to Humes High School. That way they would know that he was white.

The colour blindness worked the other way as well. Up in the far north, in Hibbing, Minnesota, fourteen-year-old Bobby Zimmerman had taken advantage of the night-time ionosphere effect to tune in to Frank 'Brother Gatemouth' Page who was playing rhythm and blues records on a station out of Shreveport, Louisiana, fully a thousand miles away. Page talked the jive and played the blues but he was no blacker than his pale Jewish listener in the frozen north. On the air you could be whoever you wanted to be.

Everybody involved in the music business knew rock and roll was happening but only Freed had seen with his own eyes the way that it was happening. Few had much hope it would turn out to be more than a fad, much as calypso and Latin had been the previous year.

When producer Bumps Blackwell had been sent from Los Angeles to New Orleans by Specialty Records to see if he could get a record out of Little Richard, a boy who had already been recorded a handful of times but had never had a hit, he didn't have anything particular in mind. The most-played record on American juke boxes that week in September 1955 was 'Maybellene', the first release by Chuck Berry, a former ladies' hairdresser from St Louis. Berry had a gimmick. He was offering something that sounded like a comical country song but with a heavy backbeat. Blackwell didn't know exactly what he had to come up with but he was alive to the possibility of making a comparable leap.

The studio they were in that day was the size of a motel room. The band squeezed into the room contained a number of the regulars in Fats Domino's outfit. When the twenty-two-year-old Richard appeared, wearing a shirt of a violent hue with a high collar that made him look like a pantomime queen, with his pompadour kept in place by lacquer of industrial strength, his natural skin tone concealed beneath a full inch of Pancake 31, the band rolled their eyes at each other but then got down to work.

'We recorded "Kansas City" and "Directly From My Heart To You",' Blackwell recalled later. 'They were OK. Good songs, and he was a good singer. But we weren't really getting anywhere.'

They took a break and went across the street to the Dew Drop Inn. This was a famous New Orleans spot where musicians hung out. According to a city ordinance it was supposed to have a partition separating the white drinkers from the black drinkers, but the owner couldn't be bothered. The Dew Drop Inn made its own law.

'All the boosters, rounders, pimps and whores were sitting around,' remembered Blackwell. 'And there was a piano. Well, all you need to do with Richard is give him an audience and the show's on.'

Richard approached the piano and called the patrons of the Dew Drop Inn to attention with a yelp that rent the frowsy lunchtime air. That yelp was pitched like a cross between a football chant and an order barked across a parade ground. Like a stone skimmed across the profound stillness of a vast pond, that yelp went on to echo around the world.

It went as follows: 'Awopbopaloobop.'

It continued: 'Alopbamboom!'

That's all it was. It was just a little riff of Richard's, an imagined percussion fill which he was in the habit of beating out on the lunch counter of the bus station in Macon. This time it tumbled without interruption into a sort of song, a song that was greeted throughout the Dew Drop Inn with the knowing smirks of those whose chosen lifestyles meant they were not readily given to indignation.

The song, if song it could be called, was a selection that could only be sung, if singing it could be called, in front of the kind of people who spent their lunchtimes in the Dew Drop Inn, an establishment louche even by the standards of Planet New Orleans. Its title, if it could be said to have one because nobody had ever considered it fit enough for publication, was 'Tutti Frutti'.

Its subject matter was, not to put too fine a point on it, anal sex.

It began 'Tutti Frutti, good booty'. It then added 'if it's tight, it's all right'. It developed that idea further with 'if it's greasy, it makes it so easy'.

As Little Richard hammered at the high keys of the piano in the way he'd learned from Esquerita, howled in the way he'd stolen from Rosetta Tharpe and made show in the way he'd seen so many artists do out on the chitlin circuit (the collo-quial name given to the road that led from the upper Midwest, New York and Washington DC down into the South, then further into the Deep South, named after the pig intestines, or 'chitterlings', enjoyed by the black customers who came to its performance venues), Bumps Blackwell found him-self wondering if it might be possible to take some of 'Tutti Frutti''s fetid energy back into the studio and clean it up a bit.

He put the idea to Richard. Now Richard was a strange combination of libertine and prude. He'd run wild in the streets during the week but submitted to the discipline of the church on Sunday. He said he didn't want to record the song 'because it's dirty'. Blackwell reckoned they might be able to fix the words. Which is where Dorothy LaBostrie came in. Dorothy was twenty-seven at the time and was working as a waitress in New Orleans while raising a couple of kids. She was tall and thin and fancied herself as a poet and songwriter. She'd been bombarding Blackwell with lyrics for some time.

Blackwell called her over to the studio and instructed Richard to sing his 'song' to her. Richard agreed to do so but only if he could sing it with his back turned. He ran through it a couple of times as she took notes. She didn't want the job but Bumps said she owed it to her children. Fifteen minutes later she returned with a clean version, in which the references to buggery had been replaced by the slang term of approval 'aw rooty' and a girl named Daisy had made an appearance, who apparently drove the singer of the song crazy.

It took them three takes but by the end of the session they had a record. It was a record that sounded like no record had ever sounded before. 'Tutti Frutti' began like a stick-up, built up to a riot, and stopped as suddenly as it had arrived. It was like a jet plane passing over your head close enough to part your hair. It was hilarious if you thought about it. The important thing was not to think about it.

When it came out a few weeks later the only people who didn't find it meaningless were teenagers, for whom its delirious exuberance meant more than mere words ever could. 'Tutti Frutti' got to number two on the rhythm and blues chart and as high as number seventeen on the main pop chart. It wasn't as big a hit as the inevitably pallid cover version served up for white radio by Pat Boone. Nevertheless the record they'd lashed together in such unseemly haste at the end of that session on Rampart Street reached around the world and electrified the people who mattered.

Richard recorded further smashes with Bumps Blackwell over the next two years: 'Lucille', 'Long Tall Sally', 'Rip It Up', 'Keep A-Knockin'', 'Good Golly Miss Molly' and 'The Girl Can't Help It', which he also sang in the movie of the same name. That run of successes made Little Richard into the first true rock star. He was a few months ahead of Elvis into the national spotlight, which gave him first-mover advantage. More than that, whereas Elvis took the conventional idea of male beauty into almost Venusian hyper-reality, Richard remained the runt of the litter, a limping, one-eyed grotesque who seemed to turn himself into a star by sheer force of will. Richard's unrestrained sexuality was doubly threatening because it wasn't clear whether it was directed at your daughter or your son. Where Chuck Berry's records seemed to be about rock and roll, Little Richard's records were the embodiment of the simultaneous rage and joy of the thing itself. That opening shout of 'Awopbopaloobop alopbamboom!' seemed like the answer to a question nobody had yet thought of posing.

Richard was young enough, unsettling enough and clearly invested enough in the revolution announced by 'Tutti Frutti' to be that figure. It helped that he looked the way he did and acted the way he did, and had a name and a persona which placed him in the appropriate category of otherness. Fats Domino, Chuck Berry and Bill Haley were all too old and too detached from the world of their music to be the standard bearer of this new crusade. With Little Richard you finally had a personality who lived up to the sound. It was this new combination of mayhem and personal magnetism, this marriage of walking and talking, the intimation that even though the record may have reached its end the consciousness from which it sprang was alive out there in the world, carrying itself in a certain way and behaving in a way that the fans would dearly like to have had the permission to behave, that made Richard the first rock star.

Richard called, and many answered. They answered from all over the world. 'Tutti Frutti' was covered by Elvis Presley in his first album the following year. It was in the vast white audience to which neither he nor Blackwell had ever given a moment's thought when they made the record that his sound had its most profound effect.

It was released in the UK in January 1957 on the B-side of 'Long Tall Sally'. David Jones, a nine-year-old at Burnt Ash Junior School in Bromley, later recalled that his 'heart burst with excitement'. Keith Richards, who was twelve and attending Dartford Technical High School for Boys, said 'it was as if, in a single instant, the world changed from monochrome to Technicolor'. And Bobby Zimmerman, the boy who'd been tuning his radio to the sound of Shreveport from up there in the Iron Range of Minnesota, led a group called the Golden Chords who appeared in a school concert playing their own version of Little Richard's song. It was an unimaginably hot, exotic sound to be attempted by anyone other than the people who made it that day in New Orleans, let alone a bunch of Jewish adolescents from the frozen north.

Regardless of that, the die was cast. The high-school yearbook entry for Bobby Zimmerman's final year at Hibbing High in 1959 announced his ambition. He didn't want to run for President. He didn't want to write the Great American Novel. He wanted one thing: 'To join Little Richard'.

26 SEPTEMBER 1956
FROM MEMPHIS TO TUPELO
The first rock idol

F ive of them were packed into the white Lincoln Continental Mark II that day. A two-door vehicle wasn't the most sensible choice for the two-hour ride between Memphis, Tennessee and Tupelo, Mississippi. However Elvis Presley had only bought the Lincoln in August. Since then he'd either been in New York, making his first appearances on the top-rating *Ed Sullivan Show* to sing 'Heartbreak Hotel' – his first hit record on RCA – for an audience of fifty million, or in Hollywood, making his first movie appearance in *Love Me Tender*. Hence he was still eager for any opportunity to take the big luxury coupé for a spin. He was all the keener since on this day he was going to show it off to the folks in his home town.

He had rehearsed this special day in his head many times. Finally it was happening. The homecoming wasn't just for Elvis's sake. The two people in the back seat had also taken the same journey in the opposite direction in 1948. At the time their chariot was a ten-year-old Plymouth and the circumstances not quite so carefree. In 1948 Elvis's parents, Vernon and Gladys, couldn't wait to get out of Tupelo. Too many people knew Vernon had served time in Parchman Farm for trying to pass a dud cheque. They feared, with some justification, that they would never escape the stratum of society respectable folks called poor white trash.

Every marriage requires at least one grown-up. In this marriage, Gladys was the adult. That wasn't only because she was four years Vernon's senior. It was also because she was a grafter, stitching shirts at the Tupelo Garment Company for $13 a week. Vernon, on the other hand, could never seem to find the job he considered worthy of his talents. She was dark-eyed, almost Spanish-looking; he was blond. She was homely; he was a rake. She was outgoing and gregarious; he was sullen and resentful. They married on the same day in 1933 that Pretty Boy Floyd killed four lawmen in the Kansas City Massacre. Unusually, Vernon was seventeen and Gladys was twenty-one.

They started a family home in the only way open to poor people in the South in those days: they built it themselves. The following year Gladys became pregnant with twins. She was so sure they were going to be boys that she had already picked out their names, Elvis Aron and Jessie Garon. She felt it was important their names rhyme. On the night of 8 January 1935, Gladys went into labour. The first boy was stillborn. The second, who arrived half an hour later, survived. The Presleys couldn't afford the $15 to pay the doctor.

The first of millions of formal pictures of Elvis Presley was in a group with his mother and father. It was taken in the Lee County Jail immediately prior to Vernon's move to Parchman. At the time it was just a standard family portrait, such as might be ordered by any mother wishing to record a precious, fleeting stage of family life. Regular publication over the years since has lent it an iconic status. It seems possible to read shame in Vernon's expression, tight-lipped exasperation in Gladys's and the shadow of perplexity across the beautiful face of the three-year-old twin who had survived.

Through his formative years Elvis came to believe that the only person he could rely on in the world was his mother. Gladys returned the compliment by actively discouraging any sign of independence in her adored boy. She walked him to school every day, took him into her bed at night when Vernon was in prison, and rarely let him out of her sight. As a child Elvis was never lonesome, particularly at night. This was a state of affairs that was to continue throughout his life. He didn't call her Mom, like the other kids did theirs. The two had an entire secret language of baby talk. His name for her was 'Satnin'.

Elvis began school in Tupelo. He was no trouble. In fact he made little impression on anyone. His first singing performance was at the age of ten when he warbled a sentimental song about a dog in front of a couple of hundred people at the Mississippi-Alabama Fair and Dairy Show. And now, a decade later, they were sitting in the back of a Lincoln Continental, a car so exclusive the dealers were instructed to sell them only to clients with the requisite prestige, returning in glory to the same event in the same town they'd had to slink out of ten years earlier with their tails between their legs. All this was because over the last couple of years Gladys's boy had had a number of regional hit records on the Sun label. These had led to regular appearances on the *Louisiana Hayride*. Next thing she knew her boy was the one everybody wanted all across the South. And now that his contract had been sold to RCA

Records he was going to New York City to make records and appear on national TV shows. For a woman who had been born into a world without radio and raised in a house without electricity, this was a dizzying transformation.

Lolling across the front seat that day was Nick Adams, a twenty-two-year-old actor Elvis had befriended on the second day of shooting *Love Me Tender* in Hollywood. Elvis was impressed that Adams had played a small part in *East of Eden*, the James Dean picture that had been released after the actor died the previous year. Adams recognized that a friendship with Presley could be beneficial to his own career. He knew Hollywood people were quicker than music business people when it came to seeing how popular Elvis could be. 'He's Marlon Brando with a guitar,' pronounced Jackie Gleason. Old hands who were bullied into the screening room to see *Love Me Tender* dailies detected a self-sufficiency in front of the camera nobody could coach.

The fifth person in the car was Barbara Hearn, a pretty nineteen-year-old girl the fan magazines had taken to calling 'Elvis's Memphis girlfriend'. The conditionality of this description recognized what was apparent to anyone in Elvis's circle at the time: that the rough equality of family life was slowly being replaced by something that operated more like a royal court, and in a royal court everything revolves around just one sovereign. Elvis was now being asked the same questions any twenty-one-year-old was being asked. His new status meant he was free to answer in a way they never would. When he was asked who he was dating at the time he would mention Barbara but also seventeen-year-old June Juanico, who lived in Biloxi. Then he would grin and tell the truth: 'I'm dating about a hundred girls.'

Barbara had few illusions about how she figured in his life.

She knew that like everyone else in his social circle the events of the last year – the hit records, the TV appearances, the screaming crowds, the sudden geyser of cash, the frenzy of renown – had relegated her to the status of supporting player. During the drive that day Elvis turned to her and asked if she'd brought the shirts he'd given her to hold back at the house. She said she hadn't. They found a payphone and made sure that somebody back at North Audubon Drive brought along the two shirts, the blue and the red velvet blouses. He didn't tell Barbara that he'd been given these shirts by his new Hollywood girlfriend Natalie Wood; Natalie had had her dressmaker run them up. Barbara already knew she wasn't the only one, but these shirts were an indication of the new competition she could expect to face. Girls with their own dressmakers.

The Mississippi-Alabama Fair generally had a theme. In September 1956 the theme was Elvis Presley. The city fathers had been hoping that the boy they had taken no notice of when he was growing up in the town would be the main attraction of a motorcade down Main Street. Colonel Tom Parker, who had recently taken over Elvis's management, had told them that would simply be too dangerous so they'd had to settle for him doing two shows, one a matinee and one in the evening, in the amphitheatre of the show ground, within sniffing distance of the new swine barn in which so much local money and pride had been invested.

It was a hot day and the Presley family were dressed more for formality than comfort, Vernon in a dark suit and tie, Gladys in a heavy brocade dress with an Elvis button, the star of the show in his heavy velvet Hollywood shirt. For Elvis this whole day was the culmination of a wish-fulfilment fantasy. In the breast of every adolescent boy burns the hope that one fine day he will get the opportunity to return to the playing field where nobody picked him, to the dance floor where the scars of his minor humiliations were first sustained, to climb the school platform to which he was never summoned to receive a prize, there to extend his wings to their fullest span and, like a butterfly in the sun, soak up the full measure of the adoration, sexual desire and throbbing envy of those who considered he would never amount to anything.

26 September 1956 was truly the day of reckoning. Little Richard may have been the first rock star but Elvis was the first rock idol, the first to take that curious, unprecedented journey from the back of the class to the cynosure of all eyes, from an existence as that boy who dressed a little strange to being the one everybody else wished to emulate, from whispered mockery to open adoration, all in what seemed like the blink of an eye.

To his new fans he had always been attractive, but those who'd grown up with him knew that in his adolescent years Elvis's looks didn't fit. As he grew into a young man he accentuated this difference by adopting the frilly shirts and tight pants of the gigolo, as if daring the good old boys in town to take exception to him. This revolution in his appearance came before any revolution in music. From early on his hair was a statement, a form of expression every bit as vital to him as music. His hair was the one non-negotiable. He lost two jobs for not getting it cut. He devoted hours to arranging it. He loved looking at himself. This wasn't mere narcissism. Narcissism is a shallow infatuation with one's own appearance. With Elvis it was far from shallow. It was the real thing.

Over the previous year in the spotlight it had slowly, miraculously dawned on Presley that he was beautiful; so beautiful indeed that it seemed to cause many women actual pain to behold him. Fortunately he loved the company of females, whether they were adolescents smelling of Spray Net who just wanted his autograph, marriageable Eisenhower girls in rustling petticoats and white gloves who wanted to introduce him to their mothers, feather-bedecked showgirls ready to show him a good time in the dressing room next door, or even neatly ironed showbusiness professionals who weren't sure whether they wished to mother him or shove him into the nearest cupboard and kiss his face off. The kissability of Elvis was more important than his vibrato. All his early girlfriends report that he was a master of the oscular art. Since this is an activity most young men are too impatient to spend time on, he was on to something here.

Even by September 1956 Elvis was the biggest male sex symbol since Rudolph Valentino. But whereas Valentino had to get into costume in order to embody the full fantasy package and was only available on the big screen, the whole point about the new rock-star celebrity as embodied by Elvis was that while he might apparently live in the clouds he was still available in the normal world if you knew where to find him. This September Wednesday in Tupelo was one of the last such occasions. Here he was, walking among the humans, in the same Tupelo fairground he'd had to con his way into as a child, only this time almost incinerating in the famished gaze of every female in the fairground.

When he mounted the stage for the 2.30 show in front of a few thousand over-stimulated girls who had flocked there from all over the South (one of them, the fourteen-year-old Wynette Pugh, would later get on stage herself as Tammy Wynette) he just toyed with them like one who took amusement from dangling himself out like a piece of raw meat before hounds. He dawdled down to the front of the stage, planted his feet where experience had already taught him it was safe to be, and then leaned over towards the girls as if he genuinely wanted to be among them. Then, as soon as they reached out to drag him into their midst he did his relieved white-shoe totter back towards the safety of the band, who duly gave him their 'What did you just do now, El?' look.

Musically it wasn't up to much. Scotty Moore and Bill Black, the boys he'd made his first records with back in Memphis, were there, Scotty's amp balanced on a garden chair. They had only recently been joined by a drummer. The Jordanaires jostled in their plaid jackets and clicked their fingers around one microphone. They played not one but two songs by Little Richard. They plugged the movie *Love Me Tender*, as the Colonel had instructed. Mainly it was about personal appearance rather than performance. Frankly the girls were at least as interested in looking at him as listening to him. Elvis was fine with this and had developed a very simple act to cater to their interest. 'I did a little more, and the more I did, the wilder they went,' is how he explained it.

One New York journalist, seeking a fresh vantage point from which to patronize Presley, said he was simply offering a new variation on an old showbiz tradition, 'the hootchie kootchie'. In a way he was. He moved like a man who had to keep tight control of his loins lest they run away and fornicate of their own free will. The throaty timbre of the girls' screams that day strongly suggested their loins wished to reciprocate. During the first Tupelo show Judy Hopper from Alamo, Tennessee was dragged from the crush at the front of the stage and got to embrace Elvis before the cordon of tubby, perspiring policemen conducted her off the stage. She met him later and had her picture taken. 'What do I like about him?' she said in a voice no longer like a teenager's; suddenly it was as carnal as Barbara Stanwyck's. 'I like all of him.' Judy was fourteen.

Elvis changed his shirt for the evening show. That show was sweatier and more adult but not a great deal longer. Nine numbers and then off into the car and back on the road to Memphis. Somewhere along that long road back the hood of the Lincoln snapped upright, making it impossible to see the road ahead. There were no seat belts and it was only Elvis's arm that prevented Barbara going through the windscreen. The Lincoln was almost a wonder of the world at the time, particularly in Mississippi. Somebody's curiosity must have got the better of them back there in the fairground; they'd taken a look under the hood and neglected to close it properly afterwards. It was another sign that Elvis could no longer walk among his people in safety. Gladys was already sick with worry at what the fans might do to her beloved boy. Tom Parker was planning to withdraw him from personal appearances and make him a figure you could only engage with for the price of a movie ticket.

That was the plan for Elvis as a business. The plan for Elvis as a person wasn't quite so clear-cut. The Colonel had very little interest in the latter. He didn't think he would need one. There were no maps for the journey that twenty-one-year-old Elvis had taken so swiftly in 1956. Like most Americans born in the early part of the twentieth century he had arrived in a world where electric light was a rarity, where dreams didn't extend far beyond those things you were able to see, touch and run your hands along the chrome trim of, where the primary form of entertainment open to decent people was some kind of church. He came of age to find that not only could he buy a car, he could even buy a new one. And not only could he buy a new one, he could have more than one, and he could also afford to buy one for everybody in his extended family as thoughtlessly as most people bestowed candy on their children. Elvis was not troubled by the thought of this. In fact he wanted it to continue. Elvis got up each morning wishing for nothing more than to be made to feel like a lottery winner all over again.

One arena in which this seemed perfectly achievable was the sexual one. For Elvis in 1956 the world was divided into nice girls, road girls and show-business girls. He was good at kissing them but he was never quite committed to the follow-through. This was less surprising then than it would be now. There was little or no contraception. The Memphis girls might have been thrilled to be seen on the arm of this god among men but they weren't about to give it away. Elvis felt that his mother was perpetually looking over his shoulder, which she probably was, and hovering above it all there was the tumescence-defeating fact that no matter how attractive the company he was in, he was generally the most beautiful one there.

By late 1956 there was no longer such a thing as a private life, had he wanted one. The next time Elvis came back to Memphis he was accompanied by Natalie Wood, his Hollywood girlfriend during the *Love Me Tender* publicity cycle. Wood expected more of Elvis sexually than his Memphis girlfriends. She complained that when he took her into the other room to show her the dailies, the only thing he showed her was the dailies.

For Elvis, that day in September 1956 was a unique interlude between normal life and the star life. This was a truce that couldn't possibly hold for long. A month or so later he gave Gladys and Vernon a budget to start looking at bigger properties where it might be possible to keep the world on the other side of the garden wall. They found Graceland. A year after they had moved in he was drafted into the army. A few months after that Gladys died. She had never had good health and was drinking. She was forty-six.

As Barbara Hearn put it, 'he was never happy again'.

1956 PLAYLIST

Elvis Presley, 'Hound Dog'
Gene Vincent, 'Be-Bop-A-Lula'
Carl Perkins, 'Blue Suede Shoes'
Grace Kelly and Bing Crosby, 'True Love'
Chuck Berry, 'Roll Over Beethoven'
Guy Mitchell, 'Singing The Blues'
Doris Day, 'Que Sera, Sera'
Bill Evans, *New Jazz Conceptions*
Clarence 'Frogman' Henry, 'Ain't Got No Home'
Johnny Cash, 'I Walk The Line'

in close-up and there was always the possibility with Elvis that something might happen. TV is at its best when it flirts with the things it fears. The producers of the Dorsey brothers' *Stage Show* certainly feared what might be going on in Elvis's trousers when he made his first appearance. Worried that not everything was stopping when the music did they urged his agent to take him to the Army & Navy on Broadway and buy him an athletic support. Further appearances on *The Steve Allen Show* and *The Ed Sullivan Show* were similarly laced with dangerous possibilities, even though the boy himself appeared as biddable as a Bible scholar and divided all adults into sirs and ma'ams.

In 1957 Elvis was twenty-two and therefore should by rights have regarded himself as an adult, but he still identified with the burgeoning army of youth. By early 1956 there were estimated to be thirteen million teenagers in the United States. This cohort could mobilize a combined income of $7 billion a year. Not many years before that what little money teenagers had been able to earn would have gone directly into the family exchequer. Now they were free to spend it on themselves. They duly exchanged $20 million a year for lipstick and even more than that on deodorants, a product their parents had managed without. Recorded music was a growing category. Teenagers spent $75 million a year on singles alone. New technology was making it possible for them to take their amusement where they pleased. The first transistor radio appeared in 1954 and 100,000 units were sold in a short time. By 1957 American companies were selling ten million portable record players a year. Manufacturers were starting to react to the teenage market, which they had never taken notice of before. Where the manufacturers went the advertising followed, where there was advertiser demand the media rushed to catch up, and where the media rushed the agents were not far behind.

The custodians of the big US TV shows were people like Ed Sullivan, a lantern-jawed undertaker figure who had made his name in the days when reporters had tickets announcing them as 'press' in their hatbands and cameras required gripping tightly in both fists. These people might not have liked rock and roll but they understood the importance of providing variety. On the night of 6 January 1957, when Sullivan introduced Elvis for his third and final appearance on the show (Colonel Parker having already raised his price too high to encourage repeat bookings), he also introduced Lonnie Satin, the Six Gutis, Sugar Ray Robinson and the British ventriloquist Arthur Worsley. Sullivan finished by giving the camera his sincere face and assuring the family audience at home that Elvis was a fine young man who had never given them a moment's trouble while doing the show. At around the same time the army draft board had announced that Presley was liable for military service and there was no reason why he wouldn't soon be in uniform. Elvis's short period as a rebellious rock star was officially at an end.

While America was enjoying the fruits of a post-war boom, Britain was coming to terms with its newly reduced circumstances. It had come out of the war on the winning side but was losing the empire it had entered the war to protect, and facing a massive bill for the cost of waging that war. Prime Minister Harold Macmillan may have said in the course of a speech at Bedford in the summer of 1957 that 'most of our people have never had it so good', but there was a feeling that Britain's days of mattering were in the past. In April a new John Osborne play had opened at the Royal Court in London. *The Entertainer* starred Laurence Olivier as a desperate down-at-heel comedian. The theatre in which he performed was similarly shabby and faded. During the interval an actress, naked except for the Union flag, occupied the stage in the pose of Britannia. She was not permitted to move a muscle in case the censor closed the show. Most critics took *The Entertainer* as a savage attack on Britain's dreaming of a warlike past, a past that wasn't nearly as glorious as the mythology made out.

For Britain's teenagers, the ones who were in their early adolescence when Elvis and Little Richard began to filter through, there was the immediate comfort of knowing that they were the first generation in years not required to do compulsory military service. Jobs were easy to find, they lived at home and they had disposable income. They had grown up in the shadow of the war and didn't want to hear any more about self-denial or patriotic duty. This generation looked to America for everything: Westerns, hard-boiled detective stories, coffee, blue jeans, chewing gum, slang, hair products, and above all an American way of carrying themselves that they were just starting to pick up from the new rock idols.

In 1957 the Canadian pop singer Paul Anka was touring the United States in the package tour called 'The Biggest Show of Stars'. At different times this caravan included everyone from Chuck Berry, Buddy Holly, the Everly Brothers and Jerry Lee Lewis to Carl Perkins, the Drifters, Frankie Lymon, Buddy Knox and Clyde McPhatter. It was a medley of the wide variety of people having rock and roll hits at the time. Anka noticed that the acts could be divided into three groups: the older black acts, the Italianate city slickers, and the Southern boys. This last group tended to drink, curse and threaten people with the consequences of stepping on their blue suede shoes. They generally played guitars, had impenetrable accents, spoke in a thick patois and had an unlearned swagger about them. These Southern boys were the men laying down the template for what would come to be thought of as rock-star style. It helped immeasurably that they played guitars. The guitars were less important as instruments than as natural extensions of their cool. Although Eddie Cochran hailed from Minnesota and had lived since 1952 in California he fitted right in with the Southern boys because he too looked the part. Whereas Chuck and Fats were too old for the audience to wish to emulate and the Italian boys were too obviously showbiz, the look of somebody like Cochran seemed achievable to the kids who were drawn to the music.

In 1957 the British cultural historian Richard Hoggart published his book *The Uses of Literacy*, which pondered the apparent decline of self-improvement among working-class males, many of whom he pictured spending their days sitting around in milk bars 'with drape suits, picture ties and an American slouch'. The American slouch was particularly appealing to those whose army-trained fathers had insisted that the only proper posture of a man was at full attention. In Britain these imported manners appealed right across the social spectrum. When *Blackboard Jungle*, with its rock and roll soundtrack, had first played in British cinemas it had unleashed something previously unsuspected in the British character. Even nice girls in Cromer had gone along and found they were screaming before they knew what had come over them. Although the sociologist Mark Abrams, researching his book *The Teenage Consumer*, came to believe that teenagers were an almost entirely working-class movement, the American way of doing things was just as popular with the young men who would have been officers as with those who would have been other ranks.

When sixteen-year-old John Lennon was being raised by his Aunt Mimi amid solid middle-class respectability in Menlove Avenue, Liverpool, the rock and roll way of behaving was almost as attractive as the music. It could be quickly achieved, at minimum expense. Men in their twenties who worked for a living might go for the full teddy boy uniform but those who were still at school and had to obey their parents' or guardians' wishes had to be more discreet about it. They could announce themselves as one of this tribe simply by taking off their ties and pulling up their shirt collars, as James Dean had done in *Rebel Without a Cause*. Fourteen-year-old Paul McCartney had spotted Lennon around Liverpool before they formally met. This was going on all over the country. The members of this emerging tribe would silently note each other well before moving along.

McCartney's father had run his own dance band. Hence Paul's first instrument was a trumpet. A trumpet was difficult to play and it didn't seem to have much of a role in rock and roll. More important than that, in the eyes of a teenage boy, it didn't make the player look as good as a guitar did. The guitar transfigured he who owned it. So he persuaded his father to let him swap the trumpet for one. There wasn't a great deal of choice. Like hundreds of teenage boys across Britain he had his nose pressed to the window of a local musical instrument supplier, searching for something that did the job musically but also looked like the kind of machine he might have seen an American rock and roller holding in a picture, rather than the type of guitar favoured by the brilliantined men who operated them from a sitting position in the old dance bands. The way this new music looked was every bit as important as the way it sounded.

In Britain the bridge between the old world of the jazz

band and the new world of rock and roll passed through skiffle. Skiffle's foremost star, Lonnie Donegan, started out as a featured turn with Chris Barber and Ken Colyer's jazz bands. He and a couple of other musicians would perform songs by the likes of Leadbelly and Woody Guthrie in the middle of the set. It was all done in a self-consciously home-made, almost comical fashion using a guitar, a bass that was improvised out of a tea chest, and percussion provided by the sound of thimbles on a washboard. This mini-act proved so popular that Donegan went out on his own and started having big hits. It's no exaggeration to say that skiffle swept the nation in 1956. Its repertoire was up-tempo and catchy, it didn't seem to require virtuosos to play it, and the tools needed to make it could be found in anyone's garden shed. Skiffle groups immediately sprang up everywhere, from workplaces to churches.

By the summer of 1957 skiffle had peaked, but not before it had galvanized teenagers all over the country. Donegan was at number one with a song called 'Puttin' On The Style'. This was the last British chart topper to be released on 78 only. It was an old novelty song which went back thirty years. It was about young people's tendency to behave in a way their parents considered outlandish. One of the most appealing things about skiffle was that it gave young people a chance to pretend they weren't English. In Newcastle, Brian Rankin and Bruce Cripps, later to be known by other names, were in a group called the Railroaders. In Manchester, Barry, Robin and Maurice Gibb, two of them still in short trousers, were preparing for a performance as the Rattlesnakes. Over in Belfast, Ivan Morrison had started the Sputniks. In the suburbs of London, thirteen-year-old James Page was in a skiffle group that got as far as appearing on a BBC talent show. Huw Wheldon, the tweedy schoolmaster figure who presented the programme, asked him what he was going to do when he grew up. 'Play skiffle?' he chortled. 'No,' James replied, 'I want to do biological research.' Nine-year-old Ron Wood made his first appearance on stage playing the washboard in his older brother's skiffle group. They played 'Puttin' On The Style'.

That same song was part of the repertoire of the Quarrymen when they played the village fete in Woolton, a comfortable suburb of Liverpool, on 6 July 1957. John Lennon's first group had been playing together a year and their set comprised all the key songs associated with skiffle, many of which had roots in the African-American experience. There were train songs, work songs, songs about men running away from a chain gang. It was the kind of stuff averagely inhibited young English males could feel comfortable playing. It didn't require them to be themselves or pretend they were in love. In fact the only song about a female they played was 'Maggie May', an old Liverpool favourite about a prostitute.

The Quarrymen played three times that day. The first performance was from the back of a lorry taking part in a procession round the streets. The second was in the field at Woolton where the fete took place. The third was an evening show at the church hall where they were billed as light relief for the youngsters in between the dance band's stints (just like Ed Sullivan, the elders of the local church understood the importance of having something for the youngsters). A photograph was taken of the band during the second performance. They are surrounded by small children who have moved to where the action is. John Lennon is the only one who has a microphone. He isn't wearing his glasses but has somehow managed to pick out the camera. His collar is turned up, his sleeves pushed back, his hair piled up and artfully mussed. It's clearly his band. He doesn't look at all apologetic. He looks as though he's found his place.

Between the afternoon show and the one in the evening the Quarrymen hung around, killing time. It was during that time that Lennon was introduced to the boy, almost two years younger, who had been watching them in the company of a mutual friend. The friend had brought him because he felt they would have plenty in common. Being teenage boys it's possible that John and Paul never did anything so formal as introducing themselves or shaking hands. They mooched around and found somewhere to smoke a cigarette. At one point McCartney asked to borrow Lennon's guitar. He then tuned it properly (Lennon had learned with banjo tuning) and proceeded to play this right-handed instrument in his usual left-handed position, rattling off a series of rock and roll songs with a facility and confidence that belied his age. One of these was Eddie Cochran's 'Twenty Flight Rock', which was significantly more complex than anything in the Quarrymen's set. Paul didn't just know all the words, he also had the stamina to perform the whole thing. Emboldened by the fact that he had clearly impressed the others, he then got on the piano in the church hall and did his Little Richard impression. This was something else. The then thirteen-year-old McCartney had studied how he did it. 'The screaming voice seemed to come from the top of his head. I tried to do it one day and found I could. You had to lose every inhibition and do it.'

The following day's *Sunday Times* had a review of the new film *Around the World in Eighty Days* and the previous evening's BBC broadcast of *Madam Butterfly*. While the Quarrymen had been playing at the Woolton village fete,

Althea Gibson of Harlem, 'the first coloured player of either sex to win the championship', had been collecting her trophy from the Queen at Wimbledon. But more than sixty years later 6 July 1957 is still most remembered for the consequences that flowed from that meeting between two Liverpool teenagers who were obsessed with rock and roll. For years afterwards each of them was asked what had impressed him the most about the other. Lennon said he was struck by how well McCartney had managed to imitate the American acts. He knew McCartney was better than he was and realized he would never improve unless he played with somebody who was better. In his company they might be able to produce something worth hearing. For his part, McCartney said he was most impressed by Lennon's confidence, the way he adapted the songs he sang to include references to the name of the vicar. Together they could first of all copy things and then change those things in all sorts of interesting ways.

A couple of weeks later they happened to run into each other in the street. After some small talk, Lennon said, almost as an afterthought, 'Do you want to join the group?'

McCartney replied distractedly, as if he too had given the idea no thought: 'OK.'

1957 PLAYLIST

Paul Anka, 'Diana'
Sam Cooke, 'You Send Me'
Everly Brothers, 'Wake Up Little Susie'
Buddy Holly, 'Everyday'
Jerry Lee Lewis, 'Great Balls Of Fire'
Little Richard, 'Lucille'
Chuck Berry, 'Rock and Roll Music'
Miles Davis, *Miles Ahead*
Johnny Duncan, 'Last Train To San Fernando'
Elvis Presley, 'Loving You'

22 MAY 1958

LONDON AIRPORT

A bad boy flies in

If success was a straightforward question of the amount of sheer musical talent, then twenty-two-year-old Jerry Lee Lewis of Ferriday, Louisiana should have had more of it than anyone. He was the first rock star to be a master of his instrument. From the age of nine he had taught himself to play, showing self-discipline at the piano not readily apparent anywhere else in his life; by the time he was in his late teens and had already dropped out of Bible College he could sing and play anything – jazz, gospel, blues, Gershwin, you name it – with an assurance that dazzled anyone, particularly anyone who thought that compared to jazzers and dance-band players, rock musicians were strictly cavemen.

Jerry Lee sounded as though he came out of the woods. His father was one of those cotton farmers who was hit by the Great Depression and never got out from under. He diversified into making moonshine, which led to a period in the penitentiary. The family, who had started off as Baptist, joined the Assembly of God, a sect that condemned drinking, dancing, fornicating and playing secular music; in fact they drew the line at pretty much everything Jerry Lee had any aptitude for, which accounted for his occasional bouts of bad conscience about the way he wound up making his living.

Jerry Lee's prodigious talent made him almost a novelty act. When, in 1956, Sam Phillips had taken his twenty-year-old charge up to New York City in an effort to get him booked on one of the big TV shows before he had even had a hit record, Jerry Lee performed for the man from NBC right there in his office. He barely got to the end of the number. 'I'll give you five hundred dollars if you don't show him to anyone else,' said the man to Sam as though the two were discussing a racehorse.

That man's confidence was not misplaced. When Jerry Lee's record came out it was a huge hit all across the country. It deserved to be. In the years since 1956 hundreds of performers have covered 'Whole Lotta Shakin' Goin' On' but not one has endowed it with the coiled power young Jerry Lee invested in it in Sam's studio on Union Avenue in Memphis. Whereas Little Richard sounded like the helpless vessel of a power too great for him to tame, Jerry Lee sang like a man with the monster on a leash. No matter how much mayhem he might have summoned in the course of a performance there was never any question that he had both hell and tarnation in reserve.

The only drawback – and here Jerry Lee could be said to have laid down a marker for the ages – was that all that talent was at the mercy of a man with the appetites of a Viking raider, the manners of a Confederate skirmisher and the tractability of a mule. Jerry Lee's problem was that he actually was the obnoxious redneck hoodlum his rock and roll peers only pretended to be. Paul Anka, the sixteen-year-old clean-living boy from Canada, never got over meeting him on that 1957 package tour. 'I can't even explain how abusively unpredictable this guy could be,' he recalled later, still white with shock. 'White trashy spew, that's what it was.' Fellow Southern boys were less easily thrown by Jerry Lee's front, preferring to say he didn't mean nothing by it, but even they were forced to concede that he would argue with a signpost.

Whereas Little Richard was professionally the show-off and Elvis was professionally modest, the self-belief of Jerry Lee Lewis went beyond the quality it takes to get up on stage and command everybody's attention with a prolonged 'weeeeeeellllll', passed directly through the braggadocio that showbiz traditionally expects of a headliner, and edged perilously close to an acute psychological condition. He was the first rock star to play up to his public image regardless of the cost. He liked to claim that he was 'born feet first with a hard-on' and that even at school he'd been known as 'The Killer'. Either this was not an act or it was such an all-encompassing act he couldn't afford to let it drop at any point.

Success certainly didn't change him. In fact he took it as overdue confirmation of his infallibility. At the end of 1956 he got a royalty cheque for $40,000. That year the average American male made less than $4,000. Jerry Lee was promised the same amount six months later. However, there are few sure things in show business and therefore it was perfectly possible that his might be a one-off windfall. Certainly his manager Sam Phillips urged him to invest at least some of it. Jerry Lee didn't do that. In fact by March 1957 he'd come back to Sam asking for another $17,000. Why did he want another $17,000? Well, said Jerry Lee, he wanted it to buy some cows.

Even though he knew it was the wrong thing to do, Sam gave him the money. He never saw it again. He didn't enquire further about the cows.

The first rock stars were not natural travellers. This particularly applied to those who came out of the South, who already regarded the rest of the United States as alien territory. Abroad was like the moon. Going abroad involved flying across a body of water, which simply didn't seem natural. In late 1957 Little Richard had abandoned an Australian tour when he took the launch of the Russian Sputnik satellite as a harbinger of the end of the world and announced that henceforth he would perform only sacred material.

Jerry Lee Lewis was not the first American rock star to have visited Britain. Bill Haley had toured in 1957. Bill was thirty-one by then and had his head firmly enough screwed on to spot the bear traps laid by British tabloids in search of a story. Jerry Lee was not made of the same timber. Furthermore, Jerry's domestic arrangements made him more vulnerable.

In looking at those arrangements from the twenty-first century it's important to bear in mind that this was the real world for many people in the Southern states of America and not a Coen Brothers fantasy. Jerry Lee had been married for the first time at the age of fifteen. His bride was the seventeen-year-old daughter of a travelling evangelist. Two years later he began running around with another woman, who became pregnant. At the strong urging of her brothers he married her. Unfortunately he did so before the divorce from his first wife had been finalized. This match was further complicated by the arrival of two sons. When Jerry Lee's music career began to take off he left the second wife and moved in with his bass player Jay Brown, a cousin of his. Jay had a pretty young daughter called Myra. Jerry Lee married her, despite the fact that she was thirteen, despite the fact that she was his cousin, and despite the fact that he was not technically divorced from his previous wife. Or the one before that.

Now here he was, flying into London airport on an early summer's day in 1958, anticipating no problems. This was in the days when all visiting entertainers would be expected to give a press conference of some sort as soon as they had gone through baggage claim. There were some friends and family in the touring party, and a hack working for the *Daily Mail*'s diary page, which went out under the name of the fictitious Paul Tanfield, fastened on the pretty young girl hovering on the edge of the melee and enquired who she might be. 'I'm Jerry Lee's wife,' she chirped, just as you would expect of a proud young bride.

Myra was to spend most of the rest of her life regretting those words. She could easily have avoided them. After all, she was also the daughter of Jerry Lee's bass player, and this would have been more than adequate cover. But by then the words were out and the antennae of this representative of Her Majesty's press had quivered into full alert. He asked for details. 'How old are you?' he enquired, pencil poised. Already sensing that she may have done something wrong, Myra attempted to cover her tracks. 'I'm fifteen,' she lied, praying this would put an end to it. It didn't. By the time the party had arrived at the Westbury Hotel in London's Mayfair the press pack was slavering and Jerry Lee, twenty-two years old and not one of nature's diplomats, was forced into crisis management mode without the help of a PR.

Jerry Lee couldn't say he hadn't been warned. Sam Phillips had told him it might not be a good idea to take Myra with him to Britain, where a nymphet would inevitably be catnip to a press pack looking for a story about the decline and fall of morals in the coffee-bar generation. Sam's brother Jud was even more forthright. His precise words were: 'If you do this you're going to flush the greatest talent that this country's ever seen right down the commode.' But Jerry was stubborn and Jerry was in love. He said that he wouldn't go if Myra didn't. Here, not for the first time, Jerry Lee was a prisoner of his own certainty. Once he'd put his foot down there was no raising it again.

It was supposed to be a six-week tour, involving thirty-seven dates all over the country. Sam had entrusted the job of running it to Oscar Davis, an old-school country music operative who had once been Hank Williams's manager and who should have known what might be involved in running a difficult client. What he reckoned without was the fact that he was dealing with a different generation of performer here, one apt to give a candid answer to a probing question, and he was in a country where the press didn't blench in the face of a sex scandal. In the face of a sex scandal it rubbed its hands together and called for more ink.

By the time Jerry Lee took to the stage of the Regal in Edmonton in his hot pink suit with sparkly lapels, any music he was playing was over shadowed by this new narrative in which he had been sent to infect the youth of New Elizabethan England with his in-bred hillbilly ways. In the audience was eighteen-year-old Harry Webb from Cheshunt in Hertford-shire. Harry had just been informed by his manager that his name was henceforth to be Cliff (in honour of rock) Richard (in honour of the singer of 'Tutti Frutti'). 'People were shout-ing "cradle-snatcher",' Cliff remembered. 'I didn't care who he was married to. I just wanted to hear the music.'

Things got worse during the other London shows. Oscar Davis didn't have the crisis management skills required and

Jerry Lee was temperamentally inclined to quell fires with gasoline, responding to the press question 'Is she really old enough to marry you?' with the perfectly incendiary line 'Just *look* at her.' Oscar tried, unsuccessfully, to interest the US Embassy in London in staging a proper wedding between this pair of American citizens on what he argued would be American soil. The columnists had a field day. Questions were even asked in the House. The public space hummed with sanctimony.

The inevitable occurred. The Rank Organisation, who ran twenty-seven of the venues Jerry Lee was due to play, leaned on the agents, Lew and Leslie Grade, to cancel the tour. Jerry Lee said he wouldn't be out of pocket anyway and there were lots of places in the States he could play. Oscar Davis stayed behind to try to reach a settlement with the Grades over the $100,000 they had expected to earn from the tour. Jerry Lee put a brave face on it back in New York, giving an interview with his arm around his gum-chewing, visibly adolescent wife, dodging questions about his marriage by drawing her near, looming in the direction of his interlocutor and saying 'Well, sir, we don't want any personal questions' with the smile of The Killer.

The blow-back was immediate in the United States. Sam Phillips found that distributors were sending back so many copies of his boy's new single it was in danger of being the first record in the history of the business to have shipped gold and returned platinum. Radio play was non-existent. Given the substance of the scandal it didn't help that the song Jerry Lee was singing was 'High School Confidential'.

Jerry Lee refused to recognize that he had done anything wrong and never once said that he was guilty of any kind of lapse of judgement in taking Myra to Britain. The two remained married for ten years, a union which featured the usual mental and physical abuse but also engendered enough love for them to be still speaking to each other at the end. Says Roland Janes, who played guitar on many of Jerry Lee's records, in a judgement that could in future be applied to many rock-star marriages, 'Myra grew up and I don't think he ever did.'

Leslie Grade, the old-school agent who had represented Jack Benny, Danny Kaye, Bob Hope and hundreds of other stars – stars who never considered it part of their job description to tell the truth about their personal lives – said afterwards, 'It seems such a great shame he had to make public his private life.' The whole point with this new generation of rock performers is there wasn't really a division between public and private.

And Jerry Lee paid the price. He said later that his earnings went down from $10,000 a night to $250, which may have been an exaggeration of the actual figures but was a reasonable representation of the trajectory. He didn't return to Europe until the next decade and never recovered his momentum as a rock and roll star in the USA. He didn't get another proper shot until he relaunched himself as a country singer, his speciality being honky tonk laments that made the most of the one quality he had taken away from his week in 1958, ruefulness.

Jerry Lee Lewis's disorderly retreat from London played into the narrative favoured by the popular press, in which rock stars were essentially characters belonging in a farce, people who couldn't find their own fundaments with a flashlight and owed their brief period in the spotlight solely to the machinations of their minders. The music was now clearly past the point of being a fad but the press certainly weren't going to take it seriously. It seemed that grown-up media had identified what *The Times* called 'the mood of self-pity and resentment which is bedevilling modern youth' and had got the number of the quacks who claimed to be able to minister to this condition. *The Phil Silvers Show* had an episode called 'Rock 'n' Roll Rookie' in which their unit was joined by a suddenly rich rock and roll star, an amiable rube called Elvin Pelvin who was of course no match for Bilko's swindles. At the same time British humorists Frank Muir and Denis Norden were writing a sketch for Peter Sellers which was a thinly veiled satire on Britain's rock svengali Larry Parnes and the stable of gormless young men who just happened to share his Mayfair apartment. This last featured the immortal reprimand from the manager to one of his intellectually challenged charges, 'How many times have I told you? The hole on the guitar points away from you!'

1958 **PLAYLIST**

Jerry Lee Lewis, 'Breathless'
Peggy Lee, 'Fever'
Chuck Berry, 'Johnny B. Goode'
Buddy Holly, 'Rave On'
Royal Teens, 'Short Shorts'
Cliff Richard, 'Move It'
Eddie Cochran, 'Summertime Blues'
The Kingston Trio, 'Tom Dooley'
South Pacific soundtrack
Duane Eddy, 'Ramrod'

3 FEBRUARY 1959
CLEAR LAKE, IOWA

A good boy flies out

Everybody liked Buddy Holly. His records, 'That'll Be The Day', 'Oh Boy', 'Peggy Sue' and 'Rave On', had been hits in the United States and all over the world. His particular strain of 'western bop' had enjoyed surprisingly wide acceptance. He had even topped the rhythm and blues charts. He had appeared on all the big TV shows: *Ed Sullivan* in the United States and *Sunday Night at the London Palladium* in the UK. He had headlined tours. He was famous. Even his glasses were famous. Nevertheless in the winter of 1958, barely a year since he had been at number one in the US Hot 100, twenty-two-year-old Buddy Holly found himself without funds.

Born in 1936, the youngest of a poor but musical family, Charles Holley had little reason to think he would ever amount to anything. In a school essay in 1953 he listed all his many shortcomings and then said, 'I have thought about making a living out of Western music if I am good enough, but I will have to wait to see how that turns out.' Gary Tollett, who sang on some of Holly's records and came from the kind of west Texas town outside Lubbock that Larry McMurtry depicted in *The Last Picture Show*, said of their entire generation, 'We thought more about work than we did about playing.' Holly was the first member of his family to graduate from high school. He thought if he was very lucky he might get work as a draughtsman.

The unhappy position he found himself in at Christmas 1958 owed something to the deals he had done in the course of his swift rise to fame. He and his group the Crickets made their hits in a studio in Clovis, New Mexico which was owned by an older musician and producer called Norman Petty. Petty had no great sympathy for rock and roll but it was he who got them a deal on two separate labels of Decca, one for the Crickets as a group and one for Buddy as a solo. Petty, a father figure without whom they may well have remained unknown in Lubbock, intervened in the creative process, sometimes to add words in the songwriting, at other times to decree the addition of radio-friendly backing vocals, and his name often ended up among the writing credits. Of course nobody argued about who had the credit and how the split worked in 1957 when they were riding high on a sequence of hits. They were too busy tearing about all over the world, making the most of the fact that everybody suddenly wanted them. They assumed that once things settled down everything would be straightened out. However, by the following year, when Buddy had done a lifetime's growing in twelve short months, got married, moved to Greenwich Village, was suddenly visiting jazz clubs, taking acting lessons and talking about recording in a different style, things, as they have a habit of doing, turned ugly.

Holly's new wife María Elena was a New Yorker. He had proposed on their first date and she had accepted. Holly's Baptist mother didn't like the idea of him being married to a Hispanic Catholic. María Elena, who worked for his publishing company, knew her way around New York. Holly, on the other hand, had grown up in a wind-blown town in Texas, a town that styled itself 'the buckle of the Bible belt'. María Elena pointed out that all the money he earned was going through Petty's bank account before being disbursed to Holly and the Crickets. This was news he didn't wish to hear. This was a classic case of a young star's new associates in the big city facing off against the allies who had helped him out of the small town, with the new star in the middle feeling it ought to be possible to please everyone.

Petty had always worried his charges would have their heads turned by success. He had seen the signs early on when they all went out and splashed money on matching brand-new motorbikes on their way home from some out-of-town dates. Now it seemed to be happening. Nevertheless Petty sat tight, thinking this all might pass.

Holly moved to sever his links with his manager, figuring in his naivety that there would be a simple accounting of the monies from which everybody would be able to walk away satisfied. This proved not to be the case and hence, until the lawyers had finished their inevitably cash-draining work, as 1958 drew to a close Holly found himself in the unenviable position of being massively famous, widely celebrated and functionally penniless.

At this point enter Irvin Feld, who had promoted 'The Biggest Show of Stars' on which Holly had appeared in 1957. Holly wanted Feld to be his agent and find him some work which could cover his expenses and pay for some studio time. Feld had been busy cooking up a tour of unpromising secondary venues in the frozen north of the country in the depths of winter. With the jaunty optimism of a promoter who doesn't actually plan to come along for the ride himself, Feld billed this as the 'Winter Dance Party'. It featured the young Latino Ritchie Valens of recent 'La Bamba' fame, the radio personality cum pop singer J. P. Richardson, otherwise known as 'the Big Bopper', and up-and-coming New York greasers Dion and the Belmonts. Advance sales had been sluggish so Feld invited Buddy to join the bill as headliner for a fee of around $3,000 a week. Holly didn't have a lot of choice. Musicians, even famous ones, had to play or starve.

The itinerary of the Winter Dance Party didn't make it sound like a cakewalk. It seemed more like an attempt to map the middle of nowhere. It began at the Million Dollar Ballroom, Milwaukee and ended at the Riverside Ballroom in Green Bay, Wisconsin. These were far from front-rank venues. These were the kind of places show-business people were traditionally sent as punishment.

The musicians travelled in two old school buses. These might have been equal to the job of taking kids on a short hop to school in the summer months but over long distances in the middle of winter they were found wanting. Most of the people on board had been born in the middle of the Great Depression so as a rule they did not tend to complain. But this was different. There were men on that bus who had served in Korea who had never expected to be that cold again. They kept warm by taking slugs of whisky which they mixed with mouthwash. What heaters the buses were fitted with had recently frozen up and now they were heading into the northernmost part of the itinerary where the mercury didn't often get above zero. When the buses broke down, which they frequently did, the huddled occupants burned newspapers in the aisles to keep warm.

Some people were going down with flu. One unfortunate member of the tour party was even hospitalized with frost-bite. By the midway stage of the tour the traditional fatigue and homesickness had been made worse by an all-pervading lack of hygiene. Following each evening's second show all the musicians would take off their sweaty stage clothes and toss them in the back of the bus, where they would ripen. This meant the bus smelled. It smelled so bad that even small boys remarked on it.

The next show was on 2 February at the Surf Ballroom in Clear Lake, Iowa. The name, redolent of cobalt skies and warm waves, mocked the venue and its location. It was far up in *Fargo* country, a thousand miles away from any warming ocean and closer to the Great Lakes where the wind was apt to gather and, in January, scythe through anyone not properly protected by multiple layers of clothing. Following the most recent bus breakdown the police came and rescued them for the simple reason that otherwise they would have died. Buddy Holly and his band, which included hometown boy Waylon Jennings, were Texans and not good with cold. But compared to Angeleno Ritchie Valens, who had arrived for the tour in just a light cotton jacket and was soon actually whimpering in pain, they showed Russian levels of forbearance.

Even at their lowest ebb nobody was thinking of calling their manager to get them off this caravan from hell. They kept buggering on. It was only the laundry that forced the issue. Buddy Holly, who as the headliner was making more money than the rest of the bill, was interested in seeing whether he might be able to rent a small plane to take him to the next show in Moorhead, Minnesota. Because Clear Lake didn't offer any laundry services his only chance of getting his clothes clean was to get to Moorhead in time to be able to do the laundry there and collect it before the show. It was agreed. They finished the second Clear Lake show that night with their version of Jerry Lee's 'Great Balls Of Fire' and then the promoter took them immediately to their plane.

They had found an airfield nearby and a twenty-one-year-old pilot who was prepared to fly them to Fargo, which was a taxi ride from Moorhead. It was supposed to be Buddy plus two members of his band but as soon as Valens and the Big Bopper heard of his plans they bought the $36 tickets from the band members and hurried with Buddy to the airfield after the show. It was dark, it was snowy, and the plane, a Beechcraft Bonanza, had room for just four people including the pilot. Either the pilot didn't get the weather report or he did but was too excited by the idea of his cargo of stars to refuse to take off.

The Beechcraft climbed out of the airfield just before one in the morning on 3 February 1959. The owner of the flight company watched it go. He saw its tail light climb, turn and then slowly descend. Subsequent attempts to make radio contact with the plane failed.

It wasn't until 9.30 the following morning that another plane took off to see if they could see any sign of what had become of the Beechcraft. They found the wreckage just eight miles north of the airfield. It had hit the ground right wing first and then ploughed into snow and earth at 170 miles per hour. The three musicians had all been thrown clear and died of massive brain trauma. The pilot was still in the wreckage.

The news spread all over the country from radio station to radio station. Holly's own family learned of it from the radio. The rest of the musicians, who hadn't been able to afford the plane ride, turned up at the next town following a bus ride that was relatively comfortable to be greeted by the news. There was no hysteria. The planned two shows were condensed into one. The promoter organized a quick audition for local talent to fill out the bill. The winners were a group from Fargo led by fifteen-year-old Robert Velline, who became better known two years later as Bobby Vee. The musicians in the tour party carried on and played the show that night. Waylon Jennings sang Buddy's parts. The crowd was swelled to two thousand by walk-ups attracted by the publicity. Within days Irvin Feld had taken a couple of the big names from one of his other tours and transferred them to the Winter Dance Party. The tour completed its final two weeks with Jimmy Clanton and Frankie Avalon as reserves.

Two months after the crash, in the first sign that this par-ticular tragic story would not die with its victims, Buddy Holly's gun was found near the site, leading to rumours that some horseplay on the plane might have led to the crash. 'Sure Buddy carried a gun,' said good old boy Jerry Allison of the Crickets. 'We all did. It's fun to have a gun.'

What nobody predicted is how good the tragedy would be for business. The day after the crash young people were seen at the site, making away with items of the dead men's cloth-ing. By Wednesday afternoon the papers were reporting heavy demand for the victims' records. Buddy Holly was buried in Lubbock, Texas a week later. A thousand people turned up. The following Monday his record company announced that they would release an album called *The Buddy Holly Story*. You need an ending to make a story. It appeared Buddy Holly would be the first rock star to have a story.

The longevity of Holly's songs is guaranteed because the sadness of his passing places every note in a melancholy light.

At the time he died he was very excited about his plans. He wanted to start his own record company back in Lubbock. He was going to do everything himself. He talked about having his own trucks. He was optimistic. Much the same was also said of most of the rock stars who died in years to come, whose deaths were inevitably linked with his as though in some sad but beautiful tradition. He was the first rock star of whom it was possible to say that he was worth more dead than alive. His heirs, his wife, his family and Norman Petty all said they didn't wish to exploit his memory and then put out almost every fragment, out-take and demo.

Unlike Elvis there was nothing supernatural about Buddy Holly, either in appearance or in terms of the sound he made. He looked like a neighbourhood boy. The glasses made him appear more studious than he was. The ideas for his songs, which came from catchphrases in movies or the names of sweethearts, seemed within the compass of anybody. His voice didn't have an unearthly range. It was the kind of noise any guy in an amateur band could imagine himself making. Furthermore, he and the Crickets were a band, far more of a band than any of the competition. You could see them playing the different roles that added up to the sound on their records. You could watch his fingers on the fretboard and then try to emulate it in your bedroom. You could practise the gently self-mocking hiccup in his voice. He was as popular with the boys as Elvis Presley was with the girls, but for different reasons. He was the most influential rock star of his time, possibly of all time. Influential is not a synonym for 'good' or 'successful'. It denotes the extent to which other people feel they can pattern themselves after you. Buddy Holly is where the do-it-yourself ethos of rock and roll begins. He inspired thousands of people to play. There wasn't a band with an electric guitar in the early sixties that didn't play at least one Buddy Holly song.

Thirteen-year-old John Fogerty in Berkeley, California looked at the cover of *The 'Chirping' Crickets* and said to himself, 'That's a group. I'd never seen a group before. I'm gonna have a group.' Although Holly and the Crickets dressed in tuxedos and bow ties and on TV at least put most of their energies into smiling, the fact that they played their own instruments was what made them huge. An electric guitar such as Holly's Fender was as much a stage prop, workman's tool and fan's totem as it was an instrument. Men who would feel self-conscious merely clustering around a microphone and singing felt the guitar provided them with just enough of an alibi. They weren't just performing. They were operating a machine. The guitar made it look as if they were there to do work.

John Lennon had sat rapt in front of the TV when Holly appeared on *Sunday Night at the London Palladium* in 1958, enthralled by his fingers, his Fender guitar and his glasses, taking in every nuance of this rare, precious, unique, three-minute, once-only demonstration of how this magical sound was accomplished. The first demo his group the Quarrymen made was their version of 'That'll Be The Day'. The Beatles took their name and their entire idea of what a group could be from the Crickets.

Even Mick Jagger, the blues snob, went to see Holly on tour in London in 1958. The Rolling Stones' first real hit was 'Not Fade Away', a Holly song.

Among the crowd watching Holly at the Duluth Armory just a few days before he died was Robert Zimmerman of Hibbing. He later said, 'He seemed to have a halo round him.' By then he did, in a sense, have a halo around him. He had the purity of a martyr. He had also left behind songs and a way of writing which lived on. When the rock and roll renaissance came along at the beginning of the sixties it was the children of Buddy Holly who would lead it.

1959 **PLAYLIST**

Buddy Holly, 'It Doesn't Matter Anymore'
Wilbert Harrison, 'Kansas City'
Bobby Darin, 'Mack The Knife'
The Clovers, 'Love Potion Number 9'
Ray Charles, 'What'd I Say'
The Drifters, 'There Goes My Baby'
Frankie Ford, 'Sea Cruise'
Brenda Lee, 'Sweet Nothin's'
Santo & Johnny, 'Sleep Walk'
Lloyd Price, 'Personality'

1 JULY 1960
LONDON

Enter the guitar hero

Brian Rankin is one of the most influential rock stars ever to have come out of Britain. The fact that his real name isn't familiar even to rock scholars doesn't make this any less the case. Neither does the fact that he's not known ever to have said or done anything particularly memorable. That he never did a great deal that was particularly original doesn't change that fact either.

Brian was born in Newcastle in 1941, when England was one of the few regions of Europe not under Hitler's rule. His father worked for the railway. The house he lived in had no bathroom. As a teenager he was keen to learn a musical instrument. The nearest to hand was a banjo, which he played in a New Orleans-style 'traditional' jazz band. On hearing Buddy Holly he traded the banjo for a Hofner Congress cello-bodied guitar, which cost sixteen guineas.

He then joined another Newcastle boy, Bruce Cripps, in a skiffle group called the Railroaders. Two hundred miles away on the opposite coast of England John Lennon had also formed a skiffle group with a similarly artisanal name. In an effort to sound more American, which they felt was naturally expected of all people who tried to play in this new idiom, Bruce Cripps changed his name to Bruce Welch and Brian Rankin coined a new identity by combining the name his school friends used to describe his cowboy's walk with the first name of a country singer who had once played in Newcastle. Thus he became Hank Marvin. This seemed the ideal name for a noble loner who carried either a gun or a guitar. It was a name that had particular resonance for boys who grew up in the 1950s. Bob Dylan, born a few months earlier than Brian, 'liked all kinds of Hanks'.

Both Hank Marvin and Bruce Welch came from modest backgrounds but they were grammar-school boys and there-fore they could potentially have gone on to further education and a career. It says a lot about the disengagement between the children who had grown up during the war and their parents, who had served in that war, that nobody tried to stop Hank and Bruce going down to London in their teens to try and get some sort of start in the music business, a business about which they knew nothing at all. The two teenagers shivered and very nearly starved until they caught a break in the shape of an Anglo-Indian kid called Harry Webb who'd just had his name changed to Cliff Richard and needed a backing group. The other two members of the group were Tony Meehan and Terence Harris, who took the name 'Jet', and they came to be known as the Shadows. Cliff Richard's career prospered immediately and some of the attention naturally spilled over to his backing band, who started to make instrumental records for the same record company.

Musicians, like golfers, tend to believe they're just one

piece of equipment away from achieving perfection. The young Hank was no exception to this rule. He persuaded Cliff that what he really needed was a guitar like the one he'd seen Buddy Holly posing with on the cover of The 'Chirping' Crickets. Cliff agreed and wrote to Leo Fender's company in faraway California. A glossy catalogue of the Fender company's products was mailed to them. The group pored over it as though it were the first Playboy. They finally decided on what added up to, with all the add-ons and refinements, the most expensive guitar in the book.

The Stratocaster was Leo Fender's development of his earlier, more functional Telecaster. There was something about the Stratocaster that seemed to belong to the world of jet-age styling. It was so sensual it should have required a licence. This was certainly the case with the model Hank ordered: flamingo pink with bird's-eye maple neck, tremolo arm and gold-plated hardware. The serial number was 34346. It cost around £120. The average man in Britain at the time would have had to work eight weeks to earn the price of that guitar. They could only get it into London at all by circumventing the strict regulations governing the supply of expensive overseas goods into the UK during post-war austerity. When Hank's Stratocaster finally arrived in the spring of 1959 it was the very first to come into Europe. As a covetable item of equipment it combined the space-age lines of a supercar with the dazzling ingeniousness of a smartphone. As a unique object from the very country where this new music was being made it was greeted in London like a religious artefact. When Hank took it out to play in the kind of clubs where musicians gathered, the faithful would draw near as though in worship.

The Strat wasn't merely for show. 'It looked like something

out of the future,' recalled Marvin. 'It was so sensual and sleek. But with the vibrato bar it enabled me to play with more expression.' With it Hank could do things he hadn't been able to do before, such as bend notes with the tremolo arm, helping him achieve his first objective, which was to make the guitar sound less like a guitar. The difference in sound was the kind of thing other musicians would note. Young men in Britain watching the Shadows play their tunes on TV were predominantly drawn to how it looked. Leo Fender said he'd thought of the contoured body before anything else. Hence it fitted on the hip like an item of clothing. With his shiny suit, windowpane spectacles (which he borrowed from Buddy Holly) and Stratocaster at the hip, Hank Marvin immediately became the most widely emulated British player.

Those who didn't have a guitar or had one but couldn't play it could take a tennis racket and mime along to his solos on Shadows records. The electric guitar was a natural extension of the war toys these same boys had grown up with. As they moved from boyhood into adolescence and their heroes turned from cowboys into rock musicians, the accompanying fascination with shiny kit was transferred from Colt 45s to Vox AC30s. At the same time the instrumental hits of guitar groups like the Shadows echoed the association with noble sacrifice traditionally at the core of *Boy's Own* entertainment.

On 1 July 1960 the Shadows released their single 'Apache'. 'Hang on to your scalps' advised the adverts. 'Apache' was a thrilling evocation of the atmosphere in a Native American encampment on the eve of battle. It was certainly thrilling to young ears who had learned most of what they knew of the world from Hollywood. It was as authentic as could be expected from its composer Jerry Lordan, an advertising man from Paddington. Lordan had got the idea from seeing Burt Lancaster play a Native American in a film of the same name. 'I wanted something noble and dramatic, reflecting the courage and savagery of the Indian,' he said. The Shadows wanted it to be the A-side of their single. Their producer, Norrie Paramor, wanted the A-side to be 'Quartermaster's Stores', an old barrack-room tune which he could anonymously claim the composing credit for by putting it down as 'traditional, arranged'. Amazingly the Shadows got their own way. 'Apache' became a number-one single in the UK and every young man in Britain suddenly wanted to be 'in a group'. It was a pivotal moment.

Whereas girls had driven the first wave of rock and roll, the second was powered by the way it renewed the relationship between young men and technology. It had been taken for granted that rock and roll was mainly about love or having a good time, but the music played by groups like the Shadows hinted that it could also be dramatic, lyrical, even heroic. The names of singles like 'FBI', 'Atlantis' and 'Man Of Mystery' reflected their identification with action and adventure. Until then rock had been primarily about charismatic individuals, but following the emergence of the Crickets in the USA and the Shadows in the UK it became about something that was even more attractive to boys – the pull of the group. No longer tethered to the bandstand as their predecessors had been, the Shadows worked out how to play while weaving intricate patterns on stage, leading with their patent chisel toes. They had picked this up from watching the visiting R&B group the Treniers who had appeared down the bill from Jerry Lee on his ill-fated 1958 tour. TV was what the Shadows were really built for. The cameras went in tight on Hank's fretboard and then travelled up to where his gaze would meet the lens with the pride of somebody who had mastered a party trick a large part of the nation were desperate to get in on. The Shadows were the boys' band par excellence. There wasn't a young male in the nation who didn't want to be one of them.

Groups weren't just efficient performing units, liberating you from the need to enlist the help of proper backing musicians; they were also gangs, and they were particularly attractive to the kind of boys who never would have got involved with a gang. Being in a rock band and being in a gang had features in common: both were founded on oaths of loyalty – oaths that were bound in time to be broken; the lion's share of the power resided in one charismatic individual, even though the others would stoutly deny this was the case; and all the members secretly believed that they would be better off without the others. The mantle of leader of the gang tended to fall on the guitarist. When it came to guitarists, the kinship with the lone gunslinger setting out down the dusty main street to do battle with an adversary in a black hat was openly acknowledged. The dreams that had germinated in the dark in front of Western movies were blossoming into a whole new dream world with rock and roll. The transformation of Robert Zimmerman, storekeeper's son from Minnesota, into Bob Dylan, poet-visionary to the world, was accomplished via a short spell during which he was known as Bob Dillon, a name he borrowed from the sheriff in TV's *Gunsmoke*. Duane Eddy's first album in 1959 was called *Have 'Twangy' Guitar Will Travel*. In 1960 Bo Diddley put out an album called *Bo Diddley Is A Gunslinger*. Rock and roll offered a new outlet for the adventure fantasies of boys and their obsession with kit. Even the guitar of folk troubadour Woody Guthrie bore the legend 'This machine kills fascists'. This was a claim few were likely to make for the saxophone.

'Apache' turned out to be one of those records that enjoyed a surprisingly long career. Long after the vogue for guitar groups had passed – it was this vogue that Decca's Dick Rowe was referring to when he turned down the Beatles – it was a tune that refused to die. Following a funk version in 1973 by the Incredible Bongo Band, it ended up being quoted in scores of records by MIA, the Roots, even Rage Against the Machine. Because 'Apache' started life as a fantasy it could never sound anachronistic. In the twenty-first century there was even a learned essay on the subject, penned by journalist Michaelangelo Matos, entitled 'All Roads Lead to Apache'.

More importantly, all roads lead to Hank Marvin. There were a million young men all around the world who would never have had it in them to swivel their hips like Elvis, who would have found the idea of actually opening their mouths and singing like Buddy Holly simply too mortifying, but who nonetheless looked at this new rock-star archetype, this stolid figure with the beautiful guitar, the non-speaking role who took the lead when mere words were no longer enough, and imagined themselves in his shoes. Forty years later writer Steve Waksman described it as 'the ideal of masculine achievement contained within the idea of the guitar hero'. Nobody would have put it in those words back then but everybody would have known the feeling. That feeling was to endure through the next decade of beat music and emerge blinking into the daylight during the virtuosity mania of progressive music.

No form of music has been quite so closely identified with one instrument as rock has been with the electric guitar. For most of the music's lifetime it was seen as not only the one necessary item of equipment but also the most potent symbol of the music. Whether we could play it or not, all of us at one time or another cradled a guitar in our arms, felt it awaken something within us, and had no difficulty imagining what it must mean to somebody who could really play it. Similarly we all knew what a band was and how these weapons could be deployed as one. We all felt we had some idea of what each individual member did. We joined bands in our dreams. Those instruments and the professionals' mastery of them, the whole ritual of a band coming on, plugging in and playing, was a huge part of what we liked about rock and a huge part of what created rock stars, from the age of Buddy Holly to the time of Nirvana. When things went digital and we could no longer see where the sounds were coming from, much of the rock star's artisan mystique began to disappear.

A whole generation of British musicians who were only just starting their journeys at the end of the 1950s – Jimmy Page, Jeff Beck, Phil Manzanera, Eric Clapton, Mark Knopfler – got their idea of what being the guitar player could amount to from watching Hank Marvin on the TV. He was the reason they sat in their rooms and practised. He was the guitar hero of the boys who would grow up to be guitar heroes. Exceptional soloists have long been revered in different forms of music, but only rock felt the need, decades after Hank Marvin had set out the prototype, to coin the expression 'guitar hero'; this might have been because the guitar had some of the characteristics of a weapon like a rifle or a sword. The guitar hero eventually became an idea so widely adopted that it was used as the brand name for a best-selling computer game, happily played by millions of people who have never been or even seen an actual guitar hero. It was adopted because everybody had subliminally taken on board the idea that the man given the honour of playing the lead guitar in the band is a figure of almost priestly specialness. When the time comes for his solo, he steps to the front of the stage, closes his eyes to denote his dedication to his sacred duty, and does battle with the darkness on our behalf. Every time he does that he's standing in the shoes of Brian Rankin.

1960 PLAYLIST

The Shadows, 'Apache'
Roy Orbison, 'Only The Lonely'
Ray Charles, 'Georgia On My Mind'
Chubby Checker, 'The Twist'
The Ventures, 'Walk Don't Run'
Joan Baez, *Joan Baez*
Elvis Presley, *G.I. Blues*
Bo Diddley, *Have Guitar Will Travel*
Everly Brothers, 'Cathy's Clown'
Maurice Williams and the Zodiacs, 'Stay'

25 SEPTEMBER 1961
GERDE'S FOLK CITY, NEW YORK CITY

A boy invents himself

The climactic scene of the 2013 Coen Brothers film *Inside Llewyn Davis* takes place in a Greenwich Village coffee house. The year is 1961. Members of the audience in the coffee house have the opportunity to come up from the floor and perform. The titular hero of the film, an ambitious young man trying, like so many at the time, to make his name in what later commentators would call the Great Folk Scare, but handicapped by the lack of any special talent, doesn't go over big. As his lousy evening culminates in a life-threatening beating in the alley outside the club, the soundtrack pulses with the sound of the man who has succeeded him on to the stage and, as we the audience instantly recognize, has achieved in reality everything Llewyn Davis dared hope for in fiction. The implication of that scene in the film is that Bob Dylan arrived in New York City in the autumn of 1961 fully formed, that his talent and originality were immediately manifest to anyone who had ears to hear and that you could no more hold back his rise to world prominence than arrest the march of time. It wasn't as simple as that.

By 1961 the rock and roll thing appeared to be done. The twist seemed to have taken over. Elvis Presley had come out of the army straight into an appearance on *The Frank Sinatra Timex Show*, appearing every bit as comfortable in a tuxedo as he did sending up his hip-swivelling past. Little Richard had done his own bizarre double by marrying and embracing the Christian ministry. Jerry Lee Lewis remained mired in the scandals of 1958. Chuck Berry was being retried on charges under the Mann Act, charges that turned on the legal point of whether he had transported a fourteen-year-old Apache girl across state lines for the purpose of rescuing her from vice or involving her further in it. The music history books recall it was the time of Fabian, of 'Wooden Heart' and the twist. Seemingly the only people keeping the old faith alive were acts like the Beatles who played rock and roll favourites because that's what worked best for their German audiences on the seamy side of Hamburg. In fact, the paucity of good music in 1961 is one of those myths on which all new beginnings in pop music are invariably predicated. It was also the year of Roy Orbison's 'Running Scared', Ben E. King doing 'Stand By Me', Ray Charles singing 'Hit The Road Jack', Jimmy Reed and 'Bright Lights Big City', Arthur Alexander's 'You Better Move On' and 'Please Mr Postman' by the Marvelettes. In a couple of years these songs would be in everybody's act. All over the world pockets of enthusiasts kept the flame burning.

But for the moment, in America at least, the thing that had apparently taken over from rock and roll among the kids was folk music. Songs with words that meant something. Songs that celebrated old values. Songs that helpfully pointed out where the world might be going wrong. Songs that could be best performed on simple wooden instruments that had no need of either the plastic or the electricity of the machine age. Songs that allowed the people who listened, who were overwhelmingly white, comfortably off and the beneficiaries of a college education, the feeling they were on the side of the angels. Everybody was adjusting to this new aesthetic. Even the Beach Boys, who were auditioning for record companies in California, were being asked if they knew any folk songs.

The arrival of this movement changed everybody. At home in Hibbing, Minnesota, Robert Zimmerman had affected the classic collar-up rocker style, even going so far as to name himself Elston Gunn when playing music in a variety of local bands. He posed on the Harley-Davidson motorcycle his indulgent parents had given him to satisfy his James Dean obsession and sported a red leather jacket around town like any other teenage fantasist. Those who heard him sing at the time report that he favoured the style of Buddy Holly. In fact he had gone into mourning after Holly's death in the 1959 crash. As well as the concern that he might be left behind by fashion, Zimmerman also understood that there was something to be said for joining the ranks of these new troubadours. Furthermore, his hometown experience of how tiresome it could be trying to hold together members of a band had alerted him to the attractions of performing as a solo in the folk style.

This also suited his self-image. In years to come Dylan would explain his youthful drive by saying he always felt the world he was born into wasn't the one he was supposed to be in. He felt Hibbing wasn't his home. The great events of history were to him more pressing than anything in the newspapers. He was destined for greater things. He said, in fact, that he'd always seen himself as a commander in the military. He was born out of time. He wasn't the only young man who dealt with the narrow world of the 1950s by escaping into daydreams. But whereas the hero of Keith Waterhouse's novel *Billy Liar*, published in 1959, was a figure of fun for his fantastical imaginings, Robert Zimmerman, suburban kid with the standard set of insecurities, found that by turning himself into Bob Dylan, folk singer, he could command the attention of a room and direct it all to himself. What Zimmerman was about to do could not possibly have been accomplished within the confines of a band. The other members would never have let him get away with what he got away with, which was nothing less than inventing himself and also inventing a life in which he could star. Young Zimmerman would transform his daydreams into epic songs and his small problems into epic battles. Early on in his career, when a hotel clerk denied him a room because he wasn't dressed appropriately, he went away and furiously composed 'When The Ship Comes In'. Alone on stage, armed with nothing more than his guitar, it was as though he was wrapped in the cape of a righteous avenger.

What started the change in his personal style was going to the University of Minnesota in 1959. It wasn't the education that brought about the transformation so much as the traditional opportunity afforded by university life to lie massively about himself. He dropped out of classes after a year. He abandoned his old rocker form of dress, adopting instead the fustian of a gentleman of the road. Dylan wore work clothes even though it was clear he had never done any hard work. This was something he shared with Bruce Springsteen, who was to sing about the working life despite never having done a hand's turn of it himself.

Like the teenage Elvis back in Memphis, Dylan's act started long before he got on stage. Dylan was acting when he was simply walking down the street. In Minnesota he developed a new way of talking that was designed to make himself seem deep in an unschooled sort of way. His answers to standard questions would be either nebulous or maddeningly specific. He smiled to himself as if he had been entrusted with some truth about human behaviour that hadn't been extended to others. He didn't go to classes. What university provided him with was a society of people his own age on whom he could work his unique genius for sucking in styles and then presenting them as his own. He was not above larceny, actual as well as aesthetic. The man on campus who knew more about folk music than anyone was Paul Nelson. The young Dylan borrowed Nelson's apartment while he was away and helped himself to twenty albums. These were never to be returned but were to help shape his style. The other lesson he was learning, the same one that lots of students learned in the days before Facebook, was that college is one of the few opportunities life affords to make the world accept your past life as whatever you wish it to be. By the time he arrived at his next stop, New York in 1961, he was well on his way to creating a comprehensive framework of legend for himself.

A large part of that legend was borrowed from others. It was Buddy Holly's music that had excited him. What excited him about Woody Guthrie was a life. He contacted the seriously ill Guthrie in hospital in New Jersey and said he was going to come out east to see him – a hint of his presumptuousness. He pored over Guthrie's autobiography *Bound for Glory* with its accounts of places visited, roads travelled and hard lessons learned; he patterned himself after the older man. Guthrie had ridden freight trains, worked in the fields, roistered and rambled and drunk all over the land. Zimmerman, by now calling himself Bob Dylan – his old cowboy handle Bob Dillon altered for no greater reason than it looked better on the chalkboard outside the basket houses where he could play – didn't bother actually doing that. He merely said that's what he had done and figured word would get around.

Bob Dylan was every bit as driven by the need to be someone as Elvis Presley had been, and similarly inclined to find the idea of settling for ordinary life intolerable. In fact, as he broke his journey to New York in Madison, Wisconsin he actually came right out and told a perfect stranger, 'I'm going to be bigger than Elvis Presley.' This was a large claim for a nineteen-year-old chubby-faced kid to make. It was a large claim to make when even Elvis Presley had only been Elvis Presley for a few years. But what Elvis had done was put the idea of rock stardom out there. What James Dean had been for Elvis, Elvis subsequently became for a far larger group of people. The success of Elvis in the fifties lit a fire in people who had no particular affinity for his music but who saw in him an escape from the ordinary. This worked just as powerfully on the educated middle class as it did on the dead-end kids. In the world of American folkies at the time, hundreds of people were obsessed with making it. Each one knew they had to be prepared to step on the neck of their brother or sister to get the break that might lead to it. Even the apparently pure-in-heart Joan Baez, who had already made enough of a career for herself to be able to earn more than $1,000 for one appearance and had invested her portion of Mammon in a Jaguar sports car, had pinched a lot of her act from a girl she was with at college. She justified it to herself by reasoning that whereas the other girl didn't have a lot of ambition, Joan was going to take the material and do something with it. Nobody becomes a star by accident. They have to want it.

Dylan arrived in New York on Tuesday, 24 January 1961, having got a lift in a 1957 Impala. He was not yet twenty. The mean temperature on the day he arrived was 20°F, which was thirteen degrees lower than usual. The weather up and down the eastern seaboard had been so severe that it had almost caused the cancellation of JFK's inauguration, which had taken place the Friday before. There was a feeling in the air that, as Kennedy had put it in his speech, 'the torch has been passed to a new generation'. If he had heard this speech, Dylan took its message literally. The city of New York certainly seemed to open up for the few people fearless enough to turn up there and demand admittance. Dylan was playing a song at the Cafe Wha? that night and already starting to spin stories about who he was and where he came from. Within a few months of arriving in New York he had networked his way around Greenwich Village, via Fred Neil at the Cafe Wha? and Izzy Young at the Folklore Center to Jac Holzman at Elektra Records, through Carla Rotolo to the folklorist Alan Lomax; he made sure he met everybody worth meeting and established a pattern he maintains to this day. Dylan has never been afraid to knock on a stranger's door and ask for what he wants. He wasn't then and he isn't now.

If we're to believe his memoirs, which he wrote forty years later, Dylan spent his spare time in the Village reading heavyweights like Faulkner, Graves and Machiavelli. This is exactly the kind of reading list a college drop-out might wish to have read. He was also remarkably successful with girls. He had the two main qualifications: he looked as though he needed mothering, and he wasn't afraid to ask. He did his first recording session playing harmonica for Texan singer Carolyn Hester. Hester had made her first record back in Texas with Buddy Holly's producer Norman Petty; indeed Holly had taken some pictures of her in the studio. Through his association with Hester, Dylan came to the attention of John Hammond of Columbia Records.

Dylan had a talent for attracting the patronage of older people. One such was Albert Grossman, who had run a club called the Gate of Horn in Chicago. Grossman knew there was money to be made in the folk boom, either by taking this talent out of the college towns and on to the nightclub circuit or, more significantly, from music publishing. Grossman had moved to New York because that's where the talent was. He had merged three solo acts into Peter, Paul & Mary and was in the process of making a lot of money with them. Grossman took Dylan on as a client. According to the account in David Hajdu's book *Positively 4th Street* he first took a little of the uncertainty out of the star-making process by buying Dylan on to a bill at Gerde's Folk City and making sure that his tame journalist Robert Shelton, a staffer at the *New York Times* who had been writing about folk music for several years, covered Dylan's appearance. Shelton was certainly one of those people who blurred the line between commentator and talent-spotter to the extent that his own fortunes were tied to those on whom he chose to put the spotlight. He was on Dylan's team from the early days.

Dylan divided opinion in the Village. Things could have gone either way for him. The older folk singers couldn't see what the fuss was about, which probably meant they could plainly see what the fuss was about but didn't like the competition one bit. The money men like Grossman and publisher

Artie Mogull smelled the possibility of profit. Lou Levy of the Leeds Music Publishing Company signed him up on the basis of one of his very few original songs, 'Song To Woody'. Mogull also signed him on the back of 'No More Auction Block', an old negro spiritual which he had modified just enough to pass off as his own.

Dylan played his historic show at Gerde's Folk City on West 4th Street on 25 September 1961. He was second on the bill to the Greenbriar Boys but the publicity announced him as 'the sensational', indicating the star-making machinery was at work even in these apparently humble surroundings. How it went down with the audience isn't recorded. Only Robert Shelton's reaction counted. Shelton didn't simply cover the performance. Within the context of a small review in that Sunday's edition of the *New York Times*, which at the time sold almost one and a half million copies, he managed to put this twenty-year-old, who hadn't been in the city for a full year, on the map in a way that an expensive PR effort would have had to work hard to match.

Alongside the ads for Paul Newman's opening in *The Hustler* and the arrival in New York of the Kirov Ballet, a headline and picture announced 'Bob Dylan: a distinctive folk-song stylist'. The picture was significant in lots of ways. There was no picture of the headliners but there was one of this kid. It was no accident. Shelton devoted as much of the review to describing Dylan's appearance as he did to his music ('he looks like a cross between a choir boy and a beatnik') – an implicit acknowledgement that what was going on here had more to do with Elvis Presley than Pete Seeger. He glossed over the stories Dylan had been telling about his antecedents and said it mattered less where he came from than where he was going. He then moved on to the Greenbriar Boys, who must have been livid that their limelight had been hijacked by this fortunate new arrival.

It was TV that had broken Elvis Presley, but it was press that would make Bob Dylan. All the way through his career he benefited from the process that only press can provide, whereby the terms of engagement are established before the artist enters the room. For Bob Dylan, this Shelton review was the first of a lifetime of reviews all of which would major on his specialness and difference. The following week he carried the review around in his pocket and would show it to anyone in the folk business without second bidding. He really didn't need to. They had all seen it and read it, many of them with gritted teeth. This was just the start of it. Shelton spent the rest of his life being 'the man who first reviewed Bob Dylan'. The review led to further interest from John Hammond Jr and a recording contract with Columbia Records. Hammond spent the rest of his life being billed as 'the man who signed Bob Dylan'. These men were hitching a ride on the boy's coat tails just as much as he was benefiting from their old-boy net-work. In the music business, confidence is key. If something's on the up, everybody gets on board.

Dylan's ascent wasn't as immediate as it might have been. Columbia sat on his first album, which was mainly traditional material, for four months before releasing it. When it came out, in March 1962, it didn't bother the chart. However there were believers and, miraculously, it found its way to them. For seventeen-year-old Rod Stewart, living in north London with his parents, these songs and this voice suddenly sounded like a new, real America. The transatlantic trade in music meant Bob Dylan was to spend the following Christmas in London, playing the same character he'd developed on the streets and in the coffee houses of Minnesota and Greenwich Village in a play for the BBC. By that time, recognizing the need to come up with material that justified the hype he had begun and the faith others had placed in him, Dylan started playing some of his own new songs. One was called 'Blowin' In The Wind', another was 'A Hard Rain's A-Gonna Fall', and a third was 'Don't Think Twice, It's All Right'. They came in such a torrent he later said he had no idea how he did it. They came in such profusion that he had no room on his new record *The Freewheelin' Bob Dylan* for 'The Death Of Emmett Till', a song about the murder that had taken place in Mississippi the same year that Little Richard had recorded 'Tutti Frutti'.

Grossman started to book shows where his boy could appear in his own right. To promote them Dylan went on WNYC's *Folksong Festival*, a radio programme presented by Oscar Brand. There he told a pack of lies about who he was and where he'd come from. 'I was raised in Gallup, New Mexico,' he deadpanned, almost putting a hillbilly quaver in his voice. 'I travelled with the carnival when I was about thirteen years old. All the way till I was nineteen. Every year off and on I'd join different carnivals.' He knew it wasn't true, wasn't even half-true, but there was nothing in his delivery to indicate that he was about to laugh. More importantly, Brand must have known it wasn't true. It didn't matter. Brand, like most of the listening audience, had such an investment in the romance of the tale that he was prepared to overlook small matters of objective truth for the sake of being able to trip down the yellow brick road the artist had laid out for them. When Robert Shelton sat down with him to write what was supposed to be his official record company biography at around the same time, Dylan extemporized what he must have thought was an ideal CV for somebody who really didn't have one. He said he'd played with Bobby Vee

and Gene Vincent, that he'd learned guitar from Mance Lip-
scomb and a one-eyed bluesman who went by the name of
Wigglefoot. He hinted at a hard life which the most cursory
inspection of his soft hands would have contradicted. He said
he'd been a farmhand and that he sometimes played slide
guitar with a switchblade. He said what people wanted to
believe. They loved him for it.

Sophisticates speak knowingly of the music business and
something they call 'hype'. In their account, hype is a dark art
employed by malign puppet masters wreathed in cigar smoke
from offices in tall buildings. In their account it involves
pulling the wool over the eyes of an audience who wish above
all to know the truth. They like to think that other people
are deceived by hype, but not them. This undersells the truth
of hype. Most hype is perpetrated by the audience on itself.
The transformation of Robert Zimmerman into Bob Dylan,
which took wing in 1961 and within two years was to girdle
the globe, was masterminded not by the puppet master but
by the puppet himself. It took wing for the simple reason that
the audience's desire to believe in the fictions it proposed was
greater than their desire to know the truth behind them.

This was because in this new form of popular music which
had been born in the wake of Elvis Presley, it was important
to be able to believe that the singer and the song were somehow indivisible. A rock star didn't perform the songs, a rock
star *was* the songs. At the precise stage in their lives when
the young audience were ceasing to believe that John Wayne
was a cowboy they were quite happy to embrace the idea that
Robert Zimmerman from Hibbing, Minnesota was a hobo
who had been blown into New York by the wind of destiny. It
was this myth that he forged in 1961, in which he was already
an old man inside a young man, that was to make Bob Dylan

the defining rock star of our time, making him not just as big as Elvis Presley but in some senses bigger. It also launched an act which at the time of writing is still flourishing, an act that has outlasted Frank Sinatra, Bing Crosby, Louis Armstrong, Woody Guthrie and Al Jolson; an act so enduring in its mystery it would have made even Houdini envious. What the career of Bob Dylan teaches is that if you develop the mystique of a great rock star then you can easily ride out any rocky stages or rough patches in your career. That's because the greatest investment is in the myth itself. It could even be more important than the songs you sing. Once the myth is established it allows you to perform a striptease act where you never need actually to take anything off – an act Robert Zimmerman has been performing for fifty years. Zimmerman's greatest creation was Bob Dylan.

Within a year of Robert Shelton's review appearing in the *New York Times* there wasn't a person in the worldwide music business who hadn't heard of Bob Dylan. Word had even got back to Hibbing. Just four years later these same early adopters, these same earnest, bespectacled undergraduates, were captured in D. A. Pennebaker's film *Dont Look Back* as they came out of theatres, recoiling from the sight and sound of their erstwhile hobo hero Bob Dylan accompanied by an electric band. Many were shocked and outraged. Here, it seemed, was Bob Dylan revealed in his true diabolical colours. The embarrassment on their faces betrayed the way they felt about the way they had been betrayed. They had come to admire a folk artist but had been caught at the feet of a rock star. Arguably the biggest rock star of all.

1961 PLAYLIST

Dion, 'The Wanderer'
The Beach Boys, 'Surfin''
The Miracles, 'Shop Around'
Ben E. King, 'Stand By Me'
Elvis Presley, 'His Latest Flame'
Gary U.S. Bonds, 'Quarter To Three'
Dave Van Ronk, *Dave Van Ronk Sings*
Joan Baez, *Vol. 2*
Ray Charles, *The Genius Sings The Blues*
Bill Evans Trio, *Sunday At The Village Vanguard*

28 SEPTEMBER 1962
SALTNEY STREET, LIVERPOOL

The man who fit in

The city of Liverpool jealously guards its reputation for toughness. Richard Starkey came from one of its tougher districts. The Dingle was a part of town better known to debt collectors and school attendance officers than respectable folk. Even by the standards of the area the Starkey family were poor. The boy's parents broke up when he was just three years old. The strongest influence on his upbringing was his grandmother, a woman of nineteenth-century superstitions. One was the belief that any child unfortunate enough to be born left-handed must be trained out of the habit. She set herself the job of making sure young Richard wrote right-handed. He subsequently played a right-handed drum kit with the inclinations of a left-hander. It's Ringo's grandmother we have to thank for the characteristic lacunae that made so many of the Beatles' drum parts impossible for other drummers to play.

In 1947, around the time of his seventh birthday, Richie

contracted peritonitis. He spent months in the hospital. On three occasions his mother was told he wouldn't last the night. When he was finally off the critical list he entered a long period of convalescence during which he was instructed to stay still and do nothing. By the time he was ready to go back to school he'd dropped far behind the rest of the class. If it hadn't been for the English lessons provided by the daughter of a neighbour the boy would have been functionally illiterate. Richie left school at fifteen. The best his teacher could say of him was he was 'honest, cheerful and willing and quite capable of making a satisfactory employee'.

The teenage Richie Starkey was keen on music. At Christmas 1956, when he was sixteen years old, his stepfather kindly got him a drum kit. This was a second-hand pre-war dance band set-up which Harry Graves had sourced a couple of hundred miles away in Essex, manhandled on to the London Underground and then transported to Liverpool by train. The educational system may have dismissed Richie but he still had a determination to make things happen in his life. He also had surprisingly big dreams. When in 1958 Johnnie Ray, the American star known as the Nabob of Sob, appeared in Liverpool, Richie Starkey, by then playing drums in the Eddie Clayton Skiffle Group, saw Ray at the upstairs window of Liverpool's best hotel, signing autographs and allowing them to flutter down to the fans below. Richie swore that one day it would be him up there.

Richie had drive. When his fiancée gave him the choice of her or the drums it was clear what answer she was going to get. He did a three-month residency at Butlin's holiday camp which earned him a Musicians' Union card. He changed his name to Ringo Starr in honour of the jewellery he wore and the role played by John Wayne in the movie *Stagecoach*. Ringo was always slightly ahead of most of his contemporaries. He wanted to travel and see the world. Even as late as 1961, when he was playing in Rory Storm and the Hurricanes and was widely regarded as Liverpool's best drummer, he wrote to the Chamber of Commerce in Houston, Texas enquiring about jobs because he was interested in emigrating. Ringo was not one to let the grass grow.

He knew the Liverpool band who called themselves the Beatles. They were younger than him, in John Lennon's case by a few months, in George Harrison's by a few years. These age differences remained significant even decades later. The Beatles had proper management in Brian Epstein, the son of a wealthy Liverpool Jewish family. They had improved and sharpened their act via long residencies in Hamburg, and they drew large crowds of mainly shop girls to their lunchtime shows at the Cavern; most importantly, they were going to go to London to make a real record for EMI. Nobody anybody knew had ever done that.

Ringo had played with the Beatles on a few occasions when their usual drummer Pete Best had not been available. Best had been in the group for two years. He was recruited because drummers were hard to find, he was good-looking, and he lived in a house big enough for them to play in. But he was a weak player, and he never fitted in with the Beatles as a social group. He spoke so rarely his reticence could almost be construed as aggression. Bands, or groups as they were commonly described in 1962, require above all things commitment. You had to be all-in. By mid-1962, partly at the prompting of EMI producer George Martin, Best was on his way out, even though he was the only one unaware of this fact.

When the band had done their test recording with EMI earlier in 1962, Martin had made it clear to John, Paul and

George that when they returned to make a proper record he would have a substitute drummer standing by. The Beatles were as hopeless as any other group when it came to managing a tricky people situation, but they were reconciled to the fact that Best had to go. They knew that if they did get rid of him there was only one drummer they could replace him with. George made the first approach to Ringo, who agreed to join, provided they got on with firing Best. The Beatles didn't do this themselves. No matter how closely their lives and Best's had been intertwined they were squeamish when it came to unpleasantness so it was left to Epstein, who was mild-mannered but accustomed to dealing with staff, to dispense with Best's services in a fashion standard in the world of business but utterly unknown in the rub-along world of rock.

Epstein invited Best to his offices. He sat him down. He asked him how he thought it was going. Pete said he thought it was going fine. Brian said, that's a shame because we've decided to fire you from the group. Pete asked why. Epstein replied, with a baldness that does him credit, 'because you aren't good enough'. He then offered him alternative employment in one of his other bands where standards presumably weren't quite so high.

While Epstein dealt with the inevitable fall-out of this decision the band gleefully got on with bringing Ringo in. John rang him at Butlin's in Skegness, where he was on a residency. He began with the important stuff. He told Ringo his teddy boy sideburns would have to go. He didn't resist. When Ringo got home he shaved them off and stood in front of the mirror to get an idea how he would look with his hair flattened on his head and brought forward.

In the previous decade male hair had been overwhelmingly

swept back. To achieve the necessary sleekness, hair cream and regular use of a comb were required. The new, more boyish style which the Beatles had copied from Parisian modernists rejected hair cream, the swept-back look and its attendant narcissism. Still, the new hair, as ever, was a statement every bit as profound as any of the music they were making. Untreated and combed forward, it instantly made them appear modern, boyish, classless, unspoilt, possibly even clever. It said Liverpool, not London. It said the sixties, not the fifties. It said cheerfulness, not slickness. Ringo had come from the teddy boy culture but nonetheless accepted they had a look, a look which he was expected to fit in with. He went along with it without complaint. By the time he arrived in the group they had unwritten rules. The other three had all come along before those rules were established. In submitting to the rules without complaint Ringo was in a sense not the last Beatle. He was the first one.

The Beatles could never have gone on to success had Best remained their drummer. Brian Epstein later described the other three's decision to install Ringo as 'a quite brilliant move'. George later said that he was the one who was responsible for Ringo joining because 'every time he played with us the band really swung'. In entertainment, people are apt to confuse the appearance of virtuosity with musical effectiveness. The layman's view of a great drummer is much like the layman's view of a great actor. That is, a person showily accomplishing a thing that appears difficult to accomplish. People think a good drummer is somebody who for a start does a great deal of drumming. What Ringo brought to the Beatles could not be seen but it could definitely be felt. If you go back and compare and contrast the recordings made before Best's departure with those made after Ringo's installation you hear the difference between somebody tim-idly trying to keep up and somebody wholeheartedly leading the way. In years to come there would be many pub conver-sations about whether Ringo was even the best drummer in the Beatles thanks to a barb misattributed to John. Was he the best drummer in the world? It didn't matter. Was he the best drummer in the Beatles? That didn't matter either. Was he the perfect drummer for the Beatles? That did matter. And he was.

In September 1962 not everything was perfectly poised for lift-off. Ringo had joined a group that clearly had many of the things the other Liverpool groups wished they had. An agree-ment to make an actual record with a proper record company for one, the patronage of Brian Epstein for another, a large following in the north-west for a third. But the record com-pany was far from convinced, and it wasn't clear whether their first single would have to be Mitch Murray's egregious 'How Do You Do It' or their own insipid Bruce Channel knock-off 'Love Me Do'. And the further they ventured from their Liverpool home the more likely people were to point out that they had voluntarily saddled themselves with one of the worst names any group ever came up with. Furthermore, people in the music industry didn't have a way to process a group all of whose members played and sang. This was a new hybrid. They gave the impression that they were making life diffi-cult for themselves. The fact that they managed to transcend these difficulties was the first hint of the melting power of their charm. This charm was magically derived from their qualities as a unit.

George Martin at Parlophone wasn't convinced about their songs or the way they did them. But he knew there was something about them as a group of people, both socially and musically, which had a winning way. Together they became something far greater than the sum of their individual parts. Musically they became a four-headed organism with a God-given talent for the generation of joy. This performance continued even when they put their instruments down. At press conferences they became a controversy-deflecting cross-talk act. When you watched them play on the television their sheer togetherness could be almost moving. In photographs they were the gang of your dreams. They were the friends you wanted to grow up to have. In the fifties the Crickets had established the prototype for a group. In September 1962 the Beatles, now with Ringo, perfected that prototype. One stand-offish member like Pete Best would have broken the spell entirely. All great groups are a picture every bit as much as they are a song. Once Ringo was there, the picture was complete.

That September Ringo played some shows with his new group and made a few records but his most important day's work was on the 28th. Brian Epstein was a successful record retailer. He had tried to become an actor, which had given him some understanding of the requirements of publicity. To that end he'd hired a local photographic firm in Liverpool to take pictures of the group to mark the release of their first single 'Love Me Do' in October. A studio session had to be junked when they refused to take the task seriously. Epstein wanted a picture that positioned them as being from Liverpool. After all, Liverpool was their gimmick. Hence for the follow-up session they were taken to a number of locations in the old industrial heart of the city. And here, against the background of soot-weathered warehouse buildings from the nineteenth century, in such a place as you would never have found Cliff Richard and the Shadows or the Everly Brothers or in fact anybody involved in the business of light entertainment, the four of them placed their Chelsea boots on the brick and shale of a wasteground and just looked at the camera, neither smiling nor frowning. They were all wearing suits, shirts and ties which had the effect of making them look the same. John and George had smart short coats over the top which had the effect of making them look different. Ringo had a cigarette between his fingers. If they looked like anything it was a bunch of northern playwrights assembled for a shoot for a newspaper.

The background of the picture says not only 'this is who we are' but also 'this is where we come from'. The background wasn't the cyclorama dreamscape of the standard Hollywood publicity pic, designed to suggest a nowhere-in-particular neverland. Here you were being invited to buy the context as much as the content. It was an image, all the more powerful because it didn't seem to be an image. And Ringo, with side-parting still hanging on from the recent makeover, grey streak in the hair behind his ear and his lugubrious bus driver's face, rendered that image complete. This was a case of the instinct of three young men being worth more than all the accumulated wisdom of show business. In replacing Pete Best with Ringo Starr, John, Paul and George had got rid of somebody who looked as if he ought to be a rock star but wasn't. They'd replaced him with somebody who didn't look like a rock star at all but was. In the process they had done something even more important: they had truly become the Beatles.

1 MAY 1963
LONDON

The man who didn't fit in

News travelled faster in the days when there were fewer channels for that news to travel down. Furthermore, that news made more impact when it landed. For young fans of specialist musical genres in the UK in 1963 the advantage of only having two channels of TV and three of radio was that if the blues, or indeed anything slightly out of the ordinary, were broadcast, the likelihood was you would catch it. Having done so, it was equally likely you would meet other people who had also caught it.

Mick Jagger came to meet up with Keith Richards in just such a way. The two had been to primary school together in Dartford, Kent when they were seven years old. But after primary school their paths had diverged. Michael Philip, being academically able and the son of a middle-class family, had gone to Dartford Grammar School, which turned out Dartford's next generation of doctors and bank managers.

Keith, not being academically inclined and coming from a family with low expectations, had gone to the Dartford Technical High School, which turned out the people who fixed the cars of the doctors and bank managers. It would have been perfectly possible for them never to have met again had it not been for the blues.

On 17 October 1961 they were both waiting for a train at Dartford station, but heading for different places and different futures. Mick was going to the London School of Economics, which offered the kind of university education available at the time to less than 4 per cent of the population. Keith was headed to Sidcup Art College, which promised at best a future designing letterheads for small businesses. But what united them was stronger than what divided them. Mick was carrying two albums under his arm. One was Chuck Berry's *Rockin' At The Hops*; the other was *The Best Of Muddy Waters*. He had bought both by sending off to Chess Records in Chicago. This was a process that involved writing letters, buying postal orders and then waiting for a long time and praying that the record wouldn't get broken in transit. Keith was lugging his hollow-bodied Epiphone guitar. The carrying of such items in a public place in the year 1961 was like a cry for help. They weren't going anywhere in particular. They were probably carrying these items to show that they had them. The two struck up a conversation. It was inconceivable they wouldn't.

This was in the days when any records, but particularly imported American blues records, were such objects of desire that enthusiasts would often embark on inconvenient cross-town trips involving bus changes in order to visit the house of somebody rumoured to have a copy of some particular gem; once there they would play both sides again and again, staring hypnotized at the spinning labels until both sight and sound had been seared into the memory. If you wanted to go beyond listening and actually play this music, as Keith and Mick did, you had to listen even harder until you could make a guess at what the guitarist had been playing at the original session. If you lived within reach of London it was of course more useful to watch the fingers of actual musicians, even if they were a few years older than you and condescending about which varieties of music they were prepared to play and which they weren't.

In and around London at that time a few score white Englishmen from widely differing backgrounds – from the lower ranks of the services to the fringes of the aristocracy, from the ivy-clad walls of Oxbridge to the municipal art colleges, from working-class panel beaters to worldly Jewish émigrés – were drawn to the blues because it afforded them a chance to sink their personal histories and lose their give-away accents in its rich fantasy world of hellhounds, bootleg whisky and Chicago-bound trains; having done so, they then went on to snipe at other English musicians for real or imagined offences against musical orthodoxy and signs of insufficient rootsiness. It would have been funny had it not been so earnest. When Keith and Mick first met Brian Jones, blond-haired father of three and only twenty years old, and he announced that he was performing under the name Elmo Lewis, they didn't laugh or point out that he really couldn't be called Elmo Lewis because he came from Cheltenham. They just nodded as if they understood.

There was no such pretence about Ian Stewart. Stewart was in many senses the key individual in the group of people gathering at the time around Mick Jagger and Keith Richards. He didn't have much interest in the mythology of the music;

he dealt with the music itself. This had led him to meet Brian Jones, and through him Jagger and Richards. In that early summer of 1962, Stewart was twenty-three. He was a man of the world. He had a real job, one that gave him access to an actual telephone during working hours. He was practical. He was the one who suggested that this loose affiliation of boys should at least get serious enough to stop rehearsing in their front rooms and cough up the fifteen shillings it cost to hire the upstairs room at the Bricklayers Arms in Broadwick Street, Soho. When Keith arrived for that first rehearsal he heard the sound of boogie woogie being coaxed from the piano upstairs. Stewart, known to all as 'Stu', was the man doing the coaxing. He was wearing his customary leather cycling shorts and keeping one eye out for his bike which was attached to a lamp post across the street. 'From the moment I walked in, went upstairs and heard him playing Albert Ammons, I always felt "this is Stu's band",' Keith recalled years later.

Stu was Scottish, which was not the only thing about him that marked him out from the rest. He was five years older than Mick and Keith and held down a proper job with ICI, which meant he spent every day undercover in the real world, a place the rest of the group knew little about. There was no possibility of Keith getting a job at the time because his hair was too long. Mick was a student and therefore didn't have to get a job. Stu's job involved wearing a collar and tie. His hair was swept back in the conventional fifties style. Stu was a doer, not a fantasist. He bought a van, which made him instantly indispensable as the band, now known as the Rollin' Stones, began to pick up work. He was sharp as well. Stu was the one to spot that the trad jazz bands who dominated the circuit could be easily upstaged by a band serving up fifteen minutes of electric blues while they took a break to refill their pipes and recharge their glasses. Ian was the one who told them they had to get Charlie Watts in to play the drums. In fact in many ways Ian Stewart was the man who formed the Rollin' Stones.

The winter of 1962/63 was when 'the whole attitude in London changed', according to Keith Richards. He, Jagger and Jones were living at the time in a state of almost medieval squalor at 102 Edith Grove, Chelsea. (Fifty years later, when this was one of the most expensive districts in the world, a replica of the verminous kitchen at Edith Grove was constructed at great expense for a smart exhibition marking the anniversary of its former occupants.) Intuiting that neither of them was quite strong enough to perform the standard soloist's role, Keith and Brian were groping their way towards a sound that involved the meshing of two or more guitars. This, together with the laconic drum sound of Charlie Watts, is what provided the texture of the Rollin' Stones' sound. It was this texture, which didn't actually sound much like the records that inspired it, that went on to conquer the world. This was also the winter of the Beatles' 'Please Please Me' going to number one, of the distant keening sound of Beatlemania coming out of the north, of a new decade beginning to walk upright, of a feeling of new possibilities. The Beatles turned up to see the Stones and promised them a song, a leg-up not even the most ardent purist could refuse. When winter began in 1962 the Rollin' Stones were a blues band. By the spring of 1963 they had their sights on being the toppermost of the poppermost.

The three men at the front of the group were excited by this. Two of the men in the back line could certainly see the appeal. Stu could not. Maybe there was no future for him in the group.

Stewart's hash was finally settled by a new kind of manager, somebody who saw a bigger picture for the group and ensured that they would live on while the hundreds of rhythm and blues groups who came in their wake would be forgotten. Again it was the lack of options that led young Andrew Loog Oldham, who was only nineteen at the time, to become the Rolling Stones' first manager. He was a teenage PR man who had been tipped off that this group were starting to attract fans to their residencies at the Station Hotel, Richmond. He was spending Sunday with his mother in Hampstead. This was in the days when London shut down on Sunday and there was nothing on TV. He worked out he could take the train from Hampstead Heath directly to Richmond station, where the Rolling Stones played their Sunday afternoon show. He did so and walked straight into a scene of great enthusiasm, much of it female. Oldham smelled oestrogen in the air. The Stones played R&B in such a way that you would dance to it, which was not something you could say about the competition. The Stones were sexual. Oldham was excited by the possibilities inherent in this. Within days he had taken them on as management clients, in partnership with Eric Easton because he was too young to sign a legally binding document, and then got them a recording contract with Decca, who were so determined to atone for having passed on the Beatles they couldn't wait to snap them up.

As soon as this had been accomplished, on 1 May 1963 Oldham and Easton got Mick and Keith in a room and told them that henceforth they would be the Rolling Stones and not the Rollin' Stones, that Mick and Keith would be the heart of the group, and that Ian Stewart could continue to drive the van (the van he had bought and paid for) and play on sessions; indeed he could take the same stage with them, just as long as he remained behind the curtain. Henceforth he would no longer be in the group. Oldham's reasons were similarly three-fold. Apart from the practical difficulties of lugging what was effectively an item of furniture around on the road, the presence of an upright piano such as many middle-class families still had in their living rooms in those days would be at odds with his preferred image of the Stones as a nimble, naughty guitar band; by having five members the band was already asking a lot of people's capacity for recall; and finally, most crushingly, most tellingly and most indicative of why Andrew Loog Oldham is remembered as a great band manager, he told them that Ian Stewart spoiled the look of the group.

The word Oldham used was 'ugly'.

Oldham was right. Stu didn't fit the picture. In fact he looked as if he came from an earlier decade. As Oldham said, Stu had a chin like the American actor William Bendix, who was a figure from an even earlier decade. In the very few early publicity pictures which include him Ian Stewart looks embarrassed at the whole business of having his picture taken. Although the Rolling Stones were not conventionally handsome, and within a year would be attracting headlines like 'Is this the ugliest group in Britain?', they had a look. It was a look that the presence of Ian Stewart simply ruined. As Keith said, 'I'm sure much of Ian's character was influenced by his looks, and people's reactions to them, from when he was a kid.'

Mick and Keith didn't fight it. Nor, to his credit, did Stu. As Keith recalled, he said, '"I'm here as long as I can still play piano and we'll hang together in the band and I'll not be in the pictures." That takes a big heart, but Stu had one of the largest hearts around.' He would continue to be the key person in their entourage and their right-hand man for the next twenty years. He died in a doctor's waiting room in 1985. Most nights between 1962 and then he would call them to the stage of some enormous arena with the words 'come on, my little shower of shit'. Nobody else could begin to talk to them the way Stu did. He was the last person to address them as if they were simple human beings and not rock gods. He could do that because he might not have been paid for it, he might not have been seen doing it, he might not have had his name on the records, but spiritually he was still in the band. Over the years they reasoned his departure away. 'I don't think Ian could imagine being a pop star,' said Mick, which was true. Stu was also only interested in playing the kind of music that didn't get above number forty-five in the charts. And his face literally didn't fit. That was as good a reason as any for putting him out of the group. The best decision the Beatles took was to bring Ringo Starr in. The best decision the Stones took was to chuck Ian Stewart out.

The standard reaction to Oldham's firing of Stewart was to wonder how he could possibly say that this man was too ugly to be in a group that seemed to be chock-full of uglies: there was Mick with his cavernous mouth, Keith with his crooked teeth, Brian with his sinister smile and Bill Wyman looking as though Cruikshank had knocked him up from a set of instructions provided by Dickens. Andrew Oldham gave up a job doing PR for the Beatles to manage the Rolling Stones; therefore he knew something. He hadn't worked with the Beatles long but it had been long enough to see how the magic within a group operated. He intuited that the magic wasn't merely musical, it was connected with how they looked at each other and beyond that to how they looked out at the world. Groups who visibly related to each other when they played were far more absorbing to look at than those who didn't. When they looked out at the world and the world looked back with the question 'Just who the hell do you think you are?' implicit in its gaze, a group, a proper group that is, needed to be able to return that gaze with interest. They needed to be able to return that gaze with a look that said, Yes, even I, former Aircraftsman Bill Perks from Penge, secretly twenty-seven years old and already married, who only got into this group because I had an amplifier, was actually raised by wolves for this purpose, and it is my very special destiny to be a rock star and a member of this group and no other.

Ian Stewart could never have done that. Ian could never have looked that way. Ian could never have portrayed what Oldham's plan called for rock stars to portray, which was a bigger version of themselves. He was just too self-effacing for that. Stu went along with them for the ride and had a view of the madness that nobody else could match. He booked them into hotels near championship golf courses so that he could follow his other passion while they were still sleeping in. He wasn't temperamentally suited to being a rock star. He was impervious to the lust for glory that drives rock stars on. He could never have been a rock star for the same simple reason that the rest of us aren't rock stars. Because we can imagine not being one.

23 DECEMBER 1964
LOS ANGELES AIRPORT

The rock star as tragic genius

I t was just two days before Christmas. Like everybody else engaged in the music business in that year of the great pop explosion the Beach Boys were nearing the end of a hectic twelve months. In that one calendar year they had recorded and released three studio albums and one in-concert recording. This rate of productivity suggested that nobody was really looking after their long-term interests. There was not a lot of reason to think these young men had any long-term interests. The group had been christened in a hurry to take advantage of the fad for surfing. Impelled by the feeling that their moment of pop success might prove to be no more than that, the Beach Boys had also toured unceasingly, hoovering up cash while they could. In 1964 they had visited Australia, New Zealand, the UK, Germany, Italy, Sweden and France, and now they were starting a two-week tour of the West that would take them into the New Year.

1964 was the year pop went wild. It was the year of the

Beatles on *The Ed Sullivan Show*, the year of *Shindig!* and *Ready Steady Go!* It was the year Motown became the sound of Young America, the year the Rolling Stones first toured the United States. Pop music seemed to be gathering itself for a moment such as it had never had before and might never have again. Songwriting, singing and production talent were converging from all points of the compass and from all over the world and aiming at the US singles charts, which were the only game in town. The Beach Boys only had to look back to their appearance on the *T.A.M.I. Show* in October to see just how competitive a year it had been. There they had lined up alongside James Brown, Marvin Gaye, Smokey Robinson, the Rolling Stones, the Supremes and Chuck Berry, who had only recently been released from prison. In their striped Pendleton shirts, with their gleaming teeth and just-so hair, they couldn't help looking and sounding tame and suburban, because that's what they were.

It was the Beach Boys' tragic misfortune to come along at the same time as the Beatles, who matched their invention, outdid them in charisma and had the further novelty value of being English. Whereas the Beach Boys' albums looked as though they were put together by the record company, the Beatles' seemed to be the work of the band. Whereas theirs had all their singles on them, the Beatles didn't feel compelled to put their hits on their albums, which was a sign of how easy they seemed to find it to keep producing smash singles like 1964's 'A Hard Day's Night' and 'I Feel Fine'. And it didn't help that the accident of the alphabet meant their being placed next to each other in record shops.

The principals of these hit-making groups of the sixties were under a new kind of pressure. Suddenly they were expected to compose the songs as well as perform them.

Elvis had always been able to rely on a stable of back-room boys. The raw materials of his hits came from songwriting factories. Somebody else did the sweating for him. Elvis could relax and assume that the best available tunes would be on his music stand when he turned up in the studio. The same didn't apply to the Beatles, the Rolling Stones, the Kinks and the Beach Boys. They had to face the new reality: good original material, songs catchy enough for the mass audience to sing along to and intriguing enough to win the tight-lipped respect of their fellow pros, ideally embedded in records that didn't sound like the records they had made only a few months earlier, records preferably embellished with some noteworthy tweak at the recording stage, records that said something that pop records hadn't said before – this was what was expected if you wanted to compete. In the great game of pop, which was suddenly afoot, brilliant 45s were the cost of entry. They were no more than table stakes.

Although other members of the Beach Boys would pitch in with words, particularly when it came to the songs about surfing and hot rodding that had made their name over the past three years, the one who had to do the heavy lifting where the songwriting was concerned was twenty-two-year-old Brian, bassist and oldest of the Wilson brothers. Brian was beginning to find this responsibility a burden. He was also beginning to find the endless live shows, when they would do their best to present their songs in front of crowds of girls who couldn't hear for their own screams, an expense of spirit he could no longer afford. Brian was the first of his generation to notice the more depressing features of this tough new school: the expectations of fans, the unquenchable hunger of radio and the business, the unanswerable questions from people jabbing microphones at you, the mortification of hearing the latest single by one of your peers and fearing it might be better than yours, the spats and squabbles within the band that you always had to referee, the constant, nauseating travel, the bad food and, hovering over it all, the unrelenting, soul-sapping, prematurely ageing effect of the fatigue.

When Brian Wilson arrived at Los Angeles airport that late December morning he wasn't sure he could go through with the trip. He rang home from the airport, not to speak to the wife he'd married only weeks before, but to his mother Audree. She tried to stiffen his resolve and told him he'd be letting his brothers down if he didn't go. Reluctantly he got on the plane, which was taking them to a show in Houston. As it gathered speed down the runway, lifted off and began to climb, all Brian's standard flight anxieties were joined by the concerns he'd been feeling about where the band was going, where the next hit was coming from, and whether he could possibly satisfy the expectations he appeared to have awoken when he'd innocently started making music in the garage of the family home a few years earlier. Once the brittle shell of Brian's confidence had been pierced, in flooded the dark waters of uncertainty, and right there in that aeroplane, still some way from its cruising altitude, his systems simply shut down. He blacked out. He was to remember very little of the events of the day. What his fellow Beach Boys saw was their mild-mannered older brother, the man who had given the world such blithesome dreams of escape as 'I Get Around', 'Surfin' USA' and 'Be True To Your School', suddenly on his knees in the aisle of the plane. Crying like a baby.

The Beach Boys had always been a drama. They came from Hawthorne, California, a lower-middle-class suburb of south Los Angeles, and had been formed around the three Wilson brothers and their cousin Mike Love. In the Beach Boys the tensions and jealousies that simmer away in every band were superimposed on a family unit with quite enough tensions of its own. They were whipped into shape as a family band by the Wilsons' martinet father Murry. Dad had the handicap of knowing just enough about music and its attendant business to wish to compete with them as well as help them. He was happy when it was the familial vocal blend capturing people's attention; once that attention turned to his eldest son's songwriting talent he was plain jealous. He was given to corporal punishment, which was not particularly unusual for a father of boys in the 1950s.

As the brothers became less dependent on Murry and identified more with their sophisticated friends in the Hollywood music business, he became resentful of the way they were having their heads turned by the bright lights. When the success of his sons brought them what appeared to him to be easy money in unimaginable amounts he could never stop himself pointing out that when his parents had come out to California from Kansas they'd been so poor that they'd lived on the beach. Those were real beach boys. The Wilson boys ended up sniggering about their own father behind his back and sometimes arguing openly with him in front of music business professionals. In 1963 they finally and painfully relieved him of his duties as their manager. He still retained the rights to their catalogue of songs. He sold them for a pittance at the end of the decade, ostensibly believing that there would be no place in the future for a bunch of songs about sun, surf and teenage escape.

Brian, the eldest, was tall and awkward and prone to putting on weight. Carl was the baby brother. The lead singer, Mike Love, introduced a number of complications. He was older, taller, thin-skinned and deeply immodest. He was also a cousin and felt that he was not dealt with fairly because Murry was jealous of his father's relative wealth. Love had married the first girl he impregnated but in 1962 was describing himself as single in fan magazine interviews just as she was giving birth to his daughter. The following year they were divorced as quietly as they had married. The middle Wilson, Dennis, was handsome, horny and a terrible judge of character. Dennis lived the life the band sang about. He was the one who surfed. He was the one who got around. Carl and Brian never went near the water. Dennis went near everything. It was Dennis who, in picking up a couple of nubile hippy hitchhikers, as was his wont, was to bring his family into uncomfortable proximity with that infamous family headed by Charles Manson.

The young women who married the young stars of the pop boom in the early sixties were quickly brought face to face with the over-arching truth of the music business. It was this. Young, virile men who sing and play in groups are offered lots of no-strings sex and in the majority of cases these are offers they take advantage of. It would be foolish to believe otherwise, no matter how much the songwriters' lyrics harp on the subject of fidelity. Any observer of the human race can see that the natural inclination of the young adult male in the wild is towards promiscuity. The rock world of the early sixties provided a whole new arena for demonstrating this truth. The opportunities presenting themselves to even the humblest bass guitarist or drummer were greater in number than for any earlier generation of entertainers. In this new world fans might actually get to meet their heroes, contraception was becoming more available, and the men themselves were often far from home and lonely as well as horny. Unconsecrated sex was bound to happen. Within the Beach

Boys the most energetic in this regard were Dennis and Mike, but they were by no means alone. Just three weeks before he got on that plane to Houston, Brian Wilson had married Marilyn Rovell. He was twenty-two, she was seventeen. They had already been seeing each other for two years when they wed. The marriage didn't seem to have brought Brian peace of mind. Already he imagined that he'd seen Marilyn and Mike exchanging meaningful looks.

That night in Houston, having got through the show as if in a dream, Brian sat and looked at the wall of his hotel room and promised himself this was the last night he was going to spend away on the road. Tomorrow he would go home to Los Angeles. Audree met Brian at the airport. He was like a kid who had come home early from camp. Session musician Glen Campbell, who had already played on some Beach Boys hits, flew out to Houston to deputize for Brian for the remainder of the tour. It was resolved that henceforth Brian wouldn't tour. He wasn't cut out for the gilded vagabond life. The rest of them were prepared to blunder on from hit to hit, from tour to tour, from dumb photo opportunity to embarrassing TV appearance, without giving a thought to the inevitable truth that the hand of fate that had plucked them from obscurity two years before would be likely to drop them back into the same position just as abruptly. Brian was different. Brian was thoughtful. Brian was the one who wondered where it could all be going. Brian was the one who realized it couldn't go on for ever, and Brian was the one who most dreaded it ending. Brian was the first of his generation of songwriters to real-ize that success inevitably meant raising expectations that at some time had to be dashed. He suffered the singular agony of the man at the top. There is nowhere to go but down.

Having resigned from touring, he and his teenage bride

took a house in Beverly Hills and he settled down to write and produce songs for the Beach Boys and others, without exposing himself to the psychic buffeting of life on the road. The year that followed Brian's incident on the plane saw a flowering of his talent. *The Beach Boys Today!*, which came out in 1965, is their best album. The second side, made up of ballads perfectly suited to the angora mood of young marrieds like the Wilsons, has a sustained feeling that even the Beatles didn't dare try, a mood sadly shattered by the inclusion at the end of a track of studio chat called 'Bull Session With The "Big Daddy"'. This is the sort of thing the Beatles would have been wise enough to keep for the Christmas flexidisc they mailed out to their fans. Throughout their career the Beach Boys could always be relied upon to let themselves down.

The fact that Brian was at home while the band were on the road meant he was free to make more use of session musicians, moving towards a situation where the band would be used as featured vocalists on records that had been effectively made before they got there. By the end of 1965 this approach had resulted in 'Good Vibrations', which was certainly his finest hour, and also a dead end masquerading as a fresh start. Pop songs couldn't usefully get much more complicated than 'Good Vibrations', which is something it took Brian a long time to realize.

Remaining at home may have freed him from the stress of touring but it brought him face to face with the pressure of the blank page. It was this that eventually led him to install a huge sandbox in his house so that he would be able to write songs evoking the carefree beach life he had once written about with such success. It also led to him spending more time in bad company. He was introduced to cannabis, which he felt unlocked his flow. He took to it as enthusiastically as food, which had always been a problem for him; in the marital home he would command his wife to magic up huge roast meals. He and his new stoner friends would sit in high-backed chairs, gorging themselves on vast bales of cannabis like noblemen back from the chase. Once he felt he'd come up with the tune for 'California Girls' after taking LSD, he convinced himself that he needed drugs in order to translate the music of the spheres into hit singles. Within a year his brain was fried and his productivity at an end. Marilyn Rovell, another child bride turned mother figure, later looked back on those years when they stayed in that house and played the piano all day. 'For Brian, sitting down at the piano and writing music is just as easy as walking. That was the easy part. Life was hard for Brian.'

Despite his success he was haunted by the fact that the Beatles seemed to do things easily that were a struggle for the Beach Boys, and obsessed with the feeling that his group would always be held back by their image. He hired the Beatles' PR man, Derek Taylor. The first thing Taylor did was tout him to the press as 'a genius'. This was the first time anyone had felt moved to make this kind of claim about a composer of pop songs. This placed even more pressure on poor Brian's shoulders. It was hard enough to match Phil Spector. Now was he expected to be Beethoven as well? The word 'genius' didn't seem the right word for a man in a Pendleton shirt grinning through 'Barbara Ann' in front of a phalanx of fruggers on TV's *Shindig!* But for an increasingly unhappy, overweight, insecure, unshaven, drug-addled rock star remaining indoors in front of his piano there seemed no better word.

1964 PLAYLIST

The Beatles, 'I Want To Hold Your Hand'
The Beatles, 'A Hard Day's Night'
The Beatles, 'I Feel Fine'
The Animals, 'House Of The Rising Sun'
The Kinks, 'All Day And All Of The Night'
The Beach Boys, 'I Get Around'
The Rolling Stones, 'It's All Over Now'
Bob Dylan, 'The Times They Are A-Changin''
Roy Orbison, 'Oh, Pretty Woman'
Them, 'Baby Please Don't Go'

the four of them, whose average age was twenty, could endure their punishing schedule was by taking drugs, the kind of drugs that in an earlier era had been provided to troops going into combat in the early hours. These amphetamines had the inevitable effect of further agitating the already quarrelsome relationships between the members of the band. The band had been formed initially by the dogged Daltrey, who had recruited the mercurial Townshend, the inscrutable Entwistle and the indescribable Moon. Unlike the Beatles, whose names were always listed in chronological order to reflect their time of joining, the hierarchy of the Who did not remain the same. The big-nosed guitarist turned out to be an enormously productive songwriter and the drummer was not only the member of the act with the most teen appeal and the biggest show-off but also the musician whose peculiar qualities led to the Who playing in a way no band had ever played before. The Who made the sound of things boiling over.

This was a musical reflection of the relationships within the band. The arguments tended to start with the same members. Townshend and Moon liked to provoke a reaction. The guitarist was made that way. He once dangled a £5 note in front of an old friend not as well off as he was. When the friend declined to take it Townshend tore it into pieces in front of him. The drummer had a similarly unpleasant streak. Back in Wembley, where Keith Moon grew up, there were rumours that he'd been treated in the local mental hospital for having physically attacked his mother while a child. They said he'd been bought the drums as a way to channel his aggression and save the wear and tear on his parents. John Entwistle was thick-skinned and apparently imperturbable. Exposed at the front of the stage without a machine of his own to hide behind, Roger Daltrey suffered the lead singer's anxiety that the others might be smirking behind his back. In the case of Moon, these worries were well-founded.

That particular night in Denmark there had been crowd trouble. A bottle was thrown at the singer of one of the support acts. The Who had only been on stage for a few minutes when the audience got up from their metal chairs, overwhelmed the inadequate security and invaded the stage. When the band withdrew and the show was halted the audience picked up their chairs and flung them at the stage. Fire hoses were turned on the crowd. By the time the audience had retreated, eye-witnesses said the hall looked as if it had been trampled by wild elephants. The trouble spread into the streets around the venue where irate longhairs smashed shop windows and pitched bicycles into fountains.

Penned in their dressing room, the band dealt with adversity in their customary way. By taking it out on each other. Daltrey, the only member of the group who didn't take speed, blamed their misfortune on their over-indulgence in pills. What he really meant was the pills made the rest of the band unbearable. To drive home the point he took Moon's substantial supply and tipped it down the lavatory. Temporarily emboldened by amphetamine sulphate and deprived of the drums on which he took out most of his frustrations, Moon launched himself at Daltrey. This was ill-advised. Neither was a big man, but whereas the drummer generally relied on inciting others to follow through on things he started, the singer could take care of himself. He was the only one of the first wave of British rock stars to cultivate a reputation for being hard, and he had the frame to back up that reputation. He punched Moon. It was only the intervention of security men that prevented the drummer from sustaining further damage and being hospitalized.

In the Who's dressing room that night something snapped, and there didn't seem to be any way of mending it. Nevertheless, like exemplary professionals the band fulfilled the terms of their contract by playing the second show in the other venue and then returned to Britain. On the way back it was agreed that Daltrey was no longer in the band.

In 1965 the Who weren't the only group having this kind of scrap. A few months earlier the Kinks had had a set-to at the Capitol Cinema in Cardiff. On that evening Dave Davies arrived sporting a black eye he'd sustained in a recent altercation with the drummer Mick Avory. That night Dave and his brother Ray took the stage from one side while the rhythm section came from the other, like negotiators arriving for difficult talks on the Korean border. Following the opening song, the reliably incendiary 'You Really Got Me', Dave Davies walked over to the drummer, spat in his direction, and kicked his drum kit apart. Roused to a fresh level of fury, Avory seized his high-hat cymbal, advanced on the gap-toothed popinjay in the hunting jacket and crowned him with the heavy brassware with sufficient force to make at least one onlooker suspect he might actually have killed him.

In the course of 1965 a sourness seemed to have entered the beat music bloodstream. There was a hint of jadedness in the air which it was possible to detect in some of the year's great singles: in Bob Dylan's 'Like A Rolling Stone', the Beatles' 'Help!', the Kinks' 'Tired Of Waiting For You', Otis Redding's 'Respect', the Animals' 'We Gotta Get Out Of This Place' and the Rolling Stones' 'Get Off Of My Cloud'. The Who's first album, *My Generation*, released at the end of 1965, was a carnival of spite. It was such a furious assertion of the rights of man, and only man, that it makes you wonder how its ideas had occurred to a bunch of boys only just old enough to legally drink. Most of its songs were about shrugging off the attentions of women clearly intent on putting their brand on you. As a matter of fact most of these women were scarcely more than schoolgirls. Daltrey had already been forced to secretly marry his sixteen-year-old girlfriend when she became pregnant. Three months after the wedding his new father-in-law turned up just as the band were about to take the stage, pulled Daltrey outside and punched him. Meanwhile Moon was spending every spare moment down in Bournemouth where he was trying to get his teenage love Kim to come across. The songs on that first album were marbled with misanthropy and misogyny but delivered with such panache that they got away with it. They had unique elements: Daltrey's genius for singing even the most far-fetched lyric as though it had just fizzed across his synapses; Pete Townshend's guitar flourishes and solos that sounded like electrical malfunctions; Entwistle's clambering, baroque bass which was busy enough to serve as the lead instrument; and through it all Keith Moon's drums, which sounded as though they were either on the way to a fire or had just escaped from one. The Who, as everybody realized, were unique. They also appeared to be coming apart.

Roger Daltrey was out of the Who for just two weeks, during which time he slept in the back of the band's van. This was a perfect metaphor for where his life choices had led him. At the age of twenty-one he had been ejected by the two families in his life, the wife and child on one hand and the band on the other. In those two weeks the Who's management gave some serious thought to how they might reshuffle the pack to come up with a better group or groups. They eventually decided this would be impossible so a meeting was called and Daltrey was invited to stay in the band provided he mended his ways.

He had to accept that he wasn't in charge and couldn't expect to tell the other members of the group how to carry on. The rational argument for how the group should continue to function had been roundly defeated. They wouldn't get rid of the troublesome member of the band because they intuited that it was the troublesome member who provided their spark. Daltrey, the stolid, reasonable one, had to swallow his pride and agree. He knew he had no choice. As he was later to say, 'If I lost the band I was dead.' Townshend recognized that they had already created something more powerful than themselves. 'It doesn't matter if you get your own way so long as the band keeps going,' he said.

It says something for the streak of anarchy running through the Who that in the event of a face-off between sobriety and chaos, they chose chaos. Faced with a choice between reorganizing the group so that it ran more smoothly and clinging on by their fingernails to the unsafe vehicle that had brought them this far, they took the latter course. Given a choice between a good lead singer who had put in the hard yards to establish the group and a drummer who seemed to be elevating attention deficit hyperactivity disorder into a branch of the performing arts, they sided with the drummer. Having done this, they released their biggest and most radical record.

In 1965 a hit single quickly brought the band to the attention of a huge general audience. If you appeared on TV shows like *Top of the Pops*, *Thank Your Lucky Stars* and *Ready Steady Go!* in the UK or *Shindig!*, *American Bandstand* and *The Ed Sullivan Show* in the USA – and everybody who got the chance did – you immediately became so famous it was impossible to walk down the street. For beat group musicians who had been rattling round in the back of vans and playing in front of initiates and ace faces, this sudden emergence into a world of fame, acclaim and ready cash was difficult to negotiate. In many cases they had entered the van years as kids from modest, often poor backgrounds and, following a period of profound disorientation and drug use, then been dropped off in a strange old world where they were suddenly expected to behave like young gentlemen about town.

When in October of that year the Beatles, who only three years earlier had been poked and prodded by a London Establishment who couldn't believe they were entirely real, were driven to no less an address than Buckingham Palace to be installed as Members of the Order of the British Empire by Her Majesty the Queen, it suddenly felt as if the hooligans of yesterday were the national heroes of today and were expected to behave as such. Pictorials in magazines like *Fabulous* and *Rave* featured these young princes making cups of tea in posh apartments they clearly saw only rarely. As a breed they were homeless, rootless and restless, waiting only for the next call to get in the back of the van, the van that gave some purpose to their lives.

In 1965 Pete Townshend was installed in a flat in Belgravia, an address no musician with a couple of hits would be able to afford in the twenty-first century. He lived for a time with the Who's manager Kit Lambert. Lambert and his business partner Chris Stamp raised funds from the banks purely on the basis of their business address. The act of being the Who had to be maintained twenty-four hours a day. In interviews Townshend claimed to be living a lavish lifestyle, boasting about cars he didn't own and saying he spent £50 a week on clothes, despite having to borrow a jacket for the photo accompanying the piece. Just for show he had bought a 1936 Packard hearse for £30 and parked it outside his flat. The vehicle soon offended traditional Belgravia residents and was towed away by the authorities; some said it was the Queen Mother who didn't like seeing the hearse because it reminded her of the funeral of her late husband. In a characteristic case of elevating a fit of pique into a matter of principle, Townshend dashed off his anthem 'My Generation' in response, with its stammering vocal and hostage-to-fortune line about hoping to die before getting old. It was to 1965 what Little Richard's 'Tutti Frutti' had been to 1955, an almost hilarious expulsion of youthful energy, this time cloaked in avant-garde seriousness. 'My Generation' became not just a big hit. It was also the defining song of the group and a token of their ongoing commitment to following chaos wherever it might take them. The record climaxed with a furious tantrum from – who else? – their drummer.

The very same things that had made Keith Moon an impossible child made him the perfect rock star. He was hopeless at school and left at the age of fourteen. Moon had such a need to be admired and noticed that it could only be satisfied by being the centre of attention all the time. Not all his school friends remembered his clowning with fondness. Some saw it as a form of bullying. Some felt he was on his way to prison. It was only by becoming a rock star that he could avoid having to grow up. He didn't want to grow up. At the age of seventeen he had already bought his own gold lamé suit because he felt that this was what rock stars did. He had 'I am the greatest' stencilled across his bass drum case. Moon wanted the world on his own terms. Being a rock star gave him the means of doing it. As a civilian he would inevitably have to find a way of maturing, fitting in with other people and curbing his excesses. If he became a rock star he wouldn't have to do any such thing. As 'Moony' he was licensed to do all the things Keith Moon would never be permitted to do.

With Daltrey back on board the Who immediately embarked on a visit to Scotland. They were due to play the Kinema Ballroom in Dunfermline and the city hall in Perth. On the way, Moon asked the new tour manager Richard Cole to stop. Moon disappeared into a shop. He emerged with some fertilizer and a large quantity of sugar. When they arrived at their five-star hotel, the drummer disappeared to his room. In due course Cole's afternoon tea was disturbed by the sound of an explosion from the room next door. He came out into the hall, and through the smoke and dust materialized the distinctive figure of Keith Moon. He appeared to be seared around the edges but elated at heart, his large round eyes blinking delightedly like a cartoon character who has lit the fuse of a fizzing bomb and lived to tell the tale.

This conflagration inevitably meant the group had to move out of their nice hotel and into a manifestly inferior one down the road. That appeared to be the price the Who had to pay for being the Who they had decided to be. Entwistle and Townshend grumbled. Daltrey kept his mouth shut. The die had been cast.

1965 PLAYLIST

The Rolling Stones, '(I Can't Get No) Satisfaction'
The Byrds, 'Mr Tambourine Man'
The Beatles, 'Help!'
The Lovin' Spoonful, 'Do You Believe In Magic'
The Who, 'I Can't Explain'
Bob Dylan, 'Like A Rolling Stone'
The Kinks, 'See My Friends'
Otis Redding, *Otis Blue*
The McCoys, 'Hang On Sloopy'
The Beatles, *Rubber Soul*

1 OCTOBER 1966
REGENT STREET POLYTECHNIC, LONDON

A new sheriff in town

A popular urban myth is that the reason ring-necked parakeets are to be found in the parks of London today is because they were brought by Jimi Hendrix in an effort to repaint the dun city in the colours of paradise. When the real James Marshall Hendrix landed at Heathrow airport in the early morning of Saturday, 24 September he was twenty-three years old. All he possessed was one change of clothes, including a recently purchased Burberry raincoat, and a jar of face cream which he used to combat his acne. Since he didn't have a work permit his guitar was carried into the country by a member of his new management team, a bunch of apparently well-connected Britishers who had promised back in New York to make something happen for his career. This was something nobody in the United

States had managed to do since he'd begun playing professionally eight years earlier.

The key person in the new management team was Chas Chandler. Chas had played bass with the Animals, the Newcastle rhythm and blues group that never graduated from a string of hit singles to the same long-playing El Dorado as the Beatles and the Rolling Stones. The Animals' recordings had been handled by Mickie Most. Their business affairs had been handled by Mike Jeffery. Both were clever men, far too clever to worry too much about whether the members of the band made any money or not. Realizing that a sturdy aldermanic figure like himself had no future as a rock star, Chas was planning to get out of the band in order to find and manage talent. He was going to do this in partnership with the aforementioned Jeffery. Better the devil he knew.

Chas had found his first client, Jimmy Hendrix, playing in New York's Greenwich Village. He had been steered in his direction by Linda Keith, who was a girlfriend of Keith Richards. She knew of Chas's plans and told him this guitarist would be worth seeing. Chas went. He was quite impressed. What clinched it was the fact that in his five-song act, alongside Bob Dylan's 'Like A Rolling Stone' and the Troggs' 'Wild Thing', Hendrix, who at the time was playing as Jimmy James and the Blue Flames, covered a song called 'Hey Joe'. Chandler was fixated on getting somebody to record a hit version of this song, a less than judgemental account of domestic violence, and now here he was faced with this guy who didn't even have to be persuaded. Plus he looked good and played the guitar with his teeth. How could he lose?

Jimmy had come from a chaotic family background in Seattle, Washington, far away from the heartlands of the blues. The first tune he learned to play all the way through on the guitar was Duane Eddy's 'Peter Gunn'. He walked into an army recruiting office in 1961 in order to avoid going to prison for stealing a car. Thus he found himself in the 101st Airborne, who flung young men out of planes and pointed them towards gunfire. Hendrix should have had the foresight to realize he wasn't cut out for this. He wrote home from Fort Ord, California asking his father to send the one thing that might stop him losing his mind, his guitar. Even though this was in the short period between the Korean and Vietnam wars, when US troops were not regularly in harm's way, Hendrix was sufficiently keen to escape to have pretended to the authorities that he had all sorts of disqualifying conditions up to and including homosexuality. When he was actually discharged in 1962 the only trade he appeared to have picked up was that of a musician. He had built the beginnings of a name for himself playing to fellow troops. Now his intention was to take that into the outside world.

It wasn't easy. Over the next four years he was at the bottom of the food chain on the most gruelling treadmill a young musician could be on, the chitlin circuit. Many of the circuit's venues were in states that preferred to act as though Civil Rights legislation had never happened. Jimmy took whatever work he could get, playing back-up for Slim Harpo, Carla Thomas, Ironing Board Sam and anybody who'd have him. Even at this low point in his career there were two poles to Jimmy's magnetism: the men admired his playing, the women admired him.

He graduated to playing with bigger names such as the Marvelettes, Curtis Mayfield, the Isley Brothers (the night the Beatles appeared on *The Ed Sullivan Show* he watched with the Isleys) and Little Richard. In due course the latter claimed that the guitarist took a lot of his style from him.

All were tough bosses. They were believers in polish and professionalism and fiercely jealous of their limelight. Jimmy played in bands where you could get fired for having different-coloured shoe laces. He played in bands that would can you for not wearing your cufflinks correctly. Little Richard would have no compunction whatsoever about throwing you off the bus in the middle of Gutbucket County if you wore a prettier shirt than the one he had on. All of them would assuredly get rid of you for repeated acts of upstaging. Over the period of his time on the chitlin circuit and further scuffling up and down the eastern seaboard with everybody from the Isley Brothers to King Curtis, Hendrix won a great reputation as a player. He had another, slightly less enviable one – as a show-stealer.

Settling in New York in August 1965, he bought Bob Dylan's 'Highway 61 Revisited', which suggested he was thinking beyond the traditional parameters of the chitlin circuit. In Harlem, he complained, he never fitted in. He never felt like one of the brothers. Instead he headed for Greenwich Village and the Cafe Wha?, the same place Dylan had targeted on his arrival in New York four years earlier. There he started to put together an act. This already featured 'Hey Joe', 'Like A Rolling Stone', 'Shotgun' and 'Wild Thing'. Lots of people saw him play during that time. Many were impressed. The guitarists among them were intimidated. Bob Dylan's guitar player Mike Bloomfield saw him and said that he didn't wish to pick up a guitar for the next year. And still nobody took him under their wing. It's not impossible that this was because of the colour of his skin.

Maybe it took the eyes and ears of an Anglo like Chandler to give him that chance. It wasn't going to be easy. When Chandler sat down with him and outlined the plan the first thing he learned was that Hendrix had already signed a deal. Actually, he'd signed two. Why should this musician, who had never left the United States in his life, agree to up sticks and go with this man with a strange accent to begin a new life in England? Chandler was persuasive. He knew how musicians' minds worked. He clinched the deal by pointing out that he was selling his bass guitars in order to buy Jimmy a ticket across the Atlantic, and what's more that ticket would be first class. He also promised that when they got to London he would introduce him to Eric Clapton. That did the trick.

When he arrived in London in late September 1966, Chas was so eager to show off his new charge to his muso mates that on the way into town from the airport they stopped off at band leader Zoot Money's place in Fulham. Thus the first British guitarist to be impressed with his playing was twenty-three-year-old Andy Summers, then a member of Money's band. The first British woman to be impressed was Money's wife Ronnie who took one look and went running to the girl in the flat upstairs saying, 'Chas has just brought this guy back from America and he looks like the Wild Man of Borneo.' The first British woman to sleep with him was the girl in the flat, Kathy Etchingham. She went back to his hotel with him that night and stayed for the next three years.

Chas's fledgling management operation was hand to mouth. He had to get the word about his client out quickly. The very night of their arrival he took him down to the Scotch of St James. This was a club in Masons Yard where after-hours musicians gathered to impress each other. He cleared it for him to jam with the house band. It was the first of a number of cameos Hendrix performed in the first few weeks he was in the country. Happily he found that the same tricks he had used to impress the people of Georgia worked just as well on the models, gangsters and pop stars of SW1. The key thing he'd learned from the chitlin circuit was 'watch your audience'. If the people liked it when you played the guitar behind your head then it was pretty obvious what you had to do: you played the guitar behind your head. If they lapped it up when you played guitar with your teeth then it was plain where your duty lay. Hendrix's professional mission was to tear up whatever room he happened to find himself in. In this he did not fail.

A few days after the Scotch of St James show Chandler contrived to bump into Eric Clapton and Jack Bruce of the recently formed Cream. Cream had been put together on the principle, long established in jazz, that if you put the best instrumentalists in a group they will produce the best music. In the world of pop music in 1966 this seemed like a very exciting idea. Furthermore, because it ministered to pop music's earnest desire to grow up it was seductive as well. The names these musicians dropped when they told the *New Musical Express* of their Lifelines were increasingly the likes of Cannonball Adderley, Roland Kirk and Tony Williams. They modelled themselves on such men, who were measured more on the quality of their chops than the excitement of their noise. In the watering holes where the music business gathered, in the Speakeasy, the Cromwellian and the Scotch of St James, players were actively encouraged to get up and show what they could do.

In this spirit Clapton asked Chas to bring his boy along to a gig they were doing that night in a basement in Little Titchfield Street (now part of the University of Westminster). Chandler duly turned up with Hendrix. Although this was supposed to be a benign meeting of brothers drawn together in the spirit of musicianly camaraderie, ground rules had to

Left: With his break-through hit 'Tutti Frutti' in 1955, Little Richard introduced a new combination of musical mayhem and personal magnetism, unwittingly inventing the rock star.

Below left and right: When rock's first idol Elvis Presley came home to headline Tupelo's State Fair in September 1956, it was a triumph for him and a vindication for parents Gladys and Vernon, whose first family photograph had been taken in the local jail.

Above: John Lennon led the Quarrymen skiffle group at the Woolton village fete on 6 July 1957, the day he first met Paul McCartney. John was impressed by Paul's musicianship; Paul was struck by John's nerve.

Left: Jerry Lee Lewis was warned not to take his thirteen-year-old bride Myra on his tour of the UK in 1958. When the British press discovered her age they whipped up the first full-scale moral panic around a rock star, causing the tour's cancellation.

Above and left: Buddy Holly only agreed to take part in 1959's Winter Dance Party because he and his new wife Maria were in serious need of the money. Young Robert Zimmerman of Minnesota saw him play a few days before his death in a plane crash, later recalling, 'He seemed to have a halo around him.'

Above: Adopting the cowboy name Hank Marvin, Buddy Holly-style glasses and the first Fender Stratocaster to be allowed into Europe, Brian Rankin (*left*) of the Shadows became the guitar hero who inspired the British guitar heroes with the 1960 hit 'Apache'.

Below: When Bob Dylan arrived in Greenwich Village in the winter of 1961, almost everything he said about himself wasn't true. This entirely fictitious backstory somehow made him seem more authentic. Nobody, least of all the press, wanted to disbelieve it.

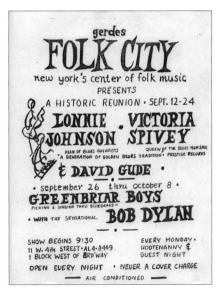

Above: Ringo Starr didn't merely make the Beatles swing for the first time, he was also the person who rendered their image complete. Before he joined in 1962, John Lennon told him he would have to restyle his hair if he was going to fit in. He didn't argue.

Below: Pianist Ian Stewart (*left*) was a driving force behind the early Rolling Stones but once they signed a record deal in 1963 it was decided that he should be demoted to tour manager because his face literally didn't fit.

Left: Days before Christmas in 1964, Brian Wilson of the Beach Boys broke down under the pressure of unrelenting road work, returning home to write his masterpieces and be with his teenage wife Wendy.

Below: A backstage argument about drugs between Roger Daltrey and Keith Moon came to blows, almost breaking up the Who in 1965 before they had really got started. The simmering resentments within the group inspired their definitive recording.

Bottom: Jimi Hendrix was introduced to the tastemakers of 1966 London through jam sessions at clubs like the Scotch of St James where musicians like Eric Clapton hung out and measured up the competition.

Between her first and second shows at the Monterey Pop Festival of 1967, Janis Joplin changed from hippie plain clothes to gold lamé pantsuit. The first show wasn't filmed. The second was.

Above: John Lennon and Paul McCartney appeared at a New York press conference on 16 May 1968 to announce that they had made quite enough money and now wished to distribute $2 million of it to artists via their Apple Corps.

Right: On the eve of a dark new decade, the members of Birmingham band Earth changed their name to Black Sabbath, galvanizing a new audience for doomy hard rock.

Above: *Teen* magazine editor Gloria Stavers took pictures of Jim Morrison in her bedroom, telling him to look at the camera as if he wanted to ravish it. In transforming this hipster into a love god in leather, Stavers invented rock-star style.

Left: In 1971 Lou Reed came out of self-imposed retirement on Long Island, setting out to exploit his own legacy via some new songs and the support of British fan David Bowie.

Below: When the Rolling Stones climaxed their American tour at Madison Square Garden on the occasion of Mick Jagger's birthday in July 1972, a giant cake was wheeled on to the stage. The original plan had called for an elephant.

Left: Mick Jagger's marriage to scene-maker Bianca Pérez-Mora Macias in 1971 had translated him from rock star to international personality, suddenly as notable for his fashion choices as his songwriting.

Below: David Bowie emerges from his limousine at the Hammersmith Odeon, London, on 3 July 1973. Schoolboy Malcolm Green can be seen between Bowie and the policeman, behind the car, wearing a dark jacket borrowed from his mother.

Bottom: Bruce Springsteen laboured long and hard to write and record his anthem 'Born To Run' in 1974 and then, with E Street Band member Clarence Clemons, to develop the stage act that could live up to its promise.

be established. Mr Hendrix would play just one number with the Cream, as they were called at the time. He would plug into Mr Bruce's bass amp, thus ensuring he couldn't sound too good. Mr Clapton would remain on the stage at all times, thereby making it clear whose group this was. In exchange Jimmy got to call the tune, which was Howlin' Wolf's 'Killing Floor'. This was a number Clapton was said to find tricky.

Many times in the future Clapton would be called upon to remember that evening. 'He brought his own guitar. He was left-handed but this was a normal right-handed guitar and so everything was upside down. He played just about every style you could think of, and not in a flashy way. He did a few of his tricks. Playing it behind his head and with his teeth. I think we did just that song. Then he walked off and my life was never the same again.'

At its most effective, hype happens among peers. It generally manifests itself in a tendency to jump aboard a bandwagon in the brief period of time before it's apparent that it is a bandwagon. Hendrix was clearly extravagantly gifted. However, it was what he represented rather than what he did that made London's musical community race to embrace him. Because he appeared to be an avatar of an entirely new musical species in that he was both black and big-haired (a look he had to work hard to maintain) it was important to approve of him whether you liked what he did or not.

Clapton and the other members of the guitarists' union responded to what he did on the instrument. The wider public, which grew wider by the week that autumn – the release of his first single, 'Hey Joe', came just in time for Christmas – responded to the way he did it. What the UK players presented as art Jimmy, by now given the comic-book name Jimi Hendrix by his manager, presented as showbiz. What the UK players made look like hard work he made look like wizardry. While for them singing was a chore they had to complete in order to earn the right to play a long solo, his singing and playing were all part of the same rippling conversation. (Here his left-handedness helped, enabling him seemingly to direct his band with his hips.) He appeared to be the first artist who had sorted out how to make the act of singing and simultaneously playing guitar a beautiful thing to watch. One became a commentary on the other, the former keeping up a channel of back chat with the latter. It was impossible to imagine Clapton saying, 'This is Jimi talking to you, baby' as Jimi would mid-performance. Where the white players gathered their features into a grimace to indicate how seriously they were taking their labour, Jimi never seemed to be able to prevent himself from laughing at his own outrageous talent.

Recalling the events of 1 October, Jack Bruce said, 'Eric was a guitar player. Jimi was a force of nature.' Although it purports to be the music of universal brotherhood the world of popular music is anything but colour blind. In the fifty years after Elvis it found scores of different ways of mapping sub-divisions of the music, most of them with at least some racial implication to them. Black musicians are far more likely to be called 'forces of nature'. This implies that they have arrived at what they do by a different route from their white counterparts. Much as it's difficult to have a white singer you would describe as a soul singer, so it's difficult to have a black star you would call a rock star. There are a handful of musicians who've walked this very fine line and they've been helped by the fact that they were directed from the beginning towards a white audience. Ultimately the thing that elevated Jimi Hendrix above Clapton, Beck, Green and all the other guitar players who came to pay tribute in October 1966 was as much stylistic as musical. It was in the three words that everybody, including Clapton, used to describe him.

The real thing.

1966 PLAYLIST

The Beach Boys, 'Good Vibrations'
The Beatles, 'Paperback Writer'
Stevie Wonder, 'Uptight (Everything's Alright)'
Bobby Fuller Four, 'I Fought The Law'
Jimi Hendrix, 'Hey Joe'
The Rolling Stones, 'Paint It, Black'
The Kinks, 'Sunny Afternoon'
The Mothers of Invention, *Freak Out!*
The Byrds, *Fifth Dimension*
Cream, *Fresh Cream*

18 JUNE 1967
MONTEREY, CALIFORNIA

The first female rock star

Before Janis Joplin there was nobody remotely like Janis Joplin.

Jazz and blues had produced female singers who sang with similar directness about their thirst or their carnal appetites, but Janis was another thing altogether. She was a white rock star, which meant she was written about in newspapers and interviewed on television. Those things that were implicit in her performances became explicit when she talked about them. When asked how she came to be the singer in her band Big Brother and the Holding Company she said she had slept with the man who was sent to ask her. Furthermore she was so impressed with him she couldn't say no. 'I was fucked into it,' she would cackle in interviews.

Nobody had ever heard a woman talk like this. Certainly not for publication. Some of it was an act. Privately she confessed she had actually made up this story as a favour to the man. She seemed oblivious to what this might say about her.

Because she was, in the argot of the day, a chick singer who behaved in a way no chick singer had behaved before, her personality was overshadowed by the way she played her gender and even that was overshadowed by the way she boasted about her sexuality.

Janis was one of those rock stars who found herself representing what appeared to be a new kind of person. By the simple act of walking on to the set of a chat show she provoked questions. These were the same questions that were going through the minds of every parent in America in the mid-sixties as they surveyed their own teenage children. Why do you dress like that? Why can't you tidy yourself up a little? Have you been taking drugs? What did you just say? Is that any way for a young lady to talk?

There had been female musical stars before Janis Joplin but they had conducted themselves like young ladies. Many of them, like Dusty Springfield and Aretha Franklin, were much admired for their artistry. None of them was permitted anything as vulgar as a personality. In the case of Sandie Shaw the fact that she sang in bare feet was considered quite sufficient. These female singers were just as prim and proper as young women were widely expected to be at the time. The idea that they might have a love life was hard enough to imagine. A sex life would be wholly out of the question.

Janis Joplin came to the fore in the age of let it all hang out. The thing she decided to let hang out was her own quite considerable pain. This was what the public expected. As she observed, audiences preferred their blues singers – and she did talk of herself as a blues singer – to be miserable. Some of her most devoted admirers were shiny-eyed, smartly turned-out Ali MacGraw lookalikes who would gaze up at Janis on stage, enthralled by the spectacle of somebody they would never have dared be, doing things they would never have dared do, things which, in their heart of cautious hearts, they feared were bound to end badly.

Janis Joplin came from a hard-working middle-class family in Port Arthur, Texas. The early part of her childhood was happy. When she was young she was pretty and enjoyed the benefits this can bring. Puberty, and more specifically acne, cruelly robbed her of her looks, inflicting a wound she spent the rest of her life trying to assuage. She did this in her own particular way. Janis met every misfortune that befell her in her teenage years by deliberately lowering her own standing in society. She gained a reputation as the school slut, a reputation she determined to live up to. Her mother fixed her first whisky sour when she was a senior at high school, reasoning this might ensure her drinking remained at home. It didn't. Janis started drinking in bars and also, as they were wont to say in Port Arthur, 'going across the river'. When she became famous she would joke that in her scuffling days she had tried turning tricks but was too ugly to find any takers. At the University of Texas a fraternity voted her the ugliest man on campus. By the time she was twenty Janis Joplin felt she had a right to sing the blues.

She found her feet as an entertainer in San Francisco in 1966, during that perfect moment when the freaks appeared to have hijacked the music business. Here there was suddenly room for people who didn't look right but evidently had their hearts in the right places. Room for a plugged-in jug band like the Grateful Dead. Room for a group who went under the name of Big Brother and the Holding Company but were soon known for having that crazy girl singer who did Big Mama Thornton and Irma Thomas numbers, took slugs from a bottle of whisky on stage and didn't always wear a bra. Janis was professional when it came to the singing but was always in danger of slipping back into drugs, particularly heroin. 'I wanted to smoke dope, take dope, lick dope, fuck dope – anything I could lay my hands on I wanted to do it,' she said.

Janis had always craved attention. She understood what she needed to do to be a star. She worked at it. She was smart enough to know that the appearance of spontaneity is something that must be worked at. Once she'd decided the precise number of apparently spontaneous imprecations to her sweet loving man to place in a particular verse of a song she could then do seventeen takes without the slightest variation. When she and the rest of Big Brother first sat down with a publicist she proceeded to dictate the larger-than-life version of herself she instinctively felt people would lap up. Janis was the one who urged her publicist to contact the makers of Southern Comfort and get them to pay her for drinking their product. She put the money they paid towards a fur coat. Janis was the one who would say in interviews that she had slept with all of the band at one time or another (this wasn't true). Janis was the one who instructed her publicist to get *Rolling Stone* magazine to publish the news that she'd had a one-night stand with star quarterback Joe Namath.

Janis was even the one who volunteered to take her clothes off for photographer Bob Seidemann. After he had draped her with just enough jewellery to cover her right nipple and she'd placed her hands over her crotch, the resulting picture eventually became a best-selling poster. She boasted that this made her 'the first hippie pin-up girl'. For the ugliest man on campus this was some kind of revenge. When she invited her parents to come out to the coast and see how well she had done for herself one of the things they found most mortifying was the ubiquitous sight of that poster based on Seidemann's picture. As far as Janis was concerned she'd shown becoming modesty by exposing just the one nipple, and besides, 'it hardly shows, mother'.

When she performed live she would encourage the audience to surround her on stage. It was as if she had to prove to herself that she had personal magnetism. When she was enveloped by ecstatic dancers she felt accepted. 'Being on stage is like making love to thousands of people,' she said, 'but then I go home alone.' Throughout her life she noisily complained about the difficulty she had attracting men. Just the men. The new candour about sex didn't extend to boasting about her lesbian lovers. Now that Janis was on stage she could and did use her position to advertise her availability. She found to her puzzlement and delight that she could attract men who would never have looked twice at her had she been a waitress. This caused her more concern than it would have caused her male counterparts, many of whom were every bit as homely. Not all Janis's boyfriends were worthless chancers. Her final one, Seth Morgan, could stand for the ones who were. After she died he admitted, 'If she was any old body, I wouldn't have looked at her.'

Sunday, 18 June 1967 was the longest day of the hippy summer, the day when all America was briefly beguiled by the novelty of peace and love. The Beatles had released *Sgt Pepper's Lonely Hearts Club Band* two weeks earlier. Lou Adler and John Phillips, two smart Los Angeles music business types, had hijacked an open-air show taking place at the same fairground that normally hosted the Monterey Jazz Festival. They brought in big acts from LA, London and New York with the idea of putting their stamp on the wild music and exotic costumes of the flower children. The deal was that if the bands wanted to play they had to allow themselves to be filmed. The managers of Jimi Hendrix, Simon & Garfunkel, the Who, Jefferson Airplane and Otis Redding signed the waiver. Big Brother and the Holding Company were too suspicious and too small-time to agree, so when they played on the Saturday they weren't filmed.

Having seen how well they went down with the crowd and how much people were talking about this band and the wild chick, Adler, Phillips and Albert Grossman, the manager of Bob Dylan, approached Big Brother and said that they would put them on again the following day if they would agree to being filmed. This was an unprecedented concession to make to a band that was largely unknown. They eventually agreed, the band reluctantly and Janis gleefully. The following day they understood why. When she had performed on the Saturday it had been in a plain top and jeans. When she returned for the Sunday night show she was arrayed in a gold lamé pant suit which she satirically described as 'lame'. She wanted to be glamorous. The members of Big Brother smelled showbiz in the air.

That very weekend Clive Davis of Columbia Records signed her up. Grossman moved in on her management and began the inevitable process of separating her from the band and launching her as a solo star. Monterey was a heady coming-out. It was less a festival than an industry party. The acts that weren't playing wandered through the crowd. Therefore she was suddenly seen by everyone from Brian Jones to Joan Baez and Mama Cass, who was seen enthusing during Janis's act when the film eventually reached cinemas. Monterey was the making of three acts: Otis Redding, who had previously been largely unknown to white American audiences, Jimi Hendrix, who had broken first in the UK and was now coming home in triumph, and Janis Joplin, whose Sunday night encore 'propelled them into the big money', as one report said, and established her as 'the best white blues singer'. For Janis it was a top-of-the-world moment.

The interesting thing about the new rock stars whose images were beginning to be sold in the wake of festivals like Monterey was that they were made of such apparently un-promising clay. Frank Zappa, Jerry Garcia, Pete Townshend and Janis Joplin would never have been stars in any other medium or at any other moment. In the case of Joplin, as in the case of Zappa, they were probably more powerful as icons than as musicians. Zappa pictured on the lavatory; Janis with the beads: both were as likely to be found on walls as on turntables. The first big-label Big Brother album did well, although it took producer John Simon months to drag a performance out of the band that he was happy with. Janis's future was as a solo star.

Janis had no remorse about jettisoning the other members of Big Brother and the Holding Company. She said she thought they were the kind of people who might find other things to do. She, on the other hand, felt the only thing she could do was be a singer. In fact the only thing she could do was be a rock star. Only as a rock star could her short-comings be repackaged as marks of authenticity. 'They're paying me $50,000 a year to be myself,' she said, delightedly. The very things that might have held her back in the main-stream entertainment business were assets in this new world which was suddenly paved with gold. The lack of polish, the straining for the right note, the disarranged outfits, the ap-pearance she gave of saying the first thing that came into her head – these were the hallmarks of a new kind of entertain-ment which had come out of the West Coast counterculture. In this world a certain level of wastedness was a badge of the sincerity suddenly prized above all things. Janis found herself being celebrated for being the same person everyone had despised back in high school.

Janis Joplin never stopped trying to get acceptance from home and family. As she was beginning to make her name out on the coast she would dutifully report back to her parents by letter. They were understandably heartbroken when she claimed in print that they threw her out when she was fourteen. This wasn't true, but it was the price you evidently had to pay for having a rock star in the family. Fans preferred the myth to the truth. She would send her parents clippings and ask whether the local paper in Port Arthur had reprinted any of the stories about her. In 1970 she got an invitation to attend her high school reunion. Amazingly she decided to accept. And she didn't accept quietly. She announced it on TV, on *The Dick Cavett Show*. 'They laughed me out of class, out of town and out of state, so I'm going home,' she said. She even told the *New York Times*, 'Man, these people hurt me. It makes me happy to know I'm making it and they're back there, plumbers just like they were.'

Having savagely patronized the people of Port Arthur in the public prints, she should not have been surprised the trip didn't turn out to be the dream vindication she had hoped for. She turned up with three handsome men, one of whom was her driver. Refusing to serve as walk-ons in this publicity opportunity, her parents left town to go to a wedding. She clashed with her siblings, both of whom were sore about the way she'd airily mentioned them in the press. All the homecoming weekend achieved was to accentuate the gap between her and her contemporaries. She was engaged in a battle for prestige, a battle they didn't seem to want to join. She actually volunteered to revisit the sites of the most painful episodes of her teenage years. Reporters asked if she had ever entertained at high school. Only when I walked down the halls, she said. At the press conference she confessed that her school days had not been happy, that she hadn't been to the prom. Why not? Because nobody had asked her.

By that point of the weekend whatever reservoir of booze and bravado kept her pain at bay had run out and she looked broken and heart-sick. This was no grand vindication. This was no triumph over the little people. She was caught between the life she had left and the life she'd found. Neither seemed to satisfy her. By the Sunday night her mother, tired of turning on the TV and seeing her eldest daughter inviting the audience to snigger at her family's straight life and quaint domestic arrangements, had had enough. According to one account she said, 'I wish you'd never been born'. If she did she probably didn't mean it, but nothing had prepared her for the experience of being an unsympathetic minor character in a drama she didn't recognize.

Janis never made it home again: just seven weeks after the reunion she was found dead in her hotel room.

1967 PLAYLIST

The Velvet Underground, *The Velvet Underground & Nico*
The Beatles, *Sgt Pepper's Lonely Hearts Club Band*
The Jimi Hendrix Experience, *Are You Experienced*
Pink Floyd, *The Piper At The Gates Of Dawn*
Sly & the Family Stone, *A Whole New Thing*
Love, *Forever Changes*
Procol Harum, 'A Whiter Shade Of Pale'
The Doors, 'Light My Fire'
Aretha Franklin, 'Respect'
Van Morrison, 'Brown Eyed Girl'

his wife would be essentially the same people they had been before being stunned by success. They might be more tanned but they would still recognizably be members of the same human race as their neighbours.

Five years later the old scale no longer applied. Five years later the first single on the Apple label, the record company the Beatles by now felt confident enough to launch, would be dedicated to the same Maureen on the occasion of her twenty-second birthday. It was called 'Maureen Is A Champ' and had been recorded (to the melody of 'The Lady Is A Tramp') as a special favour to Ringo by no less a person than Frank Sinatra. The lyrics had been rewritten by Sammy Cahn. Just one copy was pressed. That was the kind of grand gesture Maureen's birthday now demanded. A few years earlier she might have been satisfied with flowers.

Clearly the four members of the Beatles had ascended beyond the clouds on which the merely successful were perched and had now reached a terra incognita of soft power and magical prestige on which there was neither footprint nor flag. Rising so high so quickly induces a special kind of vertigo. The realization that for them there would be no going back to the world they'd known must have stolen upon the Beatles in instalments over the previous five years as they hit milestones that were at first thrilling, then hilarious, and finally intimidating. It might have truly come home to them when they had so many singles on the American chart there was scarcely room for anyone else. The moment could have come in 1965, when they were awarded the MBE by Her Majesty the Queen. It could have been in 1966, when they were forced to give up touring because they simply could no longer be heard above the loudly expressed enthusiasm of their fans. It could have been as late as 1967, when they realized that the hippy kids they bumped into on the street seemed to believe they were encountering not people but deities.

At some stage on the journey they must have understood there never would be any going back, that this gig, this lark, this last mad shout of youth they had taken up because, back in the struggling days, it was infinitely preferable to reality, was their new permanent state and therefore they had to find a way of dealing with it.

Hence on 15 May 1968, as an alliance of workers and students put a million people on the streets of Paris and brought the French state perilously close to breakdown, Paul McCartney blandly informed a press conference in New York City that he and his bandmates were 'in the happy position of not really needing any more money'.

He said this because, despite all he had been through and seen since 1963, he was still only twenty-five. He said this because, like all the Beatles and indeed like all their peers, he didn't pay overly close attention to the details of their financial affairs and trusted the people he had in place to deal with that sort of thing. He said this because it was 1968 and the air felt full of possibilities. He said this because it was not yet apparent that even the largest sum of money can be reduced at first steadily by too many outgoings and then dramatically by any time at all spent in the company of lawyers. He said this because he had been smoking lorry-loads of weed. He said this because the band's accountants had told them that they had a $2 million surplus which they could either give to the government in tax or spend on a project. He said this because he and John were in New York City to announce the project they had decided on, which was to be called Apple Corps.

Lined up in front of journalists at the Americana Hotel in

New York's Times Square, he and John explained the concept. They didn't wish to compete; they simply proposed to invent a new paradigm. Apple would be a new kind of entertainment and arts company, one that was not just looking for new talent but actively flinging its door open and asking anyone who felt they had the spark of inspiration about their person to send them their ideas, their demos and their tapes. Here, finally, they promised, was a place where they would no longer have to get down on bended knee. Here was a place where their stuff would get not just a hearing but a sympathetic hearing, and not just a sympathetic hearing but possibly even a Beatle hearing.

Such an appeal was asking for a response that would have been difficult to contain had the request come from the members of, say, the Hollies. Coming from the Beatles it was tantamount to publishing their unlisted numbers on the front page of the *Daily News*. In all they placed just two advertisements asking for material, one in *Rolling Stone* and the other in the *New Musical Express*. Apple were immediately buried under an avalanche of tapes, biographies, scripts, photos, green-ink letters, eight-by-ten glossies, reception squatters and nuisance calls. They never advertised again.

The only person who might have called a halt to this madness before it achieved escape velocity was gone. Their manager Brian Epstein, the man who had taken every bullet aimed in their direction since 1962, had died from an accidental overdose of sleeping pills the previous year. The news had reached them when they were in Bangor, north Wales, sitting at the feet of the Maharishi Mahesh Yogi, who'd promised to teach them how to meditate their way through all their trials. Thus they appeared to have exchanged one father figure, who traditionally dealt with matters temporal, for another, who purported to restrict himself to the spiritual. During the time they spent with him in his ashram in Rishikesh earlier in 1968 they'd come to believe that he was not above the desires of the flesh, deciding on flimsy evidence that he had made advances to fellow meditating celeb Mia Farrow. Although the Maharishi had taken root in their lives when they felt the need for spiritual nourishment, they were not the kind of people content to stare into the middle distance for very long. The scuttlebutt about the Yogi's wandering hands simply freed John, Paul and Ringo to disavow him every bit as quickly as they had taken him up the previous year.

Now that meditation had been relegated to the mental box labelled 'last year', the Beatles, who were culturally obliged to have the shortest of attention spans, devoted their thoughts to the new project, which was Apple Corps. The focus of this company meant it restricted itself to films, records and electronics, which should have been more than enough. John didn't tell the journalists that only a couple of days earlier he'd had a meeting to discuss the prospect of some kind of free school which could be run by his friend Ivan Vaughan, who happened to be a teacher. They glossed over the fact that the first product of the film division, their own *Magical Mystery Tour*, was being quietly buried because it had been so disastrously received when it was screened on British television the previous Christmas. They gave no indication that the Apple boutique in the West End of London, which had been opened with such fanfare the previous year, was about to be closed, having swiftly racked up losses of £200,000. The boutique had been run by John's friend Pete Shotton and George's sister-in-law Jenny Boyd. The A&R man of their label was Pete Asher, the brother of Paul's girlfriend Jane

Asher. One of the first acts signed to the label was George's old Liverpool mate Jackie Lomax. The declared philosophy of Apple might have been to give an outlet to maverick talent who otherwise would have no chance. In practice they were more comfortable with the old-fashioned networking favoured by the music business they were loudly determined not to copy.

Like all young princes who had been fabulously successful in one field they were prone to thinking they could be equally successful in others. They had not yet absorbed the lesson that when it goes well it doesn't mean you're a genius, and when it goes badly it doesn't follow that you're a dunderhead. During their months in Rishikesh they had written lots of new material which they were already recording. Indeed there seemed to be enough for a double album. Paul was producing the first single by TV talent competition winner Mary Hopkin. George's soundtrack to the film *Wonderwall* had just been released. If you looked in that direction all was going well. So that was the direction they chose to look in. That day in the middle of May 1968 saw the Beatles at the pinnacle of their omniscience, calling the world to order and blandly using words that no human being had used before: 'We're in the happy position of not really needing any more money.'

At the same time, though they may not have realized it, the group was coming to the end of its natural life. In their new, post-touring situation they had the leisure to think about things that previously they had never thought about. They had achieved most when they had no choices. The relentless forward motion of touring had maintained them in the upright position. Now they had to face the difficulty of having options, some of which involved other people doing the hard work and the Beatles lending their name or their image. John's

In His Own Write was being produced for the stage at the Old Vic. Paul was recording with the Black Dyke Mills Band. The animated film *Yellow Submarine*, in which their voices were imitated by actors, was opening in July. George was appearing in a film called *Raga*. There was nothing here that exactly burned to be accomplished.

The Johnny Carson Show that May night in New York was presented not by the titular mirth-master but by professional baseball catcher turned TV personality Joe Garagiola. Palming them off with a substitute seemed disrespectful to stars of their magnitude. Garagiola made a desultory attempt to keep the conversation going. Did they still get asked about their hair? Was it really true that they'd been in Central Park and nobody had recognized them? Some girls in the studio audience screamed, which suddenly seemed inappropriate. John was asked what he wanted to do next and he said 'films', by which he didn't mean what Cliff Richard and Elvis Presley meant when they said the same thing. Neither of them shared with Garagiola, or his other guest, the veteran movie star Tallulah Bankhead, who was three sheets to the wind by the time they appeared and wouldn't have understood anyway, what was really occupying their minds that week.

As Paul was speaking at the press conference earlier that day in the Americana Hotel at least half his attention had been on the woman sitting in the front row taking pictures of the proceedings. Linda Eastman was twenty-six at the time. She lived in New York on an allowance provided by her late mother, with her daughter from her first marriage, devoting much of her time to hanging around with and taking pictures of rock stars. She was familiar with wealth and status. Linda was born on the right side of the red rope. She had been introduced to McCartney at a club in St James the previous year. She had talked her way into the party at Brian Epstein's flat to mark the release of *Sgt Pepper's Lonely Hearts Club Band* and there they'd talked further. As he was leaving the press conference in New York McCartney asked her for her number. She wrote it on a cheque. By the time she got back to her apartment he had called.

Lennon was similarly preoccupied with his love life. His wife Cynthia was away on holiday, which meant he had the family home in Weybridge to himself for the coming weekend. He was not planning to be alone. He was making arrangements to be visited by Yoko Ono, the Japanese avant-garde artist he had been contacting off and on for the past two years. She was older than him, more sophisticated, and like Eastman had a child by a previous marriage. She came to the Lennon family home on the Sunday and, according to their own legend, the couple spent the night recording sound collages before marking the dawn by making love. When Cynthia arrived back from her holiday Yoko was still there. A scene ensued. John was unapologetic. Cynthia filed for divorce soon afterwards. At around the same time Jane Asher announced that she and Paul McCartney were no longer engaged.

Neither Lennon nor McCartney was prepared for the backlash the announcements of these changes to their domestic arrangements would attract. Over the previous five years Beatle Nation had developed such a powerful identification with its favourites that any upheaval they were going through seemed bound to involve the fans as well. It was as if that nice couple next door suddenly started having rows. The fact that both of the new partners were from overseas left the United Kingdom feeling slighted, as if Britannia was no longer good enough for the boys she had nourished at her breast. The fact that neither of the new partners was as pretty and photogenic and young as their predecessors tarnished the fairy tale that was so close to the fans' heart. People never felt the same about the Beatles again.

McCartney didn't get the flak that Lennon did. A lot of the attacks aimed at Yoko were racist and sexist, though neither term was used at the time. The next Beatles album would see the four individuals increasingly working on their own, using other members as they saw fit. One of John's tracks would be a brutal sound montage that was obviously done as a Valentine to his new love. At first the other members of the group tolerated the fact that Lennon insisted on bringing her along to every session. It took them a while to realize that as far as he was concerned, if she wasn't in the group there wasn't going to be a group.

It had always been John's group so if anyone was going to bring it to a close it would be him. He felt his involvement with Yoko, both romantic and artistic, was changing him; if this new expanded, improved version of Lennon could no longer fit into the mould of the Beatles then he would have no problem cracking that mould. There never has been and there probably never will be a band whose gossamer internal balance can survive the introduction of one member's husband or wife.

In this week in May 1968 the two key Beatles started out on new lives and effectively brought to an end the gang that was the Beatles. They had passed through five years that had utterly transformed their lives and now some of them at least were prepared to throw all that in the air for love. Through the decade up until then their greatest intimacies had been shared between themselves; their primary loyalty had always been to the people who stood alongside them on stage, their greatest confidants and most important critics.

That had applied no matter what it said on the certificate of marriage. Now John and Paul were embarking on new lives with new partners. They were behaving like men who no longer needed each other in the way they had since meeting at Woolton village fete eleven years before. They now identified as strongly with the women in their lives as they had once done with each other. One of them thought he could take the Beatles with him into this next phase of his life. The other already knew he couldn't. One cared. The other didn't.

1968 PLAYLIST

The Rolling Stones, 'Jumpin' Jack Flash'
The Beatles, 'Hey Jude'
Joni Mitchell, *Song To A Seagull*
Simon & Garfunkel, *Bookends*
Led Zeppelin, *Led Zeppelin*
Van Morrison, *Astral Weeks*
Otis Redding, '(Sittin' On) The Dock Of The Bay'
Jimi Hendrix, 'All Along The Watchtower'
The Byrds, *Sweetheart Of The Rodeo*
Hair soundtrack (Broadway cast)

9 AUGUST 1969

BIRMINGHAM, ENGLAND

The devil's business

Four doleful longhairs, all around the age of twenty, were unloading their ancient Commer van outside the Newtown Community Centre in Aston, Birmingham, in the middle of England's industrial heartland. All four were members of a band called Earth. Earth was not a particularly striking name. They had recently discovered to their dismay that they weren't the only band to have chosen it. Of the two skill sets involved in running a band, these four longhairs were more comfortable with the tangible side of things, such as dealing with the equipment, than with image, which was harder to get a grip on.

All four men, each with a naturally defensive expression framed by a curtain of unmanageable hair, came from homes and schools which in the usual run of things held out few prospects. All four came from the kind of backgrounds from which the only traditional escape was war. They had all left school at the age of fifteen to follow the only occupations open to unqualified youths with strong backs and low expectations: abattoir worker, machine operator, plumber's apprentice. As they pursued these tough, dirty jobs they daydreamed about their real passion, which was playing the kind of loud rock and roll that made the players feel they were settling scores with the world.

The four were neither gilded youth nor nature's flower children. Guitarist Tony Iommi had changed his playing style after losing the tips of his fingers in an industrial accident and had spent a short time in Jethro Tull; singer John 'Ozzy' Osbourne, who was clean-shaven and, next to the rest of them, pretty, had spent a few weeks in prison after his father decided to teach him a lesson by not paying the fine he'd incurred for a bungled burglary; bassist Geezer Butler wasn't given a guitar for Christmas so he took out his tool kit and made one himself; and drummer Bill Ward smoked the residue from banana skins in the belief that this would get him high. In Birmingham you made your own entertainment.

For the four members of Earth, who at the beginning of August 1969, just as the stage for the Woodstock Music and Arts Festival was being erected thousands of miles away, had recently returned from playing a village hall in the wilds of Cumbria, nothing had come easily. But fate was about to vouchsafe them one single, self-sufficient thought, one transformational shaft of insight that would eventually make them rich and famous. On the 9th, as they were loading their equipment into the local community centre where they assiduously rehearsed, Geezer Butler pointed to the title of a movie on the marquee of a nearby cinema. It was the English name of an Italian schlock horror film that some sharpie in the marketing department had decided would do better in the UK if it were called not *Three Faces of Fear* but *Black Sabbath*.

It's funny, Tony Iommi remarked, contemplating the sign, how people will pay money to be frightened. The actual expression he used was 'shit scared'. Standing on that Birmingham pavement, Tony had the key insight of a lifetime. An insight that led directly to other thoughts. What if you could prosper by making music that didn't set out to delight the audience in the traditional way? What if you took a darker route? What if you made music that dealt in something different? What if you made music that at least pretended to strike fear into an audience's heart, much as Hammer Films had done for a generation of British moviegoers? What if, like the best-selling thriller writer Dennis Wheatley, you placed a chill hand on the cosy English soul? What if, like Screamin' Jay Hawkins, you arrayed yourselves in the habiliment of horror? Wouldn't that be a thing?

In their rehearsal hall Earth set to work on transforming that thought into a song. Actually, to call it a song was underselling it. Earth had already learned that they didn't deal in tunes milkmen could whistle or sentiments housewives could share. The composition they came up with was less a song than a short drama, a penny-dreadful playlet such as might have provided Edwardian music-hall audiences with a salutary shudder between the soprano and the patriotic finale. It began slowly and ominously. It took its time, to ensure its signature riff had bludgeoned its way into the listener's subconscious well before the vocal began. The lyrics, when they arrived, were delivered as if by one who stared, wide-eyed with terror, at a ghastly apparition. As this apparition drew near the tension in the music built until the guitars went fortissimo. At this point Ozzy screamed, 'No, no, please God help me!' The way he screamed it caused you either to laugh out loud or nod in sage recognition, depending on what age you happened to be. The song was called 'Black Sabbath'. The members of Earth looked back on their day's work and were well pleased.

Two days later they set off to play a series of dates in Germany, at Hamburg's Star-Club, where many English groups, including the Beatles, had developed their act in front of audiences who demanded little more than to be taken out of themselves. That morning Tony pulled up outside Ozzy's home to pick him up for the trip. The singer emerged wearing a T-shirt and a pair of jeans. He was carrying his entire touring wardrobe, which amounted to a single shirt, on a hanger. Tony, who had already spent enough time with Ozzy to know that he could be as daft as a brush, asked him if he was aware they were going overseas. Ozzy said he was. Tony asked him if in that case he had enough clothes for the trip. Ozzy said he did. Tony shrugged, slipped the clutch, and pointed the Commer at the port.

On the ferry across the Channel the four men sat around a small table that was bolted to the deck and loaded with pints, much as thousands of English visitors had done before them. Here they entertained a further thought. What if they gave the group the same name as the song? There and then they decided they would become Black Sabbath. In practical terms they didn't announce the new name until later in the month when they played a show in Workington, Cumbria, but their new identity did give them a renewed sense of purpose and the six shows a day they were contracted to play in Hamburg provided an invaluable opportunity to temper their new material on the anvil of performance. By the time they got into the studio in October they were so settled on what that sound should be that Tony overruled any attempts to correct the distortion in his guitar. The distortion, he pointed out, was what he was after. The sound he was after was the opposite of uplifting. It was defiantly morose. It was innocent of ornamentation. It didn't go anywhere. It wasn't meant to bloody go anywhere. Instead it lent itself perfectly to planting your feet, bowing your head, closing your eyes and swishing your curtain of hair from side to side in blessed incognizance as the music simply swallowed you up. Most of the time these people were communing with their boots. If they did look up they saw Ozzy stationed at the side of the stage, getting out of the audience's eye-line so that they could get an unimpeded view of what this performance was all about, which was serious young men operating heavy machinery, much as they had done in this part of the world since the industrial revolution.

Black Sabbath. It was the combination of name and sound that did the trick. In the late sixties the shape of band names was changing to reflect the shifting pretensions of both musicians and fans. A band's name can be more instructive than the actual music when it comes to describing what's in that band's collective head. While the actual music will always be restricted by the abilities of the players, a band's name is the one spot on the aesthetic spectrum where imagination can be permitted to run wild. Whereas sixties groups once had names like the Beatles or the Byrds or the Beach Boys, pairing the definite article with a category of person or creature for the chipper, matey vibe consonant with the age, the bands of this hairier era leaned towards terse single-word statement names like Earth or Cactus or Cream, names that also hinted at previously unplumbed depths of heaviosity. It was either that or deliberately incongruous conjunctions of noun and adjective like Grateful Dead, Led Zeppelin and Black Sabbath. Such names sent off the warning message that this music was masonic in nature and primarily for initiates. Bands with names like these were not setting out to woo you. They were not there to entertain. They were animated by an altogether more serious purpose. The best you could hope for is that you would relish the experience of having them roll over you like so many tanks, that you would be pathetically grateful to them for doing you the service of blunting your senses, that you would stagger away from any live encounter feeling you had been ravished and would not have had it any other way.

Names like these were at the other end of the scale from African-American rhythm and blues acts. The Miracles, the Supremes, the Temptations – these hinted at a sensuality and delight any audience might share; names like Moby Grape, Blodwyn Pig and Frumpy hung out the shingle reading 'members only', ushering in a new era when both rock band and rock fans prided themselves on marking out a territory that no longer sought public approval. The change in name style was significant. In a period of six years bands had gone from being groups of musicians with broad repertoires, capable of entertaining most audiences they might be faced with, to highly specialized units who were proud of the fact that they purveyed one thing and one thing only. As Black Sabbath went forward in their new incarnation, playing exclusively material that came from the same well of fear, loathing and terror as that first song, they worked a narrower and narrower seam. The trick was to find the audiences who were quite happy with the narrowness of the seam and not to waste time on anybody else.

Their first album, recorded later in 1969, was of course called *Black Sabbath*. The members of the group hadn't heard of branding but that's nonetheless what it was. That first album was a stake in the ground from which they never wandered far. It came packaged in a cover featuring the ghostly figure of a woman standing in front of an ancient watermill. It began with the sound of rainfall and a bell notionally tolling in the background of this scene and then became the song called 'Black Sabbath'. The imaginative world of Black Sabbath was not a reflection of the real world at all. It didn't set out to reflect anything that the fans might experience. With Sabbath we move from the recognizable world of teenagers and teenage concerns, from dating and dancing and driving cars and learning how to fit in with your fellow man, to an entirely confected world of gloomy castles, passing bells and white-faced figures of foreboding. It was a world that played into the young male feeling that his troubles are greater than they actually are, that his emotional responses are more profound than they actually are, and that the greatest problems of life can be dealt with through the military application of sheer sensation. It was non-sexual, anti-glamour, and, best of all, nobody was going to ask you to dance to it. It was the point at which rock was successfully converted into ritual by giving a twist to some of the oldest and best-established rituals of all. Inside the cover of *Black Sabbath* was a picture of an inverted cross. This was just another symbol stirred into the prog rock pot by an art department that probably thought this one would be forgotten as quickly as the latest album by Juicy Lucy. Only this one wasn't. Tony Iommi, who was (nominally at least) a Catholic, never stopped answering questions about that cross.

As the sixties turned into the seventies the times conspired to make their change of image seem spookily prescient. On the night of 9 August 1969, the same day that Sabbath glimpsed their future on a movie theatre marquee, four members of the so-called family that had gathered around jailbird and would-be musician Charles Manson broke into the Hollywood home occupied by film star Sharon Tate, wife of Roman Polanski, and three of her friends. They were acting on the instructions of Manson, who was motivated by malice, madness and the bitterness of seeing a potential record contract snatched away from him. He told them to slaughter everyone in the house. This they did, though not without terrorizing them first. Their leader that night, Tex Watson, woke up one of the people sleeping on the sofa. When asked what he was doing there he replied, with that combination of hideous malevolence and ghastly pretension which was to become the hallmark of the urban terrorist, 'I'm the devil and I'm here to do the devil's business.'

1969 PLAYLIST

The Rolling Stones, 'Honky Tonk Women'
Bob Dylan, *Nashville Skyline*
Led Zeppelin, *II*
The Band, *The Band*
Neil Young, *Everybody Knows This Is Nowhere*
Black Sabbath, *Black Sabbath*
Leonard Cohen, *Songs From A Room*
The Who, 'Pinball Wizard'
Peter Sarstedt, 'Where Do You Go To (My Lovely)?'
The Temptations, *Cloud Nine*

chalice was at hand to catch and mingle the drops of their blood when the time came.

Officiating at this pseudo-marital rite of 'handfasting', which had its roots in Celtic lore and the practices of the Wiccans, were a couple of Kennealy's friends. They were going, for the day, by the names Lady Maura and Lord Brân. They described the circle in the air into which the couple were invited to step in order to plight their troth. Jim was apparently startled by the change that came over him the instant he stepped through this very particular hole in the air. If it's true that he and his Wiccan bride made love no fewer than six times in swift succession in the immediate aftermath of the ceremony we can take it that he also found the circle to have energizing properties. This was the minimum expected of Jim Morrison, who was said by the *Village Voice* to be 'the biggest thing to hit the mass libido in a long time'.

Jim Morrison was actually a film-school graduate who had drifted into music. What put his group the Doors on the chart back in 1967 was a song called 'Light My Fire'. This was written by the band's guitarist Robbie Krieger and boasted a trippy organ part over which Jim sang about what he took to be a higher state of consciousness but most of those listening took to be sexual intercourse, which, conveniently, seemed as if it had only just been invented. The Doors would have been consigned to the column marked 'rock' and long articles about their influences in *Rolling Stone* or *Crawdaddy* had it not been for Gloria Stavers. Gloria was a former model turned photo-journalist who edited *16* magazine, which was the most powerful conduit in the United States for the muffled thoughts and quickening desires of teenage girls. She had form. Gloria had been instrumental in establishing the personalities of the Beatles in print. Gloria was the one who made Peter Noone into the country's most popular teddy-bear substitute. She could do a lot even with unpromising timber. When she saw Jim Morrison she realized she was looking at the most lubricious figure in American popular music since Elvis Presley.

Before he left the West Coast to fly to New York for a major publicity blitz off the back of 'Light My Fire', Morrison visited the celebrity hairdresser Jay Sebring, handed him a clipping of a photograph of a statue of Alexander the Great and announced that this was what he wanted to look like. Morrison was not handicapped by modesty. In New York, Elektra publicity man Danny Fields took the band to Gloria's East Side apartment to shoot some pictures for *16*. The other three were efficiently processed and let go. Stavers then took the singer into the bedroom where many of her most memorable pictures were taken and there she told him that the more he looked at the camera as if he wanted to ravish it, the better the photograph would turn out. She further encouraged him to adopt poses he never would have had the band been there to inhibit him. It was in her apartment that Morrison threw on her fur coat over his leather trousers. This single frame struck the androgynous note that secured him a picture session with *Vogue* – his first step to rock godliness.

Three years later few things were more utterly vanished than that summer of 1967. Sebring had died at the hands of Manson's murderers in 1969. Morrison's drinking, which nobody was yet characterizing as an illness, had become at least a distraction for the band. This unfortunate state of affairs had had its most public airing at a concert that took place at the Dinner Key Auditorium in Miami on 1 March 1969. By this point Morrison was operating at arm's length from the rest of the band. He would fly to the city where they were due to play, rent a car at the airport, buy a case of beer and then just drive around until it was time for the show. His flight to Miami that day had been diverted and he had passed the time in various airport bars. By the time he got on stage at the auditorium, which was over-filled and inadequately air-conditioned, he was in no fit state to perform. The performance he did deliver combined rock-star petulance with avant-garde pretension and would have been wholly unmemorable had he not threatened to take out his penis.

The police, who seemed always to be there when the Doors played, drew proceedings to a premature end. Following the show Morrison was charged with two counts of indecent exposure, two of public profanity and one of public drunkenness, but the real capper was 'lewd and lascivious behaviour in public by exposing his private parts and by simulating masturbation and oral copulation'. These charges, theoretically at least, carried a penalty of three years and 150 days in an exceptionally unpleasant jail – a prospect that would have been worrying enough for a rock star who didn't look, as *Rolling Stone* had said of Morrison, 'as if he was made up over the phone by two fags'. Following the charges the band were said by *Rolling Stone* to be vacationing on the Bahamas. Each member was said to be on his own island.

In 1970 rock music was increasingly focused on the crotch. Naturally exhibitionist lead singers were leading with this area. They had been courting trouser catastrophes and the headlines that tended to follow ever since P. J. Proby split his pants on every stop of his 1965 tour. Now that the music was louder and the lyrics more overt, and the lemons openly advertised their need for squeezing, it seemed only logical that some of the clothes should begin to tumble off. From Mick

Jagger's coy 'You don't want my trousers to fall down, now do you?' at Madison Square Garden, captured on the live album *Get Yer Ya-Ya's Out!*, to Robert Plant's apparently overstocked loons, the new generation of lead-singer princelings dressed like Cavaliers from the waist up and rent boys from the waist down. This was the most body-conscious of times. Even Rod Stewart wore blouses. Roger Daltrey's chest was as integral to the Who's act as Pete Townshend's assault on his amplifier. A large part of the appeal of Free was down to the fact that Paul Rodgers was the college girl's preferred bit of rough.

Morrison wasn't as easy with the call for bump and grind to enliven the performance as the Brits. His threat to produce his member from the dark recesses of his leather trousers was rooted more in his desire to provoke the baser instincts of the crowd in the confrontational spirit of Julian Beck's Living Theatre than it was to show them what Elvis Presley had only hinted at. When he gave evidence he had to endure the shrivelling indignity of describing his underwear. They were boxers, he said, which was unusual, he added, because usually he didn't bother with any. This particular pair were unusually large, which necessitated rolling them over the belt of his pants to keep them up.

There were seven thousand in the Dinner Key Auditorium that night. Nothing speaks more eloquently of the dehumanizing effect of the increased scale of the rock spectacular than the fact that people in the audience couldn't agree whether Morrison had actually taken his penis out or not. Clearly a penis large enough to impress itself on spectators in the far reaches of a cavernous auditorium would have already found its way into medical textbooks. Flashing is traditionally a close-quarters activity for good reason. It has never become part of the standard repertoire of the rock performer.

The court case, which took place in Miami in September 1970, hinged on whether Morrison had done so or merely threatened to do so. When a love god goes to the trouble of taking it out he likes to feel that at the very least everyone will agree that it is out. In this case they never quite did.

While waiting for the trial Morrison did his best to re-position himself as a man whose motivations were artistic rather than base. There's a filmed interview around this time of the four Doors talking to early rock journalist Richard Goldstein in which they talk about shamanism, the role of the artist and the sense of community at a rock show. They speak like men who have already learned that the filmed rock interview is a new medium in which it is possible to embark on a sentence without the slightest idea where that same sentence might end up. Here they are pioneering the monotonous, affectless ribbon of musing that became the standard way in which alternative rock acts communicated with their fans and absolutely nobody else at all. At one stage Morrison launches into a poem and then retreats, worried about the absence of the backbeat.

During this time Lillian Roxon was putting the finishing touches to her *Rock Encyclopedia*, the pioneer of a whole new genre. Her entry on the Doors finished: 'Things are looking up for the Doors. One more bust and they'll be back in favour with the underground.' Roxon was recognizing the fact that somebody like Morrison was playing to two crowds. One was the public. The other was the community of taste-makers who liked to feel that they controlled admission to the pantheon of real stars.

When the jury returned its verdicts on 20 September Morrison was given a pass on the most serious charge of 'lewd and lascivious behaviour' and convicted on the public drunkenness and indecent exposure charges. It didn't really add up, but that didn't matter, because the law had flexed its muscles by forcing the Doors to abandon plans for a European tour, the elected officials had been seen to be holding back the tsunami of permissiveness which threatened to debauch Florida's sons and daughters, and Morrison was relatively free to resume his life and profession. By then Kennealy had joined his retinue in Florida and was claiming to be pregnant with Jim's baby. She said that she and Jim had been married at a Wiccan ceremony back in June. This came as a complete surprise to the band. It was also a bit of a turn-up for Pamela Courson, who liked to announce herself as Morrison's wife.

Two days before the verdict was delivered Jimi Hendrix died in London at the age of twenty-seven. Al Wilson of Canned Heat had died just two weeks earlier. He was also twenty-seven. Two weeks later Janis Joplin was to die. She too was twenty-seven. All were the result of accidents with drink and drugs. It was a dangerous time to be a rock star. Clearly nobody was going to protect them from themselves. In an interview in the *New York Times* in October Eric Clapton said that every time he stepped on stage he was terrified. Talking of Hendrix and Joplin, both of whom had 'phased themselves out of a situation that became intolerable', he said, 'All we want to do is be left alone to make music, but because we are called "rock stars" a whole different set of expectancies are thrust upon us – that we have instant opinions about everything, that we should set an example to the youth of today by making public statements about drugs, that we should dress and behave like the freaks we're supposed to be. I just wish 1970 would hurry up and go away. It's all been a disaster.' Clapton had just discovered that the woman he thought was his sister was actually his mother. He

1970 PLAYLIST

Simon & Garfunkel, *Bridge Over Troubled Water*
Led Zeppelin, 'Whole Lotta Love'
Free, 'All Right Now'
The Doors, *Morrison Hotel*
James Taylor, *Sweet Baby James*
Elton John, *Elton John*
Todd Rundgren, *Runt*
The Stooges, *Fun House*
George Harrison, *All Things Must Pass*
Derek and the Dominos, 'Layla'

16 MAY 1971
NEW YORK CITY

The comeback

When Lou Reed left the Velvet Underground on 23 August 1970 his parents had driven into the city of New York to collect him from his last gig and taken him back to their home in Freeport, Long Island. This seemed a reversal of the natural order of things. Normally rock stars left home once and for all in their teens and after that they discouraged any speculation about their home life, preferring to leave the impression they had been raised by wolves. This was particularly the case for the generation born, as Lewis Reed had been, during the war. His parents could have been forgiven for thinking that at the age of twenty-eight their son might have finally given up on his dreams of making it as a rock star. Rock star was plainly a young man's occupation. Experience was not any kind of advantage. Certainly his erstwhile group seemed to be getting on without him. *Loaded*, the last album he had made with them, had come out in late 1970. On the back it had a picture of bass player Doug Yule at the piano, giving the impression that it had been mainly his work, which it wasn't. Lou's songs, such as 'Sweet Jane', were credited to the entire band, which was equally incorrect.

That appeared to be behind him now. Lou's father gave his son some work as a typist in his accountancy business. Lou's downtown friends back in the city were amazed that he seemed happy to do this, at least for a while. Nonetheless they continued to circle Lou as though he were an IED.

Lou had had an unhappy childhood. His misguided but loving parents thought electric shock treatment might snap him out of his adolescent unhappiness. Throughout his life it was difficult to know where his psychiatric problems ended and his overbearing personality began. Almost all the professional relationships Reed had in his career involved at least the threat of physical violence. This was the case in some of his personal relationships as well. Glenn O'Brien, who edited Warhol's magazine *Interview*, knew him at this time and commented that 'he was brilliant, but had a lot of bitterness in him that fed a mean streak. A mean mean streak that alternated with empathy and great humour.' He remembers him ordering double Bloody Marys before noon and pills 'that pushed him in different directions, up and down'.

He had met a girl, a pretty undergraduate at Columbia University called Bettye Kronstad. His downtown friends called her 'the cocktail waitress' or 'the stewardess' behind her back. They did standard boyfriend and girlfriend stuff together. They spent the day in the park, drinking sangria, and then going to a movie. Lou related the details of the time they spent together in the song 'Perfect Day' in the same matter-of-fact way he had described the life of a junkie in 'I'm Waiting For The Man'. Bettye had no interest in his old dark life; she didn't do drugs and her priority was to keep Lou away from strong drink. For Lou she was the latest in a long line of surrogate mother/nurse/secretary figures who would deal with all the aspects of the world that were beneath his dignity and also be on hand to admire him when he was temporarily removed from the sunshine of his admirers' acclaim.

The Velvet Underground had originally been put before the public in the middle of the previous decade via the patronage of Andy Warhol. For every potential record buyer excited by the idea that they were an art project as much as a band there were many more people who were put off by just the same thing. Their admirers were well-placed rather than numerous. If all the journalists who liked them were gathered in one place then they could fill a small venue. If it were left to the wider public they were a failure. The standard Velvet Underground review recounted their latest misadventure with the music business, described the state of the tensions within the band and ended by being slightly disappointed with how unadventurous record buyers were not supporting them as they had supported Led Zeppelin or the Doors. The Velvet Underground seemed to have missed the bus. The one after that as well.

Nonetheless they had admirers overseas. On 27 January 1971 one of their biggest fans from London was in New York as the Doug Yule-led version of Velvet Underground played the Electric Circus. After the show this long-haired Limey talked to Yule for fifteen minutes, enthusing about how inspirational he found the band and how distinctive their sound was. Puzzled as to why the visitor kept calling him Lou, Yule felt he ought to make it clear that he wasn't Lou Reed. He was Doug Yule. The visitor from Britain withdrew, faintly embarrassed. He would be back later in the year. His name was David Bowie.

Having apparently failed to make it as a rock star Reed was attempting to reposition himself as a man of letters. He published poems as Lewis Reed. On 10 March he took part in a poetry reading with Jim Carroll at St Mark's. He wrote a piece for *Crawdaddy* magazine. In this he seemed to be taking advantage of the unique vantage point of the retired rock star. The piece was headlined 'Why I Wouldn't Want My Son to be a Rock Star or a Dog Even'. Like many pieces of prose penned by musicians it had clearly not been edited, either by its author or anyone else, and was consequently near unreadable. The central thrust seemed to be that only a person with no proper sense of self would ever wish to be a rock and roll star. 'But a real star can go in Max's and have everybody say hello and live in the Castle in Los Angeles and know the right people and be interviewed in Rolling Stone, perhaps even the cover, bitch and yell in public, discuss politics, ride in limousines, have styled hair and perhaps a private make-up man, smoke the best dope, be arrested and make headlines, be featured in the very best gossip columns, and be a candidate for the Plaster Casters.'

The tone of this passage suggested that Lou considered the life of the rock star beneath his dignity. At the same time the close attention to detail in that list suggested that there wasn't a single facet of the rock-star life he didn't ache to experience. He also wrote a piece for a book called *No One Waved Goodbye*, which had been inspired by the recent deaths of Janis Joplin, Jimi Hendrix and Jim Morrison, where he observed, perceptively, 'It simply requires a very secure ego to allow yourself to be loved for what you do rather than what you are, and an even larger one to realize you are what you do. The singer has a soul but realizes he isn't loved off stage. Or perhaps, he feels he only shines on stage . . . but we are all as common as snowflakes, aren't we?'

Lou could no more renounce the life he had left than fly to the moon. He had a need for the spotlight that could only be satisfied by living out the rock star's life. He might have been enjoying the short holiday from the bohemian limelight back in his parents' home in the suburbs but the rage for repute was building inside. His contradictory nature cried out for expression. His need for attention meant that he could never pass up the opportunity to extemporize into a reporter's tape machine. The more he derided journalists the more he sought their company. This applied throughout his life. And the more he insisted that what he was doing was art, the more he desperately sought the approbation of the market in the only kind of coin he truly understood. This was the same one he had been chasing since starting as a jobbing songwriter of dumb ditties back in the sixties – chart success. Lou Reed wouldn't admit it but he wanted a hit record every bit as badly as Marc Bolan or Three Dog Night wanted a hit record. His first record had been a celebration of a non-existent dance craze called 'Do The Ostrich'. He never lost his belief in the power and beauty of near-moronic simplicity and the monetary rewards it could bring.

On 16 May 1971 he was at the New York City apartment of Richard and Lisa Robinson. She was a journalist and friend of the stars; he had recently signed on as an A&R man with RCA Records. Bettye Kronstad, who was included in these evenings, told author Howard Sounes 'all these people in the music business would hang out and all sit around in a circle and listen to Lou pontificate. We just all sat around and gazed adoringly at Lou.' There are no recorded instances of this state of affairs ever bothering Lou. On this occasion he played them a number of songs he had been working on, including a new one called 'Walk On The Wild Side'. This had been inspired by Nelson Algren's novel of the same name, but had grown into an unblinking account of the back stories of the key people in Andy Warhol's Factory. Without the girlie backing vocals and the swooning string bass 'Walk On The Wild Side' didn't yet have the qualities that might make it a hit. Nonetheless there was enough there for Richard to suggest to Lou that he should put his poetry career on hold and have another tilt at making a record, this time with RCA. The same record company, which hadn't made any significant signings in the last few years, had just done a deal with the manager of that English guy David Bowie who was, interestingly, a big admirer of Lou's, and indeed was said to include some of his songs in his stage act. Robinson might even be able to arrange for Reed to have artistic control and to make the record in London, far away from his bad experiences in New York. Lewis Reed didn't need any second bidding.

Over the summer, as Robinson sold the deal to his masters at RCA and Reed took steps to assert his right to be credited as the composer of the songs on the Velvet Underground's *Loaded*, the second coming of Lou Reed took shape. It was to have one crowning moment of coming-out. On 9 September David Bowie was in New York to officially sign his deal with RCA, who would release his new album *Hunky Dory* before Christmas. Flushed with the rare experience of being the centre of attention, RCA threw a party for their new signing at a club called The Ginger Man. Among the guests were Lou Reed and Bettye Kronstad, who appeared in the midst of Bowie's carefully cultivated fabulousness like the suburban figures they had become. Assured this time that he was talking to the right person, Bowie allowed the older man to take the limelight. It was a curious meeting. Neither was anything like as big a noise as the people around them fervently hoped they could become. Reed was the elder statesman nobody had heard of. Bowie was the hot young thing nobody knew from Adam. They performed the familiar courtly dance of rock luminaries seeking to avoid at all costs deferring to each other. At the end of the evening Bowie's party went on to another venue where they were introduced to another of the American performers Bowie liked to advertise his approval of, Iggy Pop.

Thus began the strange joint life of this unholy trinity, who would circle each other for the rest of their lives, using each other and in turn being used to their mutual benefit. There was a crackle about and around them. Lou could go off at a moment's notice, Iggy was in the grip of heroin and gave the impression that he had already flamed out, David was shrewd and controlled but was inclined to turn up for interviews in a gown and claim, despite a paucity of evidence, that he was gay. Above all they were copy. They had no PRs telling them what to say. They thought like journalists. They were a three-headed attention-grabbing device. In the year that the Rolling Stones had gone into tax exile in France, George Harrison had achieved a form of rock sainthood by spearheading the Concert for Bangla Desh, the charts were dominated by singer-songwriters hymning the attractions of bucolic domesticity, and the rock establishment was still mourning the rock gods who had fallen by the wayside, this urban conspiracy of lairy transgressives, this same-sex marriage of convenience based on three chords and a shared mascara, this trio who had nothing to lose and everything to gain, were perfectly placed to wrench away the spotlight and fix it firmly on themselves.

1971 PLAYLIST

George Harrison, 'My Sweet Lord'
Marvin Gaye, *What's Going On*
Carole King, *Tapestry*
The Who, *Who's Next*
Sly & the Family Stone, 'Family Affair'
Rod Stewart, 'Maggie May'
T. Rex, 'Jeepster'
Joni Mitchell, *Blue*
Badfinger, 'Baby Blue'
David Bowie, *Hunky Dory*

26 JULY 1972

MADISON SQUARE GARDEN, NEW YORK CITY

Rock goes high society

The Rolling Stones' American tour of 1972, which was on a grander scale than any of the tours that had come before it, was accomplished without computers, mobile phones or the internet. It was a low-tech world; in 1972 sixteen-year-old Bill Gates was still tinkering with the school computer to make sure he got to share his lessons with attractive girls. Before this tour very few rock and roll people had much call to rent a plane. Before this tour promoters didn't try to get a country's head of government on the phone to smooth out bureaucratic hold-ups. Before this tour the bands didn't pretend that they were the only thing between the state and disorder on the streets. Before this tour bands hadn't thought about actually rehearsing for their live shows, let alone hiring practice venues which were as big as the ones they intended to play. It was only at this point that people started comparing tours in terms of numbers: the number of people played for, the number of dollars grossed, the number of people begging to get on the guest list, the number of trucks it took to get the show from A to B. Everything about the Stones' two-month American tour of 1972 was on an unprecedented scale. In fact it was the scale, which invoked regular comparisons with the military, that added to the self-importance of all those involved in the enterprise. This is where rock started to get an inflated sense of its own significance. It increased the lustre of the five men at its centre and particularly the two men at the centre of the five. It fixed an idea of how it is appropriate to conduct oneself at the pinnacle of rock and roll stardom that has resounded down the decades.

The Rolling Stones knew they were setting new standards and therefore as the tour wound its way to New York City it was only meet and right that the birthday of the leading artiste should be marked by a gesture as unprecedented as the tour. The production manager's plan was that this special birthday should be celebrated in front of a large crowd at Madison Square Garden and therefore it should be on an arena scale. To that end he had hired an elephant. This beast cost $700. His plan was that at the very pinnacle of the noise and chaos of a Rolling Stones tour reaching New York, immediately following 'Street Fighting Man', said pachyderm should take to the stage. In its trunk it would be carrying a single red rose. It would bow and present the flower to Mick. Everyone would sing 'Happy Birthday'.

Of course it didn't quite happen that way. The elephant was vetoed by the management of the Garden, as were further plans to shower the audience with confetti and balloons. The production manager eventually moderated his demands and instead bought five hundred chickens, intending that they should be released during 'Street Fighting Man'. The Garden also vetoed this. He then ordered over 150 cream pies, intending that the show should climax in a finale worthy of Mack Sennett. The Garden found out about this too and confiscated all the pies in sight.

Inevitably they missed the pies the production manager had taken the precaution of hiding away. The big night came. As the Stones returned to the stage for an encore a cake was produced, and as Bianca Jagger was kissing her husband and presenting him with a large stuffed panda the first pie landed on the singer. Pies were then launched in every direction, at the other members of the band, at support act Stevie Wonder's backing singers, and at key members of the Stones organization. Finally Ian Stewart stole up on the fastidious Charlie Watts, who had thus far managed to avoid the flying patisserie, and clamped one over each ear of his Buster Keaton head.

Following the show there was a party in the roof garden of the St Regis Sheraton. Security was so tight that paying guests at the luxury hotel had to show their room keys in order to be allowed access to their beds – an indication of the demands big bands could suddenly make. The standard privileges that came with luxury accommodation were no longer sufficient for the Rolling Stones. The caution was based not only on the justifiable concern that fans might try to penetrate the private party but also the less grounded feeling that since more and more Americans were turning to guns to make their points it was clearly only a matter of time before somebody took a pop at Mick Jagger. It was a question Mick had been asked more than once during the tour. He said that if the recent death of King Curtis was anything to go by, you were in just as much danger of being eliminated by your neighbour as by a member of the crowd.

The party seemed an appropriate culmination for a tour that had been in many senses a move upmarket. The Stones' press people targeted *Time*, *Newsweek* and *Esquire* rather than the magazines and papers read by their fans. There was clearly a need to prove this was a grown-up business run by grown-up people. *Rolling Stone* magazine played along by commissioning Truman Capote to be their correspondent on the road with the band. Capote took his New York socialite pals Peter Beard and Jackie Kennedy's sister Princess Lee Radziwill with him. This didn't go down well. In the end Capote couldn't bring himself to write about the Stones. He said they didn't interest him as a subject. They should have interested him because this was the tour when they emerged as a new branch of high society, which was Truman's specialist subject. He might have been miffed that he had been blindsided by this sudden rise of the rock-star class. When he had thrown his famous Black and White Ball in New York in 1966, around the same time that Jimi Hendrix arrived in London, the five hundred names on the guest list were supposed to be a faithful representation of all the movers and shakers in everything from politics to the arts. The musicians included Frank Sinatra, Stephen Sondheim and Leonard Bernstein. There wasn't a single rock star. By 1972 this had all changed. This time the Stones' progress around the country was much like that of the Elizabethan court, trailing courtiers and mountebanks, rousing, exciting and provoking the countryside as it went on its way; taking advantage of whichever local nobs felt they might benefit from putting them up for a night, and leaving in their wake unsettled debts, ravished daughters and furniture in the moat.

The Rolling Stones tour of 1972 has a special place in the folk memory of rock because it was so closely documented. All the major organs of the media were given their little sliver of access and went away moist with excitement. With one eye on their own place in history, the band hired film maker Robert Frank to document the debauchery. When he complained after a while that he hadn't managed to get any orgy footage they staged one for him on an aeroplane between shows. They dutifully threw a television set out of a hotel-room window for the cameras, a process which, as the film showed, was a good deal more tiring than it ought to be. The Stones felt they had to act up to what the straight world was coming to expect of rock princes. (When Capote was with the tour he was roused from his hotel room in the middle of the night by Keith Richards, who said he wanted to show him what a rock and roll band was all about. Truman explained through the door that he was quite content he already knew what a rock and roll band was all about.) The finished film was only given the most limited release – the traditional fate of all the behind-the-scenes peeks the Rolling Stones insist on having total control over.

In a conversation with Andy Warhol which was published in *Rolling Stone* the following year, Truman Capote spoke about how he had noticed that all the people in the Stones' orbit seemed to draw sustenance from their proximity to the spotlight in which the Stones operated. You could see this in the pictures. The Rolling Stones were starting to have a disturbing effect on the men who flocked around them. At their most serious this meant they tried to keep pace with Keith Richards. In its mildest form this was just people who looked roughly like the Rolling Stones but weren't the Rolling Stones. Mick Jagger already had that peculiar quality of being able to change any room he entered purely by virtue of entering it. Keith Richards was the bad boy that all the good boys seek approval from – approval which will always be withheld. Such is the nature of the Mick and Keith act, and the reason why they call themselves the Glimmer Twins. All they owe to other people is the merest glimmer. Much of the coverage in the press was bathed in a glow of admiration, however, verging on the homoerotic. Interviewing Mick Jagger backstage, the *New York Times* noted that his pants were tailored of 'a silk-like material that clings so tightly that his genitalia are pushed up and out – a sexual display as aggressively protuberant as a fifties teenager in a push-up bra'.

The guest list for the party had been put together by Ahmet Ertegun and his wife Mica. Ahmet believed in parties because they got written about in the newspapers. He also liked going to them. The Erteguns were New York royalty and this list reflected that. Zsa Zsa Gabor, Gianni Bulgari and Oscar de la Renta rubbed shoulders with Woody Allen, Carly Simon, Andy Warhol and Tennessee Williams. Entertainment was provided by Muddy Waters and his band, Count Basie and his big band, and some hoofers from a Broadway show. The Stones were somewhat sheepish about the fact that such veterans were apparently at the beck and call of a bunch of musicians who were by comparison mere children. The inevitable cake was produced, the inevitable live nude girl emerged from it, and she performed the inevitable bump and grind in the direction of the birthday boy. The *New York Times* thought that it was evident a new era of rock chic had begun. Their reporter asked guest Bob Dylan what he made of the party and he replied, 'It's encompassing . . . it's the beginning of cosmic consciousness.' Keith Richards was

1972 PLAYLIST

Neil Young, *Harvest*
Paul Simon, *Paul Simon*
Todd Rundgren, *Something/Anything?*
Rolling Stones, *Exile On Main St*
Randy Newman, *Sail Away*
David Bowie, *The Rise And Fall Of Ziggy Stardust And The Spiders From Mars*
Jimmy Cliff, *The Harder They Come*
Yes, *Close To The Edge*
Stevie Wonder, *Talking Book*
Steely Dan, *Can't Buy A Thrill*

3 JULY 1973

HAMMERSMITH ODEON, LONDON

A 'rock star' retires

The erstwhile David Jones, twenty-six-year-old son of a charity worker from Brixton, south London, had devoted ten years to getting the kind of recognition that had finally come his way after he appeared on *Top of the Pops* playing his hit single 'Starman' just twelve months earlier. This song came from his then new album *The Rise And Fall Of Ziggy Stardust And The Spiders From Mars*. This depicted the career of a fictional rock star. This division between actor and role was anything but neat. The same month his management company MainMan had produced a PR dossier clearly announcing their client as 'Rock star David Bowie'.

A year earlier this would have seemed presumptuous certainly, possibly even funny. In the twelve months since *Top of the Pops* it appeared that this perennial trier, this strolling player, this dilettante who seemed fated to be forever just ahead of or behind the beat, had snapped into sync with the times. He was thus able to bank an entire lifetime of acceptance. And this currency could be exchanged everywhere. It was artistic success, as measured in the uniformly favourable reviews for his record. It was fashionable acceptance, as could be seen in the notables who suddenly expected to get into his shows without paying. It was teen enthusiasm, as he could detect in the keening sound rising from the auditorium floor at his shows. This last was particularly calculated to warm the heart of an old pop picker who'd been burning to be famous since he was sixteen years old.

But in the beginning David wasn't meant to be Ziggy Stardust. Somebody else was going to take on that role. The first person he'd lined up was Freddi Burretti, originally plain Fred Burrett, a miniature gay guy he'd happened upon during one of his R&D trips to gay hang-out El Sombrero. He'd cooked up the Ziggy idea in the course of the life-changing trip to the USA in early 1971. Over the months many things had fed into it: the wasp-in-a-bottle sound of the Stooges (from whose singer he also lifted the name); the legend of Vince Taylor, the British rock and roller whose self-destructive streak prevented him from making it; the limping figure of Gene Vincent, whom he'd encountered trying to make a comeback while on his first trip to Hollywood; the bright orange tonsure which he'd spotted on a model on the cover of UK women's magazine *Honey*; the uniform of Malcolm McDowell and his 'droogs' in Stanley Kubrick's version of Anthony Burgess's *A Clockwork Orange*, released in the US at the end of 1971. It was all coming together like an art project played out in the real world.

Multi-sourced though it was, Ziggy Stardust was also the perfect invention for its moment. It was a moment when the heads of both the new generation of seventies kids and the old sixties kids felt tugged back to a pre-Woodstock world of cheap formica glamour and nasty hair products, a world which the hippies had draped over with their cheese-cloth and suede and obsession with authenticity, a world which seemed to pulse through the lurid dreamscapes of Guy Peellaert, the books of Nik Cohn and the clothes of Mr-Freedom.

In the decade just passed, it had seemed reasonable to assume the personalities projected by rock stars were either true to their real ones or had grown from them naturally. Bowie's Ziggy Stardust was a product of a new age, when the figures on stage seemed just as likely to be characters in a musical play. On Bowie's first post-Ziggy tour he was supported by the new band Roxy Music, whose singer Bryan Ferry carried himself like Jack Buchanan (a popular British musical comedy artist of the inter-war years); in 1972 they vied for radio play with Alice Cooper, as portrayed by Vincent Furnier, a preacher's son from Michigan, who climaxed an evening's entertainment by having himself hanged.

Nobody seemed content any longer with being who they were. Nobody was singing their heart's desire. Nobody was writing personal-pronoun pop. This was a new era of gleeful self-consciousness, of stratagems and ruses you were invited to see coming from miles away. The edges of the picture were different, the trousers tighter, the speech newly guarded and self-consciously hard-bitten, the hair colour anything but the natural shade. It was like so many moments in rock a revenge on the recent past.

Bowie's manners may have been different but the music beneath them was reassuringly square. 'The Jean Genie', the big hit single Bowie had used to bridge the gap between Ziggy Stardust and the follow-up album, started out as a vamp on the Yardbirds' 'I'm A Man', a riff so bred in the bone of every rock soldier on the M1 that Mick Ronson feared it was beyond redemption. The public didn't care about that. On the scale of catchiness, it sat comfortably between Led Zeppelin's 'Whole Lotta Love' and Sweet's 'Ballroom Blitz'. Bowie already liked to tart up his work with noteworthy accents, such as Mike Garson's avant-garde piano interjections. The basic menu might be meat-and-potatoes hard rock, which was a standard part of the British diet, but he was always sure to spice it with a soupçon of strange.

It doesn't matter how long has been spent on the planning, the scheming and dreaming: fame inevitably arrives with violent suddenness and catches its victims unprepared. When it begins to break out, as it did for David Bowie in June 1972, the only thing to do is hang on for dear life. The music business has two forms of demand: non-existent and impossible to satisfy. Either nobody wants you at all or everybody needs you yesterday. For the six months after the 'Starman' breakout Bowie played anywhere his management could book him. Some of the choices were poor. He did a show at the cavernous Earls Court arena for which he was woefully ill-equipped. MainMan believed that if you wished to be big you had to behave big. Some suspected the artist's well-publicized fear of flying was just one of his Hollywood affectations. They indulged him nonetheless. After touring the UK in 1972 he sailed to the United States, touring there by bus and train, through whose windows his jaded gaze was confronted and songwriter's ears pricked by the licentious passing show from which he would fashion his next record 'Aladdin Sane'.

By the time the record was ready in April 1973 its title would be all too apposite. The experience of the contemporary rock and roll tour, with its seductive combination of alienation and indulgence, made even the people who weren't actually driven mad by it behave as though they were. Bowie's manager Tony DeFries, who had promised he would make his client famous but didn't specify whose money he would spend doing it, drove them on during the US leg of the tour with no thought for the collateral damage. Spending was out of control. They did everything big style, staying in the best hotels and swishing in and out of town like the stars they hoped they would one day be. They booked venues they couldn't fill and swallowed the shortfall. At one stage there were no fewer than fifty people in the tour's caravanserai, charging all their personal expenses to Bowie as though he were a cash-generating operation rather than a massive punt on black, underwritten by RCA's profits from all those Elvis Presley discs.

But, happily, everyone wanted a shake of his glitter dust. In 1973 Bowie was having a moment when he seemed magically able to help not only himself but others as well. Mott the Hoople did his 'All The Young Dudes' better than he could have done it himself. If there was any irony in the lyrics Ian Hunter went right past it and sent the song humming to the sentimental heart of England young and old, enjoying the rare thrill of seeing it sung back to him by all those enraptured up-tilted adolescent faces half-illuminated in the footlights. With Bowie's help Lou Reed had the hit record that previously he had only been able to theorize about. Bowie was even dusting off his old songs, like 'The Man Who Sold The World' for his pal Lulu. He was suddenly the junction through which the majority of British pop music seemed to be routed. Anything Bowie showed any interest in was swept under the MainMan umbrella as though it were an established empire. The Stooges, of all people, were actually put in a MainMan house in the Hollywood Hills to await Bowie's benediction.

All this largesse was scattered in haste. It was subsequently withdrawn just as abruptly.

Another form of currency on the 1972 tour was flesh. In Los Angeles the tour party were entertained by the girls from Rodney Bingenheimer's English disco, many of whom were perilously close to the age of consent. During this tour Bowie was reported as having slept with Lulu, Cyrinda Foxe, Lori Maddox, Ava Cherry, sundry others whose names were not recorded and even, on occasion, his wife Angie. There was a great deal of retaliatory fornication going on. During this time Angie Bowie also had affairs with Ron Asheton and James Williamson of the Stooges. She and the star's young son Joe were eventually 'let go' from the tour like any other troublesome component. Bowie wielded power every bit as ruthlessly as any star. He travelled with more minders than stars of far greater magnitude. The effect may have been other-worldly, alienated and wan, but there didn't appear to be a great deal wrong with his libido. They say the only touring musician who doesn't want sex is the touring musician who's just had some; in this respect Bowie behaved like the standard touring musician. Here his public musing about his bisexuality may have brought him the small dividend of making some women even more determined to stamp his card.

Bowie returned from the tour of the United States in December 1972 to find himself being hailed as a superstar – a sure sign of the hip establishment hyping itself. The enthusiasm was certainly running well ahead of the receipts. Bowie's manager was more than happy to paper the houses on the US tour just to increase the noise around his boy because it was the noise he planned to monetize. During this time he even had talks with a company that proposed to manufacture David Bowie dolls. This giddy sensation of something happening fed on itself. In an end-of-the-year piece in *NME*, Charles Shaar Murray raised an eyebrow at the fact that the kids were starting to scream at David Bowie. Was it David they were screaming at or Ziggy, the character he'd made up as a vehicle for his fantasies of being a rock star? Could they recognize any difference? Did it matter?

Even when he came back to the Hammersmith Odeon in London in July as the conquering hero the show wasn't actually sold out. There were enough tickets for schoolboys Malcolm Green and his friends from Wembley to turn up in the afternoon and buy some from a tout. The art students may have taken him up but his heartland fans were kids like Malcolm for whom he was the ideal worldly older-brother figure.

One of the attractive features of this new generation of rock stars for a new generation of fans was that if they were allowed to dress up as rock stars, then so were you. You might not be able to afford the same finery but with cheap hair colour, artfully applied cosmetics and well-chosen jewellery the desired alien effect could be achieved and taken out on your local high street. Starting with Bowie, the attraction of arraying yourself in the feathers of your favourite added another dimension to the relationship between a rock star and his people. It was a way you could participate in their fabulousness.

Malcolm and his friends were gathering in the alley round the side of the Odeon when a large Bentley drew up. One security man appeared to hold the crowd back while Bowie got out, wearing a pair of dungarees without a shirt, a cigarette jammed, as it always was, between his teeth. (This picture is on the jacket of this book.) He stopped and addressed the crowd in a voice that, Malcolm remembers, sounded quaintly like it had come from a post-war British movie. 'He seemed very down to earth.'

After saying goodbye, David Bowie entered the theatre and prepared to meet his public. This was now a time-consuming business. He had to make ready a number of costumes. His make-up took hours. As it was being prepared, his wife Angie turned up and loudly enthused about the limos and Rolls-Royces which were disgorging their fabulous cargo outside. Bowie was being filmed at the time by D. A. Pennebaker, who had created Bob Dylan's myth in his film *Dont Look Back*. What Angie evidently liked about it, what everybody in his circle liked about it, was the fuss, the hoopla, the minders, the opportunities to extend or withdraw favours, the trappings of being a rock star. They loved the trappings.

Bowie did the standard show that evening. He started with 'Hang On To Yourself'. Significantly, this was the first Ziggy song he had come up with. He flung in some songs from the new album and some from his old ones. He did 'Let's Spend The Night Together' by the Rolling Stones and then, after 'White Light/White Heat', the increasingly obligatory Velvet Underground tune, he approached the microphone and made his announcement. Tony DeFries was prepared for it but none of his team were; Mick Ronson knew what to expect but the other Spiders from Mars were taken by surprise. 'This show will stay with us the longest,' Bowie said, 'because not only is it the last show of the tour it's the last show we'll ever do.'

The crowd were shocked. Even these fans, who had only been fans for a few months, felt they had been promised an open-ended commitment – a standard fan reaction. Malcolm and his friends took it that this would be not just the end of Ziggy Stardust but the end of David Bowie as a live performer. Showing the showman's weakness for the ripple of shock he is capable of producing, Bowie had included the word 'ever', thereby allowing fans and press alike to overheat in speculation after the show.

Bowie needed a rest, either to pick up what remained of his old life or to adapt to this new one. He also knew what Tony DeFries knew, that this tour was starting to bleed money and he could no longer be certain that anyone would underwrite it. They played 'Rock And Roll Suicide' and then the Ziggy Stardust episode was theoretically over, just about a year after it had begun.

After the show Malcolm and his friends got on the train back to Wembley. Bowie and his wife got dressed in the last outfit of the evening to make a grand entrance at a special end-of-tour 'retirement' party that had been organized at the Café Royal, erstwhile haunt of Oscar Wilde. They played the part of the happy couple and mingled with guests including Mick and Bianca Jagger, Ringo Starr, Elliott Gould and Barbra Streisand, Tony Curtis, Paul and Linda McCartney, Keith Moon and Sonny Bono. The music was provided by Doctor John, then celebrating the release of his album *In The Right Place*.

There was much photographic evidence of this occasion, which was useful because Bowie himself didn't remember anything about the party. Two days later he felt better and began to regret his announcement. It was too late.

When Chuck Berry sang of Johnny B. Goode getting his name in lights, that seemed a benign daydream such as we all might share. Twenty years later in David Bowie's vision the rock star was a tragic figure, doomed to enact his own suicide on stage as the only way to placate the ravening hordes. The subtleties of such long-form ideas soon get lost in a telegrammatic medium like rock. His true text was stardom, which suddenly became fascinating to everyone. Within the next year it had all but replaced teen romance as a primary subject for pop, in David Essex's 'Gonna Make You A Star', the Raspberries' 'Overnight Sensation (Hit Record)', the Kinks' *Everybody's In Show-Biz – Everybody's A Star* and even the Rolling Stones' 'Starfucker'. The up-and-coming Bruce Springsteen also had his mock-boastful line about the record company giving him a big advance in 'Rosalita'. Suddenly rock was a legitimate subject for rock and stardom was something stars sang about.

The Ziggy Stardust project seeded the idea that it might be possible to invent a rock star. This rock star wouldn't have to be the person who did the inventing. He or she could be as distinct from their creator as a novel from the novelist. This kind of figure would be a vehicle for ideas and fancies that no right mind could entertain and no human frame could sustain. It was an idea that appealed to the growing number of musicians who had read a handful of books and wanted to feel that they could indulge themselves in the world of limelight while still retaining some intellectual standing. It ought to be possible for anyone to play the part of the rock star for a while and then walk away without a scratch on them.

Many rock stars would find that this was increasingly unlikely to be the case. No matter how many costumes David Bowie may have adopted, no matter how painstakingly he had pointed out the parentheses around the pop star persona, the audience out there in the dark was, and remains, essentially a simple soul. It wants its pound of flesh and is apt to get it. The Ziggy project had started with its most prescient song. Hang on to yourself. That would be the hardest thing for any rock star to do.

6 AUGUST 1974
914 STUDIOS, BLAUVELT, NEW YORK STATE

Rock in a complicated world

Great records are often made very quickly. Little Richard's 'Tutti Frutti' was bashed out against the clock at the end of a long day. The Rolling Stones' 'Satisfaction' was at the top of the charts all over the world within a few weeks of Keith Richards being woken in the middle of the night with its riff going through his head. The first Black Sabbath album was recorded on one day, mixed on the next, and on the third day it was pretty much in the shops. If popular music history has one thing to teach, it is that time spent polishing records is usually time spent ruining them.

By the time twenty-four-year-old Bruce Springsteen got round to making the third and, unless something miraculous was to come to pass, final album under the terms of his contract with Columbia Records, his world no longer looked quite as simple as it had looked to his heroes of the fifties and sixties. It seemed he was now operating in an era when the sheer amount of competition was intimidating and the people who regulated access to wider acceptance were at best blasé and at worst openly hostile. Whichever direction he took he was reminded that somebody had gone before. The wordiness of the songs on his first album meant that he had recently been included on the long list of potential new Bob Dylans, alongside John Prine, Loudon Wainwright and Elliott Murphy. By the age of twenty-four his heroes the Beatles, the Stones, Bob Dylan and Elvis Presley had already done their best work, and here he was, yet to begin. Maybe he'd left it too late to be unique.

Though the record-buying public had been underwhelmed by his efforts, he was still in demand as a live performer. His band, which at the time comprised Danny Federici, Garry Tallent, Clarence Clemons, David Sancious and, on the drums, Ernest 'Boom' Carter, had, thanks to its instrumental line-up, more colours and textures at its disposal than the average outfit; its line-up was also multi-racial, which was noteworthy; of even greater importance was the fact that the singer was a frontman in the soul tradition, every bit as engaged with the audience as he was with the songs. It was Springsteen's ability to rock whatever house he was put in front of that kept his date book full. This much was gratifying, but it would never be quite enough for a young man possessed by such a lust for glory.

In the spring of 1974 Springsteen had two sorts of supporters. There were rock critics, who were aching for him to be as good as he looked as if he ought to be. The enthusiastic support of rock critics is not always a good thing. It's often a sign that an artist's potential appeal is restricted to ill-coordinated white males who stayed at home committing

B-sides to memory when they could've been out kissing real live girls. In 1973 and 1974 the alternative and local press was studded with features about Springsteen, all trying to describe the combination of rock energy, vernacular lyricism and All-American get-up-and-go of his shows. These pieces also expressed their fervent hope that he might be able to put all that promise together into something fit to take its place in what was increasingly being seen as a rock tradition. The crowning example of this strand of music journalism appeared in Boston's *Real Paper* on 22 May 1974. It got more attention than most because it was written by Jon Landau, well-known for his reviews in *Rolling Stone* and also his dabbling in record production with the MC5 and Livingston Taylor. Landau was reviewing a Springsteen show that had taken place earlier in the month at the Harvard Square Theater. His review was unusually personal. The first half of it was taken up with a description of what music had meant to him when he was a teenager and about how nowadays he tended to appreciate it in a more detached way, as befits somebody who has to listen to it for work. This had changed, he said, in the course of Bruce Springsteen's show at the Harvard Square Theater. On that night, he wrote, he saw his rock and roll past flash before his eyes. 'And I saw something else. I saw rock and roll future and its name is Bruce Springsteen.'

Not surprisingly, the record company seized upon this and, displaying their usual scant regard for subtleties, turned it into the slightly more user-friendly 'I have seen the future of rock 'n' roll and his name is Bruce Springsteen'. It didn't make much difference. With that article the die was cast and now Landau was on Springsteen's team. The two began spending time together. Springsteen had a difficult relationship with his own father – both his parents had left to start a new life on the West Coast – and Landau was that important couple of years older and university-educated enough to be able to act as his mentor. For his part Landau looked at Springsteen and saw the true clay of a real rock star, the kind of person he would never be no matter how much he practised.

The second group of people whose support held out hope that Springsteen might graduate from the ranks of the also-rans were the women who came to his shows. They devoured his tough but tender act with a spoon, seeing at last a way they could stay invested in rock into adulthood. One of the few journalists to notice this was Paul Williams, who teased the singer, 'I got word from New York that you're a real sex star now.' He went on to quote a friend of his who was twenty-six. 'I guess twenty-six-year-old women haven't found anything for years they can get off on. A friend of mine said, "He knows that you know that he knows what he's doing."' Springsteen tried to get off the point by saying that there were 'a lot of different energies' on stage but the fact was he knew exactly what Williams was talking about. Like the vaudeville entertainer Bert Lahr who had devoted most of his early years in the trade to simply watching the audience, Springsteen learned from every interaction with an audience. One of his most profound insights was if you get the women on side the men will very quickly follow. He was already projecting a slightly bruised maleness which was all the more powerful for not being talked about. Like the mainly male rock critics the women in the audience gazed upon him and hoped he could rekindle the way they had once felt. The headline of Landau's piece had been 'Growing young with rock & roll'. The women felt the same.

In 1974 Springsteen was living on his own in a shabby two-bedroom cottage at 7½ West End Court in Long Branch,

New Jersey, just along the shore from Asbury Park. The place had few home comforts. There was an old sofa that had been rescued from the alley. There was an old Aeolian piano in the room looking out on to the street. There was a bed, and on a table beside it was an old-fashioned record player. Every night he would drift off to sleep listening to masterpieces by the likes of Roy Orbison, Phil Spector and Duane Eddy, hoping he might wake to find himself capable of writing the one song that could define him the way 'Running Scared' had defined Roy, 'Be My Baby' had defined Phil and 'Rebel Rouser' had defined Duane.

He felt he might have the germ of a song fresh enough to make an impact in 1974 but also classic enough to live alongside the fifties hits pulsing on the soundtrack of the recently released movie *American Graffiti*. It was a song that could both soundtrack and celebrate young America's profound need for movement. It could magically transform him into something more than the sum of his influences. He wrote and rewrote its words endlessly, trying to put into it everything he felt he had to offer while also leaving it spare enough to become a hit. Landau's advice had been to take note of how classic movies made their point. Springsteen was particularly keen on the way B-pictures haunted the imagination while wearing their implications lightly. His song 'Thunder Road', which he was developing at the same time, has a title from an old Robert Mitchum movie and an opening line that might have come from a screenplay. Some of the lyrics of this song betrayed the amount he had riding on it. 'We've got one last chance to make it real' was ostensibly about the young innocents in the song but at the same time about someone no longer young trying to make music that didn't collapse under the weight of its own self-consciousness. He also prayed it might become that one thing in the pursuit of which all sins of taste and plagiarism are forgiven, that eternally retreating mirage in exchange for which all artists, regardless of their pretensions, their background or their haircuts, would sell all they had – a real hit single.

The song was 'Born To Run'. It took the best part of six months for Bruce Springsteen to finish it and record it. He and his manager/ producer Mike Appel had booked time in August at a studio in Blauvelt, an unlikely location north of New York City which had the advantage of being affordable. They did the basic track quickly. The drums, which were thunderous, were played by Ernest 'Boom' Carter. It was the only time he recorded with Springsteen. The keyboards, which provide the record's lyricism, were played by David Sancious, who left the band soon afterwards. Months were then spent in the studio over-laying guitars, keyboards, backing vocals, even strings. By then it had acquired the density of a Phil Spector record. Heard at a certain angle it sounded like some lost masterpiece that had been awaiting discovery for decades. It was the sound of lost youth. It was so dense that when he played it to his old friend and fellow guitar player Steve Van Zandt the latter could no longer hear the fact that at the end of the signature riff he bent up to the major note, which had been his intention. Springsteen recorded it again to make it clear. They played it to the record company, who made the suggestion they felt was expected of them, to boost the vocal. They tried to do that but found it couldn't be done without sacrificing the titanic thrust of the original track.

They were so thrilled with it that foolishly they released it to college radio, which ensured that the shine had come off it by the time they were ready with the rest of the album, in the summer of 1975. Eventually it was a hit. It was never as big a hit as 'Pretty Woman' or 'Be My Baby' or any of the records that inspired it but in many senses it was a wholly new kind of hit, the kind that lasted for years.

Landau's review of Springsteen's live show had said that 'every gesture, every syllable adds something to his ultimate goal – to liberate our spirit while he liberates his by baring his soul through music'. Reading that repeatedly as he clearly did must have had a transformational effect on Springsteen. It told him who he was, how he already came over to people, and hinted at what he could hope to achieve. It gave this most self-conscious of rock stars one kind of validation. The other validation came from the four and a half minutes of the record he had just spent months labouring over. 'Born To Run' was the record that justified Landau's review. Now Springsteen had to live up to the record.

When the album came out, Springsteen was famously on the cover of both *Time* and *Newsweek*. This was unheard of for a relative unknown. At that time the so-called 'straight press' was only just getting comfortable with the idea of featuring the people who played loud music. They preferred to cover this story as a cultural phenomenon. The cover line on *Time* promised a look at 'the making of a rock star'. That was how it was. It was a process, rather than some magical accident. So that's what he was now. A rock star. He found the attention terrifying because he knew what he expected a rock star to be. He didn't see playing the rock star as an art project. He saw it as something more like a sacred duty. He wanted to build on what he'd seen in Roy Orbison, the Beatles, Bob Dylan and Creedence Clearwater Revival. He wanted to be able to tell the whole story. He wanted an act that encompassed politics as well as romance, drama as well as dancing, sermons as well as sex. His vision of a rock star stood on the shoulders of all the rock stars that had gone before.

Springsteen was sitting around the pool at the Sunset Marquis in Hollywood when he first saw those covers. It was twenty years since 'Tutti Frutti', twenty years since Little Richard had invented being a rock star and now the responsibilities of the role seemed heavier. Years later he recalled his feelings. 'I was just going to have to be good enough, as good as I promised, as good as I thought I was, for all this to make sense.'

1974 PLAYLIST

Steve Miller Band, 'The Joker'
Joni Mitchell, *Court and Spark*
Van Morrison, *It's Too Late To Stop Now*
David Bowie, *Diamond Dogs*
The Beach Boys, *Endless Summer*
Neil Young, *On The Beach*
Jackson Browne, *Late For The Sky*
Gram Parsons, *Grievous Angel*
Bob Dylan, *Planet Waves*
The Eagles, *On The Border*

18 JULY 1975
THE LYCEUM, LONDON
The best rock isn't always rock

The books of rock history, which were just beginning to appear in numbers in the music's third decade, have tended to agree that not much was happening in 1975. It didn't feel like that at the time.

In 1975 I was working in a record shop in London's West End. Most weeks brought some kind of event. In January there was Bob Dylan's *Blood On The Tracks*, which was widely regarded as a return to his glory days. In February there was John Lennon's *Rock 'N' Roll*, a reverential re-run of the music that had inspired him twenty years earlier, made so that he could pay off a debt to the shady publisher Morris Levy, whose properties he had misappropriated for tracks like 'Come Together'. In the same month Led Zeppelin released a double album containing 'Kashmir' and 'Trampled Under Foot', which were at least as good as anything they had yet done, and David Bowie put out *Young Americans*, which would give him his first bona fide hit in the USA. Over the summer these were joined by *Fleetwood Mac*, Rod Stewart's *Atlantic Crossing*, the Eagles' *One Of These Nights* and Paul Simon's *Still Crazy After All These Years*, records which were to linger longer than most. If those came from the easier-to-listen-to end of the spectrum they were more than matched by Neil Young's *Tonight's The Night*, Patti Smith's *Horses* and Joni Mitchell's *The Hissing Of Summer Lawns*, which provided all the red meat one could require.

Steve and I worked at HMV in London, at the time the biggest record shop in the world. We saw some special shows in 1975. In January the Warner Brothers Music Show came to town and we went to see it at the Rainbow on a Sunday afternoon. The headliners were the Doobie Brothers but most of the two thousand in the theatre that afternoon had come to see the support act, Little Feat, at the time the most fashionable band among those of us who considered ourselves taste-makers. Stumbling jet-lagged on to the stage at a most unlikely time of the week, anticipating no more than a perfunctory run through their set before getting back on the bus and yielding the stage to their senior label mates, the six Californians were met with a crowd who were already standing and roaring their approval before they had played a note. An hour later, when they were brought back for their third encore, their leader Lowell George surveyed the cheering throng, shook his head and said, 'You people are crazy.' He'd come halfway round the world with no expectation of being anything but a supporting player, found himself in the curious position of being unrecognized on the street, unplayed on the radio and unreported in the press, and yet here he was being acclaimed as some kind of a rock star.

The rock music industry was now big enough to boast many mansions. It could accommodate cult stars as well as superstars. It could find room for many different versions of the standard rock star. In February we went to see the last night of the Naughty Rhythms Tour, which was a tongue-in-cheek name for a line-up that was in itself a tongue-in-cheek version of the package tours of the previous decade. The final act was Dr Feelgood, a wilfully retro beat band who performed as if the year was 1962 and the place was Hamburg. Their clockwork-mouse guitar player Wilko Johnson was a new kind of rock star for people old enough to get the retro gag. Dr Feelgood were nothing if not self-conscious, and in that sense they were the UK equivalent of Bruce Springsteen's E Street Band (still getting ready to release, at last, the album *Born To Run*). Beneath it all there was a feeling that rock might be running out of new heroes in new moulds, that there was no longer a ready supply of people who were charismatic and self-invented, who stood for something others might want to emulate, could come up with songs that everybody could sing and might also work on the big stage.

On Thursday, 18 July, after drinking two pints of Young's in the Marquess of Anglesey on Bow Street in Covent Garden, Steve and I crossed the road, handed in our tickets, made our way into the throng and witnessed the best show either of us had ever seen. Because the Rolling Stones Mobile Studio recording truck was parked outside, the concerts were captured for a recording which made the argument for us: *Live!*

Like many of the best venues for amplified live music the Lyceum was not designed for the purpose. It had previously hosted everything from Victorian productions of Shakespeare to the glory days of the dance bands. That night's entertainment emanated from the intersection of high and low culture. There was no seating in the place for the evening, which was just as well because it would've been out of the question to remain still in the presence of the music Bob Marley played that night. The crowd included curious rock fans, volatile rude boys, London scene-makers and middle-aged Africans all in unaccustomed proximity. Although the music being played spoke of unity and transcendence the experience of being in the audience was spiced with danger, as gig-going so often was in those days, when things could go off at a moment's notice. There was certainly more at stake in this music than we were used to. It was there in the titles of songs like 'Burnin' And Lootin'', 'Them Belly Full (But We Hungry)' and 'Get Up, Stand Up'. It was there in the words: stern, unbending school-room words like 'hypocrites', 'tribulation', 'curfew', 'brutalization' and 'sufferation'. It was there in the way the music of the rhythm section seemed to be redistributing massive columns of hot summer air around the Lyceum. It was there in the way the figure of Marley, high-stepping on the spot like the leader of his own guerrilla infantry, his dreadlocks rolling back and forth, seemed to sway suspended in the strobe light's glare. This was the night when Chris Blackwell's plan came to pass. The boss of Island Records wished to reposition a form of music previously regarded by smart opinion as good only for novelty hits and skinhead dance parties into the stuff of serious rebellion, and at the same time anoint Bob Marley as the first rock star of the Third World.

Some say Elvis Presley was the invention of Sam Phillips; that he was looking out for a white boy who could sing in the black style and that he knew that when he found one he would be able to write his own cheque. He may have entertained the thought, but it's most likely it was just one of many that went through his mind as he found himself with a huge hit on his hands and wondered just how long he could hang on to it before handing it on to somebody bigger. Few grand schemes survive first contact with the enemy. This applies in show business as much as it does in battle.

In the post-war years the West Indies, seen from the point of view of most in Great Britain, was the sun-kissed source of many of the world's greatest cricketers and a great deal of London's bus conductors and railway porters, who had arrived in the city in the fifties and sixties in search of a better life. Chris Blackwell was a smart, polished, handsome, connected young man from Jamaica's white ruling class, a class that had prospered on the back of a slavery-driven economy which in its time was even more savage than the one that prevailed in the southern United States. Blackwell set up Island Records in order to sell records from Jamaica's small but vibrant music industry to the Caribbean diaspora in London. He believed talent needed to be moulded. He found the fifteen-year-old Millie Small and signed on as her guardian in order to bring her to Britain. She was given elocution and presentation lessons before cutting 'My Boy Lollipop' in Forest Hill in east London. It was an enormous hit and gave him the money to set up Island as Britain's premier independent label, and position it to take advantage of the rock album gold rush of the late sixties and early seventies. Thanks to Island's success with King Crimson, Emerson, Lake & Palmer and Free, Blackwell knew how to sell records to longhairs. When he signed the Wailers in 1972 his plan was to sell their records not to Jamaicans living in London, who knew about their hits in the Caribbean, but to white college students in Europe and the United States.

He was warned off signing them. Everybody in Jamaica knew the Wailers were trouble. There was always fighting in the captain's tower, between Marley, Bunny Livingston and

Peter Tosh. They had entered into loose arrangements with every company in Jamaica's legendarily loose record business and now didn't trust anybody. Their Rastafarian beliefs meant they regarded all commerce as the devil's work and made them duty-bound to spend their waking hours in a marijuana miasma, couching their words in a patois that few but initiates could comprehend.

Blackwell didn't waste his time trying to change their behaviour. He gave them some money to make a whole album in Jamaica. They sent the tapes to him in London where he sweetened them with instruments reassuring to the rock ear. He excluded one track in order to make the LP just nine tracks long, as befitted a rock album. Then he burst the budget packaging *Catch A Fire* in a cover in the shape of a cigarette lighter, which announced that for the first time this music was being treated with just as much respect as the prog rock of King Crimson or the art rock of Roxy Music. They toured overseas to support the record but Bunny Livingston wasn't keen so he was eased out. After the next album, *Burnin'*, Peter Tosh went off and took his hair-trigger temper with him. When *Natty Dread* appeared in late 1974 it was credited to Bob Marley and the Wailers and the front cover was dominated by a painting of Bob as a super-hero, the rough planes of his face replaced by a comic-book sheen. Blackwell's plan was to make him the first rock star of reggae.

In the Lyceum the Wailers lined up in front of a picture of Haile Selassie, the recently deposed head of the Ethiopian state revered by Rastafarians as the living son of God. The rhythm section of Aston and Carlton Barrett meted out rhythms you could rest your drink on, American guitarist Al Anderson pealed off phosphorescent leads, the I-Threes, including Marley's wife Rita, who felt her presence on tour might control some of her husband's tendency to spread his seed like a sovereign, chanted back every line, while Marley, the man at the centre of this maelstrom, hit all his marks, despite giving every appearance of broadcasting from the furthest reaches of a trance-like state of abandon. I've still never seen a better show.

This was the thing about Marley. He had drive that nobody else around him did. Something back in his childhood, possibly back in the days when the other children made his life difficult because his father had been a British army captain, had equipped him with the discipline it takes to drill a band so that they can play at the top of their game without apparent effort. He had the ear to know what was a catchy tune. He had a flair for slogans. As Chris Blackwell realized, his voice was on the right frequency to cut through the airwaves, which was what made him not just a master of the long-form album but also the hit single, of which the version of 'No Woman No Cry' recorded at the Lyceum that night was one of the first.

Within the small, febrile world of Jamaica he was a very big man indeed, one upon whom politicians danced attendance, one who could click his fingers and have any woman come running, one whose disdain for earthly wealth didn't prevent him announcing that he wanted a new BMW because the initials stood for 'Bob Marley and the Wailers', one whose patronage every other musician on the island desperately sought. He was a player. The stakes he played for would prove to be very dangerous indeed.

Steve and I went home from the Lyceum with our senses humming. For days afterwards those songs crowded out everything else in our heads. Their biblical sentiments had smuggled themselves into our consciousness via the songs' earworm properties, the combination of their most militant urgency with springy rhythms that were the apotheosis of soon-come. We also had the unique sensation that we had been present when something of great significance had come to pass. Furthermore it had gone past at the right speed to allow one to take full note. We had never previously heard reggae played with such divine heaviness. We had never before seen such a figure arise as if from out of Israel to smite the unrighteous with the rod of correction. We had certainly never heard anyone arrive with this many new ideas enshrined in this many memorable tunes. Bob Marley wasn't a mere reggae star. He was actually the biggest rock star since Bob Dylan plugged in.

A bare month after the Lyceum concert, when Marley was back in Jamaica, the news of the death of Haile Selassie was announced from Addis Ababa. The former Ethiopian ruler had been deposed in a military coup a year before and had been in custody ever since. Some loyalists believe he was murdered. More likely his captors didn't make the efforts they might have made to save this inconvenient, elderly man. Thanks to Marley and other Jamaican musicians Selassie's fame was about to grow in the years following his death. Marley, in whose belief system this frail old man was a living deity, did not believe that death would be the end. His view, expressed in 'Jah Live', the single which he swiftly recorded and released on hearing the news, was as trenchant as the world had already come to expect. It promised that, now that the enemies were scattered, Selassie would arise from the dead. Nobody laughed.

1975 PLAYLIST

10cc, 'I'm Not In Love'
Bob Marley and the Wailers, *Live!*
Bruce Springsteen, *Born To Run*
Bob Dylan, *Blood On The Tracks*
Neil Young, *Tonight's The Night*
Patti Smith, *Horses*
Joni Mitchell, *The Hissing Of Summer Lawns*
Led Zeppelin, *Physical Graffiti*
David Bowie, *Young Americans*
Dr Feelgood, *Malpractice*

4 JULY 1976
TAMPA, FLORIDA

The X factor

In 1970 Peter Green left Fleetwood Mac, the group he'd begun in 1967. He turned his back on every aspect of the rock-star life and worked as a gravedigger. He wanted no part of the money that Fleetwood Mac earned. This wasn't much of a problem in the early seventies because the group were usually in the red. It became more problematic around 1975, when *Fleetwood Mac*, the first album his old friends Mick Fleetwood, John McVie and Christine McVie had made with the newly recruited American duo Lindsey Buckingham and Stevie Nicks, began selling in unprecedented quantities. They called it their 'White Album', and at the time it was the biggest seller in the history of Warner Brothers Records. This had the knock-on effect of growing the sales of their back catalogue, which meant Green kept receiving royalty cheques. He was so bothered by this influx of cash that he visited his accountant's office to remonstrate. To emphasize his point he brandished a pump-action shotgun. Green was subsequently sent to a mental hospital for his own protection as well as his accountant's.

In the early seventies it appeared that all the men who had previously stood out front in Fleetwood Mac had suffered misadventures from which they were unlikely to recover. Both Green and fellow guitarist Danny Kirwan suffered from mental illness which some attributed to an incident with bad acid in Munich. The other guitarist, the previously genial Jeremy Spencer, had gone out for a walk before a gig in California in 1971, joined the Children of God and never come back.

But whereas the men at the front fell out of the fray in different ways, the two men who formed the rhythm section, and had the good fortune to share their names with the band's, ploughed on determinedly, managing the band themselves and engaging different musicians to do the singing and guitar playing. This leadership from the back line was without precedent; the biggest show-offs usually did the leading. Fleetwood and McVie were blessed in their latest recruits. A recording engineer had introduced them to Buckingham Nicks, a romantically linked double act who were young, looked good and could sing and write songs. Before they decided to merge the two acts they asked Christine McVie whether she was worried about the danger of being upstaged by having the group fronted by a younger woman. She said she wasn't. The fact that they asked this question was a hint of what a complex organization the new group was to become. All successful groups have some of the features of a family. In Fleetwood Mac's case the complexities within the group were almost royal in scale.

These came to the fore in February 1976 as Fleetwood Mac entered the studio to begin recording the follow-up to their breakthrough album. This was a record that carried the expectations of the company and all its senior executives on its back. Record-making is an activity that expands to fill the time available for it and the budget apportioned to it. When the Beatles made *Sgt Pepper's Lonely Hearts Club Band* in 1967 the PR line was that it had taken an unprecedented seven hundred hours to record. It wasn't as many as that but it was more than they would have devoted to previous albums, when the quest for perfection had to be kept within bounds. By 1976 the rewards of getting it right were so apparent that it was considered worth any amount of trouble.

In the case of Fleetwood Mac the trouble could be considerable. The power was distributed evenly across the five of them. Fleetwood and McVie had tenure but they weren't the ones who were expected to come up with the songs. They were expected to supply the rhythm tracks early on in the process. The simple matter of getting a distinctive drum sound in the mid-seventies was a process that could stretch for days with the drummer relentlessly bashing a snare or tom-tom as the engineers experimented with microphone placement and echo. They had to supply the base on which the other three would build their tracks but they understandably preferred to hold back their final decisions until they heard the vocal. Often they couldn't hear the vocal until later in the process because whichever of the other three had written the words either hadn't finished them yet or didn't wish to share them with the others. As Fleetwood was to recall, 'the problem was the songwriters were bringing no words because the words were in the room'.

The reason the words were in the room was because all three people supplying them were preoccupied with the fact that they had recently broken up with other members of the group. Christine McVie, who had married John in order to please her dying mother, had recently announced their marriage was at an end and started sleeping with the tall, handsome young lighting designer. McVie found solace wherever he could, spending a year on the yacht he'd bought with the royalties from *Fleetwood Mac* and entertaining fantasies of winning the favours of Linda Ronstadt, then at the apogee of her pulchritude and about to make the first of a number of appearances on the cover of *Rolling Stone* in her lingerie.

When Nicks and Buckingham were in a band called Fritz there had been an agreement that none of the men in the band could sleep with the girl out front, for fear this would be the end of the band. As soon as Buckingham and Nicks left the group and started being a duo they became a couple. As soon as they started recording the new Fleetwood Mac album, which was to be called *Rumours*, they split up. The tensions of being in close proximity in the studio had been aggravated by the fact that they were going home together. Calling it a day didn't relieve the pressure. Each was furiously jealous of any moves the other made to see anyone else.

The good thing about all this hoarded heartache was that ideas for songs came spilling out of them as if they were lovelorn teenagers exposed to their first book of poetry. The difficult thing was that the first person they would in the normal run of things sing it for was often the person who had inflicted the chest wound that inspired it. Christine wrote 'Don't Stop' about John, 'Oh Daddy' about Mick and his wife Jenny, and 'You Make Loving Fun' about her new boyfriend, the lighting man. (He was swiftly let go.) For most of the time it took them to record 'The Chain' it had no words. It only became the band's anthem at the very last minute. Lindsey wrote 'Go Your Own Way' about Stevie, who took offence at the lines about somebody 'packing up and shacking up'. She wrote 'Silver Springs' about him. Much to her fury this was left off the final album, though it was made the B-side of the first single 'Go Your Own Way', thereby ensuring that she made as much money out of profiling her ex as he made out of his musical kiss-off to her.

The fifth member of the group, its drummer and manager Mick Fleetwood, had trouble keeping his marriage together. His wife, the former Jenny Boyd, was the sister of Pattie Boyd, wife of George Harrison. She'd been with the Beatles and the Maharishi at Rishikesh. The new profile the band enjoyed meant she was often called on to be the plus-one in formal situations. To get through this she self-medicated with alcohol and cocaine, somehow still managing to get up in the morning to look after their children. After succumbing to stress she decided to divorce Mick and went to live in Surrey, not far from where Pattie was now living with Eric Clapton in a similar state of opulent unhappiness. After two months she returned to Los Angeles where she and Fleetwood remarried in order to ensure that their children's immigration status was guaranteed. In time they divorced again.

Fleetwood Mac started recording in February at a carefully chosen studio in Sausalito, north of San Francisco. The Record Plant was the last word in comfort and convenience for the new breed of recording stars with their multi-platinum expectations and highly developed taste for luxury. It had its own hot tub, a vending machine that dispensed cold cans of Coors at twenty-five cents a time, a nearby hacienda that the bands could choose to stay in while they recorded, and a studio called 'The Pit', which had been designed by Sly Stone so that the engineers could sit surrounded by the musicians and the music. Stevie Nicks retreated here one day and came up with the basic idea of 'Dreams' in fifteen minutes. The sessions did not go smoothly. They had three grand pianos, none of which would stay in tune. Studio costs were $135 an hour. They racked up three thousand of those hours at the Record Plant, in the course of which the winding and rewinding of the original tape meant that it lost much of its quality and they eventually decided that the only thing that could be rescued was the basic rhythm tracks. The record was supposed to be finished in nine weeks. In the end it took the best part of a year.

Some of this delay was down to their tastes, which had become more expensive in direct proportion to their success. The members of the original band were in their early thirties; Buckingham and Nicks were still in their twenties. Neither group had yet reached the realization that drinking five-star brandy in the studio might be impairing their performance. They also relied on cocaine to get them through the long sessions. (On stage a member of the road crew circulated among the musicians after every number, carrying a silver tray full of bottle caps of cocaine for those members who needed a small lift.) This had the unfortunate side effect of convincing them that the take they had just done was the perfect one, an impression of which they were disabused the following day when they heard it sober. With mass-market acceptance whatever starry tendencies they had were given free rein. Nicks in particular developed some of the habits of a theatrical leading lady, arriving for each day's studio work in a fresh outfit as if she was going on stage, accompanied by her pet poodle.

The record company was not in any position to put pressure on them to hurry because the manager figure was also the drummer and he refused to listen to them. Every last creative decision about *Rumours* was made by the band and its producer and engineer. John McVie came up with the name *Rumours*. When the time came to do the cover they called on an old hippy friend and shot a bizarre image of the 6ft 6in drummer and the 5ft 1in singer posing balletically with a pair of rhythm balls in his testicular zone. This was an indication of the latitude granted to rock stars and only rock stars. Even the biggest-name writers and film actors would never have been given the same control over such a crucial part of the package. It was just assumed that rock stars knew best.

One of their last duties in 1976 was to pose for the cover of *Rolling Stone*. Such a photo session was now a job of work requiring as much commitment as another song. *Rolling Stone*, once the organ of the alternative society, was about to move from San Francisco to New York in order to be nearer its real customers, the agencies that bought colour ads for cigarettes, drink and cars which were aimed at its free-spending thirty-something readership. The editorial had simultaneously smartened up to provide a more seductive environment. The photographers were more upmarket, which meant they brought with them their customary armies of stylists, make-up artists, hairdressers and miscellaneous ministers of the arts of vanity to make sure that their subjects looked reassuringly rich as well as edgily stylish. The look of 1976 was expensive and dissolute. It was the Rolling Stones' *Black and Blue*; Peter Frampton, his chest glowing on the cover of his live record; Rod Stewart, with trophy girlfriend Britt Ekland wrapped around him. The image of the members of Fleetwood Mac, swaddled in expensive silk sheets, Fleetwood with his arm around Nicks (a pose that was to prove prophetic), Buckingham snuggling up with Christine McVie, and her ex-husband upside down reading a magazine, announced what the market was already suspecting, that with this band you didn't just get radio-friendly hits and stereo sheen, you also got a surrogate family whose interpersonal relationships you could gossip about.

Although the talent within Fleetwood Mac was evenly distributed – Buckingham was the inventive musician, Christine probably the best natural voice, Mick and John the driving wheel that kept the band on the rails in both musical and practical terms – the member who cast the greatest spell and catalysed the other four was Stevie Nicks. When they were in the studio she was in danger of being passed over because she was the only one who didn't play an instrument, but it was a different story on stage. Since the only instrument she played was a tambourine which had been carefully taped up to make sure that it would be seen but not heard, she was free to act as the band's focal point, a task she took every bit as seriously as if she had been the lead guitarist. In close-up she had the Bambi eyes, Cupid's bow lips, Farrah Fawcett hair and flawless skin of the girl you would never dare ask to the prom. At a distance she was a blur of gauzy fabric. There was nothing of the standard sex kitten about her. Nevertheless, out there in the dark thousands of young men were stirred. Many felt they would scale the steepest castle walls with a rose in their teeth in exchange for just one of her sidelong looks. The Stevie Nicks persona was an imaginative invention every bit as integral to the appeal of the group as her songs or her singing. The way she moved was a significant addition to the gestural arts of rock.

On 4 July 1976 the United States of America celebrated its bicentennial. Fleetwood Mac took a break from work in the latest of a series of studios in which they were still wrestling with their new album in order to play a show at the Tampa Stadium in Florida. On this day in the sun $12.50 bought people the cream of the newly popular soft rock from Dan Fogelberg, Loggins and Messina, Fleetwood Mac and the Eagles. These were all people who sold a lot of records. But of all the people on stage that day only Stevie Nicks among them could already claim to be a rock star.

From his vantage point on the drum stool Mick Fleetwood looked out at the crowd as Stevie went into her big number 'Rhiannon'. 'I looked out of the crowd and saw a field of Stevie Nicks devotees; wispy, witchy black dresses, top hats, just everything Stevie incorporated into her stage attire.' These were Stevie's people: thousands of everyday girls who saw something in her look that was coquettish enough to attract the male gaze and inscrutable enough to send it bouncing off into space. Many more would join Stevie's tribe over the years.

This was some transformation. Just two Independence Days earlier she had been earning $1.50 an hour waitressing at a Beverly Hills restaurant called Clementine's. Buckingham Nicks had made one album together for Polydor and then been dropped. She had to work to eat. She felt it was more important that she worked while Lindsey devoted himself to staying at home, perfecting his guitar. She even worked as a housekeeper for their producer Keith Olsen. She applied herself to these mundane tasks because she was determined to postpone the day when she had to go back to her mother and father and admit that her dream of making it in show business had come to nothing.

Now there was no danger of that. Two years after the waitressing days Stevie Nicks was in a group that had gone platinum and was about to go higher, much higher. She had her face on the covers of magazines, and handsome millionaire Don Henley of the Eagles dancing attendance on her, even sending cranberry-coloured Lear jets to whisk her to his side and having limo drivers turn up as she was breakfasting with the rest of the band to strew armfuls of flowers and items of expensive hi-fi at her feet. There is no indication that she did anything but luxuriate in all this fresh attention. This could be what Glenn Frey of the Eagles had in mind when he encountered the new girl in Henley's luxurious hilltop house in 1976 and, with the newly minted world-weariness of somebody who had made it to the top of this particular mountain a whole year earlier, acidly enquired of Stevie, 'Spoiled yet?'

1976 PLAYLIST

Queen, 'Bohemian Rhapsody'
The Eagles, *Hotel California*
Peter Frampton, *Frampton Comes Alive!*
The Ramones, *Ramones*
Boz Scaggs, *Silk Degrees*
Rolling Stones, *Black and Blue*
The Isley Brothers, 'Harvest For The World'
Tom Petty and the Heartbreakers,
Tom Petty And The Heartbreakers
Eric Clapton, *No Reason To Cry*
The Runaways, *The Runaways*

16 AUGUST 1977
GRACELAND, MEMPHIS

Death is good for business

The girls who shared Elvis Presley's bed knew the drill. They had to listen for his breathing, which had on occasion seemed to stop in the night. If he got up to go to the bathroom they should knock on the door after a while and ask if he was all right. There were members of his personal entourage around the house at all times. Further staff, including a nurse who worked for his personal doctor George Nichopoulos, known to all as 'Doctor Nick', lived in trailers behind the house. Nonetheless the women he slept with were his last defence against the thing he feared most, loneliness.

Since he was a small child Elvis had hated to sleep alone. Once he was famous he no longer needed to. If he wasn't with one of his longer-term girlfriends, willing women could be brought to him. They would often be referred to him by his Memphis friend, the DJ George Klein. His Graceland people would vet them before they got to his bedroom. Anyone with dirty fingernails or opinions of her own would not proceed far beyond the ground floor. The ones who met with his approval would in due course be given money to spend on improving their appearance so that it approached his ideal. That meant big hair, pretty outfits, anything that contributed to the impress of virginal freshness and white underwear. Elvis liked women designed with display in mind. Their primary function in his life was to reflect his glory. Nobody took being the King more seriously than the King.

In August 1977 his bed was shared with Ginger Alden. Ginger was a former holder of the Miss Traffic Safety title. Elvis was forty-two, Ginger was twenty. She had been introduced to Presley's court initially in the capacity of a first reserve. Once she had passed muster he told his people to send Linda Thompson, the incumbent girlfriend of the previous few years, home. Alden was then promoted from her own bedroom to the master suite. This was the sole area of the court of Elvis where there appeared to be a succession plan.

Elvis's mother had died in 1958. His wife had left him in 1972. By 1977 Elvis had grown steadily more needy. Like a small child he had his bedtime routine. Before settling down he had to have his hair washed and blow-dried by one of his body servants. Members of his staff would be commanded to sit with him and talk, often disregarding whichever girl happened to be in bed with him at the time. Jo Smith, the wife of Elvis's cousin Billy, who lived in one of the trailers out back, was even called upon from time to time. She remembered, 'The girls would just lie there and smile, with their little negligees on.' One of her jobs might be to explain to the girl that there would be no sex, because Elvis needed to preserve 'his bodily fluids' because of an upcoming tour.

Elvis Presley had a pressing need to own people body and

soul. He couldn't bear the idea that anybody might need anything he couldn't provide. In 1977 he even cajoled his Palm Springs dentist into marrying his fiancée, providing the officiant from among his circle of friends and standing as witness himself; then, apparently overcome by the emotion of the ceremony, he announced to Ginger that he would like to marry her. By that time he had inveigled his way into the affections of her parents, even offering to pay for their impending divorce. Ginger's mother, like the relatives of many of his girlfriends over the years, was very much alive to his cash-dispensing qualities. In March he extended huge loans to Doctor Nick. While he was in the mood he made out a new will. His plan was to take Ginger away for a short trip to Hawaii. It was intended to be just the two of them. That didn't quite work out. They ended up taking thirty people.

Ginger didn't have any overpowering interest in getting married. She didn't love Elvis. She didn't wish to spend her life in this gilded prison. She was of a different generation. For her, 1977 was the year of Donna Summer's 'I Feel Love', Woody Allen's *Annie Hall* and Bill Murray in the cast of *Saturday Night Live*. This was a world Elvis knew not. However, Ginger was not immune to the attractions of having a fuss made over her. Elvis had been planning to get married anything but quietly, as he had been required to do when marrying his first wife Priscilla in 1967. His idea was to announce it during the string of dates which were due to start in the middle of August. There was much talk of new beginnings, most of which didn't get beyond talk. He knew he had to get his weight down from the 200lb he was carrying in order to get into the jumpsuits he wore on stage. His idea was to go on a diet. An all-jelly diet.

Elvis was incapable of imagining a life different from the

one he had designed for himself. When Linda Thompson made the unexpected suggestion that the two of them should turn their backs on the show-business lifestyle and go away and live on a farm, he had said, 'Now why the hell would I want to do that?' Similarly, when one of his boys suggested he might be happier dating women nearer his own age, he said, 'Now what could a forty-two-year-old woman do for me?' Everything that needed fixing in Elvis's life required Elvis giving up something. Slimming would mean curbing his appetite. Marriage would involve fidelity. He wanted to be closer to his young daughter Lisa Marie but resented any demand she made on his time. If he stopped doing live shows he would no longer have the funds that financed the expensive business of simply being Elvis. He couldn't get by without the downers that Doctor Nick prescribed to get him to sleep at night. Therefore he made sure Doctor Nick increased the dose. The real answer to his problems lay in having less of everything. Elvis's preferred solution always involved his having more of everything.

On the night of 16 August 1977 he had the usual three packets of pills prescribed by Doctor Nick. In the middle of the night, when he was starting to think about settling down, he called Doctor Nick, complaining of pain in his teeth following a recent dental procedure. The doctor gave him a prescription for six doses of Dilaudid, a powerful painkiller often given to patients in the later stages of cancer. Ricky, the personal factotum who was on the night-time shift at Graceland, was sent to the all-night pharmacy to collect it.

Among the people closest to Elvis there was a feeling that a form of slow suicide might be being acted out before their very eyes. When he had left a Nashville recording session earlier in the year blaming a throat problem for not having put anything on tape many of the musicians assumed that this would be the last time they worked with him. Linda Thompson had greeted the end of their affair with secret relief: she knew he would never change and thought it likely he would kill himself. Around the same time Colonel Tom Parker, in an unguarded moment, told some fans from the UK, 'My artist is out of control.' Columnist Bill Burk, who had been covering Elvis for the *Memphis Press-Scimitar* for twenty years, went to see his Vegas shows at the end of 1976 and wrote, 'One walks away wondering how much longer it can be before the end comes, perhaps suddenly, and why the King of Rock and Roll would subject himself to possible ridicule by going on stage so ill-prepared.' Among the diminishing number of people who actually cared about Elvis Presley there was a feeling he was running out of road.

Hovering above it all was the prospect of the imminent publication of what was known to all in Graceland as 'the book'. Three of Presley's bodyguards, all of whom had been let go in a round of cost-cutting the year before, had signed a deal to tell their stories. The book was called *Elvis: What Happened?*, and the blurb went as follows: 'A devoted son. A generous friend. A model Army recruit. A gifted entertainer. A beloved hero to millions. This is the Elvis Presley the world knew – and cherished. Brooding. Violent. Obsessed with death. Strung out. Sexually driven. This is the other side of Elvis – according to the three men who lived with him through it all.'

Elvis knew the implications. A lurid but fundamentally reliable account of the secrets he kept from the world would finally be in the public domain. His biggest secret was his utter dependence on drugs. Of all the untruths on which the Presley myth had been based, the most serious one was the drugs. Here the gap between the message he sent out to his public and the reality of his nocturnal life was big enough to drive a reputation-destroying bus through. His public posturing about drugs was so far removed from the reality of his habits that it almost amounted to a form of grim comedy. When Presley had talked his way into an audience with President Nixon at the White House in 1970 he had assured his Commander-in-Chief of his steadfastness in the war on illegal stimulants. Furthermore he had almost refused to leave the Oval Office until he'd been given a badge which he could claim identified him as a government agent fighting against the pharmaceutical tide. Now the truth was about to come out. He sent an intermediary to offer the ex-employees $50,000 each not to publish. They declined. Their declared line was that by going public they were staging a high-profile intervention that might have the effect of saving him from himself.

Elvis felt personally betrayed. In addition he was distraught over the damage about to be done to his image, an image of perfection so huge and all-pervading he almost believed in it himself. These revelations would finally allow daylight to flood in on the magic in which he had dealt since he'd stopped driving a truck. When it came to drugs his heartland audience would not be of a mind to cut him any slack. What worried him more than the absence of any close friends in his life, the manager he didn't trust, the father he didn't like, the girlfriend who had her thoughts on a man nearer to her own age, his gathering health problems, his money troubles and his damned weight was the thought that the people whose love sustained him, the millions out there in the dark who had worshipped him for the last twenty years, whose adoration had lit his way, might finally fall out of love with him.

Like all superstars Elvis alternated between utter certainty and crippling doubt, spending very little time in the region between the two where normal human beings live out their lives. Elvis had always been vain. Vanity was his driving force. Vanity was something he understood. Now that he looked in the mirror and saw the ruin he had become his vanity suffered a wound that would never heal. He had always judged by appearances. He knew full well his fans did the same. During his live performances the one minute that truly mattered was the one when he walked on stage. In that moment his audience coldly weighed up the damage time had wrought and decided whether they could live with it or not. He could see it in their eyes. He knew he was slipping.

He was on an almost never-ending tour, generally to cities in secondary markets: Palm Beach, Johnson City, Savannah, Montgomery, even Duluth, where Buddy Holly had played on his last tour almost twenty years earlier. People wondered why he put himself through a ritual he seemed to find wearing and irritating. Surely he couldn't need the money? People always need the money. Record royalties were not flowing as they once had (in 1973 he had sold RCA all his rights in all his recordings up to that year for a paltry $5 million) and expenses grew all the time. His incomings were still massive but they were no match for his outgoings. He lived an existence that was both opulent and hand-to-mouth. For every dollar he made the Colonel made the same, which he needed to fund his massive gambling addiction. But even the Colonel knew that he couldn't milk his cash cow indefinitely. He would drop in occasionally to see a show or receive reports from members of the entourage that the show was slipping to a point where promoters might stop accepting his money demands. He would call off a few dates and Elvis would fly back to Memphis to recuperate. He would manage a few reasonable shows after that, then follow them with a performance that seemed to have been phoned in from some distant planet.

Before he turned in, just as 16 August was dawning in Memphis, Tennessee, Elvis assured his cousin Billy Smith that the forthcoming tour, beginning that night in Maine, was going to be the best ever. There was no reason to believe this but he said it all the same. Billy left him and Ginger together in the bedroom. After a while Elvis said he couldn't sleep and was going to read in the bathroom.

The next Ginger knew it was two in the afternoon and she was alone in the bed. After phoning a friend for a chat and doing her make-up she decided to find out where Elvis was. She opened the bathroom door. Elvis was on the floor as if in the act of prayer. His pyjamas were around his knees. He wasn't breathing. Beside him on the floor was the book he'd been reading: *The Scientific Search for the Face of Jesus*.

The Colonel was contacted in Maine, where he was with the team preparing for Elvis's two-night stand. When he was given the news he said nothing for thirty seconds. Then, like the stone-hearted carny he was, he switched into action mode and issued orders. The plane bringing the band from Los Angeles was contacted in Las Vegas and sent back. The promoters were told the shows were off. Then he flew not to Memphis but directly to New York, where he had meetings with executives at Elvis's record company RCA and his merchandising partners. The message to both was the same: the King is dead, long live the King – prepare for unprecedented demand. (The resulting boom was so great that an RCA factory in the UK that was on the brink of closure was reprieved and put on full capacity.)

When he arrived at Graceland the following day Parker's hard-headed practicality was in marked contrast to the tears, wailing, frantic efforts to cover personal tracks and inevitable jockeying for position of everyone in the wider Presley family. (When the medical investigator had arrived on the day of Presley's death he found the bathroom had been tidied up. There wasn't even an aspirin to be seen.) There were some who were surprised to see Parker at all. Nobody could remember him ever having attended a funeral before. He took Elvis's father Vernon aside and impressed upon him the paramount importance of securing the rights to the sound and image of his late son at this delicate moment when all kinds of other sharks might be getting ready to make a move. 'Elvis didn't die,' he said, 'the body did. This changes nothing. It's just like when he went in the army.'

The passing of Elvis Presley was a surprise rather than a shock. It wasn't a shock because most people rarely thought about him. Only the people who had tickets to see him on his upcoming tour had him on their radar. Even when he was dead, *Time* magazine didn't put him on their cover. Nor did *People*. They didn't think he was big enough, in the sense that they felt he no longer reached into people's hearts. Elvis was just a rock star who wasn't hot any more. Then, as the days turned into weeks and the news programmes continued to run footage of distraught middle-aged people talking about what Elvis had meant to them, the reality began to sink in. The late Elvis, as opposed to the living Elvis, was the one thing they could agree on.

Now that he was dead everyone was free to worship the Elvis of their choice. The music magazines venerated the great American originator whose heart was always in the right place no matter what strange places his head might have wandered to. The tabloids mourned the bejewelled figure in the white jumpsuit. The high-end fashion magazines celebrated the young style icon. Even the punk rockers who were the story du jour in the UK claimed him as the originator of the mayhem they sought to perpetuate.

Jimmy Carter, making the first of many statements US Presidents would be called upon to make following the deaths of rock stars in the future, gave a statement that served to elevate him from the tawdriness of the master bedroom at Graceland and put this rock and roll singer in the same category as Mark Twain, Louis Armstrong and F. Scott Fitzgerald. 'Elvis Presley's death deprives our country of a part of itself,' he intoned. 'He was unique and irreplaceable.'

Carter didn't mention that only a month earlier he'd had to take a call from an incoherent Presley. At the time Elvis was trying to get him to pardon his friend George Klein, who was facing charges of fiddling radio ratings numbers. Elvis was worried. Elvis felt he ought to do something. He asked himself, what would Elvis do? He decided Elvis would phone the President of the United States. Only a rock star would have placed that call to a President. Only a rock star could have made the President take the call.

9 DECEMBER 1978
LONDON

A raspberry on top of the charts

In 1963 American journalist Michael Braun went to Sunderland to write about a new group called the Beatles. As he observed how these four men interacted with the world he began to recognize that their appeal went beyond just music. 'I began suspecting,' he wrote later, 'that I was in the presence of a new kind of person.'

Over the years pop music has unwittingly introduced many new kinds of people to a wider world. From Little Richard and Jerry Lee Lewis through Pete Townshend and Janis Joplin to Lou Reed and Bob Marley, pop has introduced young people to personalities they might never have encountered any other way. While the infatuation with punk raging through London's taste-making community in 1978 wasn't quite the popular uprising that is commonly painted – the pre-eminent music of this period was actually disco – it certainly brought plenty of new kinds of people to the fore.

These people were walking, talking, acting-out repudiations of the blow-dried stereotype of superstardom then represented by stars like Peter Frampton, John Travolta and Olivia Newton-John. These characters seemed to have risen from below. They were promoted from the street rather than handed down from on high. They sprang from the same world as the fans. They were on a human rather than a show-business scale. They were of the people. You couldn't easily imagine them stepping out of limos.

In 1978 in the UK everybody seemed to have been issued with a new set of Happy Families playing cards in which all the old types had been replaced by new types, many of whom had apparently been slightly bent out of shape by life. In this new world Debbie Harry was the neighbourhood Bardot, Johnny Rotten its twisted playground iconoclast, Poly Styrene its proto-feminist with the mouth full of metal, Bob Geldof the garrulous older-brother figure hammering out his many opinions on the family dinner table. All these people were perfectly balanced in the traditional British sense of having chips on both shoulders. All of them challenged conventional notions of glamour. But nobody in 1978 did this more than Ian Dury. He was the very last person anyone would have predicted would turn out to be Britain's key rock star of 1978, or start 1979 with a million-selling dance-floor hit.

Ian Dury was thirty-six years old when he finally became a rock star. Those people who had known him in the music business assumed he'd had his chance and missed it with his previous band Kilburn and the High Roads. Dury was certainly a one-off. His upbringing had been initially disrupted by the war and his parents' turbulent marriage, then by something worse. At the age of six he contracted polio after swallowing infected water at a public swimming pool in Southend. He was immediately put in an isolation hospital.

His mother was not allowed to visit him. She could only look at him through the window of the hut where he slept. Polio was one of those risks all parents ran when they had children in the forties and early fifties. Ian was not expected to live, let alone achieve any kind of public prominence. The idea that he might be a star in a trade where the standard currency was glamour of the most able-bodied kind was quite beyond anyone's imagining.

Young Ian came through the polio but didn't come out of hospital for two years. By that time the right side of his body had developed normally while his left had to be supported by calipers. His mother, knowing her way around the world of healthcare, did her best for him but in the 1950s anyone with a handicap was expected to be content with whatever they were given. His education, first at a special school for children with disabilities, then as the odd man out at a boys' boarding school, was testing. He was bullied, which planted within him a talent for bullying others. He went to art college first as a student and then did some teaching. He affected a walking stick long before he actually needed it. He made himself into a bit of a character.

In the early seventies he emerged as the singer of Kilburn and the High Roads, an unlikely-looking and -sounding group that was part of London's so-called 'pub rock' movement, which was trying to make music that was more idiosyncratic and human-scaled. By 1977 he was part of the independent label Stiff's stable of mavericks, which also included Elvis Costello. The two were put on tour together, along with Nick Lowe, Wreckless Eric and Larry Wallis. The idea was that the headliner would rotate from night to night. In the end it was a direct contest between Dury and Costello, both of whom had the killer instincts of rock stars awaiting the moment of their coronation. By the end of the tour Dury and his experienced backing band the Blockheads were justifiably regarded as the best live attraction in the country. When their first album *New Boots And Panties!!* came out in the latter part of the year it didn't do what celebrated 'new wave' albums did, which was fall out of contention after a couple of weeks in the limelight. It kept on selling by word of mouth. Given the nature of the music on it, *New Boots And Panties!!* could justifiably claim to be the most radical best-seller in British music-business history.

Dury couldn't sing in the conventional sense but he could sell a song like few others and he knew how to capture and hold the attention. His disability meant he couldn't traverse the stage as well as some but nobody else in the entire history of rock and roll has known half as well how to work that notional square between the top of the head and the waist. He would deliberately position the microphone above him so that when he sang the song was projected upwards as if to a higher power. He produced brightly coloured scarves from his sleeves like an end-of-the-pier magician. His facial features blinked, twitched and gurned as though in the power of an indecisive illustrator. He drew invisible threads through the air. His face would be lit from below so that he looked as threatening as Bill Sikes, his features flickering between child-like wonder and glittering malice. On stage or off there was nothing about him that wasn't fascinating. He was a genuine performance artist.

Dury's father had been a humble bus driver. His mother was educated. They broke up before he was born. Like fellow English geniuses Vivian Stanshall, Peter Sellers and Noël Coward, the axis Dury moved along was that constantly modulating, never far from mocking tone that passes for speech in England. Much as Stanshall played the aristo, Dury gave us a geezer. Whereas Coward had given himself the airs of a duke in order to distance himself from his suburban roots and become the vessel that could carry his songs, Dury found his character by going downmarket, turning himself into a vernacular philosopher from whom songs like 'Billericay Dickie' seemed to flow naturally. It was an act, of course. A brilliant act, but an act nonetheless. 'I'm a Mockney,' he told his biographer Will Birch, 'in the sense that my mum spoke so beautifully and my dad didn't.' His act chimed with the punk moment, which was all about aspiring to move down the social scale.

By the middle of 1978 the whole nation knew all the words of his first album *New Boots And Panties!!*, a record as dense with allusions as a book of comic poetry and as full of catchy business as a record by the Isley Brothers. This was the album in every living room in 1978, the unlikely inheritor of the mantle of general acceptance which had previously fallen on Carole King's *Tapestry*. This was despite the fact that its language was considerably more than frank. It contained one song in praise of an early-morning erection, another about how his father graduated from driving buses to chauffeuring for foreign gents, a further ode to 'Sweet Gene Vincent' (Dury was born in 1942, hence his heroes were greasers, jazzers and music-hall comics), and hidden away uncredited the song that became his battle cry, 'Sex & Drugs & Rock & Roll'.

The Dury character was the perfect vehicle for using his key quality, which was a remarkable power to make people love him. This was often in spite of the way he had treated those people. He left his first wife to bring up two children on her own. He wrote a sentimental song about his father but didn't go to see him in his final years when he was dying alone. Within his professional sphere he exhibited the talent that Kenneth Tynan referred to as 's'imposer', which is the ability to make those in his immediate circle uncertain whether their next remark would be met with a smile or a vicious put-down. Once he became the centre of attention, which had always been his overpowering need, he liked to surround himself with retainers who, justified or not, gave off the distinct whiff of villainy. This was catnip for university-educated journalists who loved to talk to Dury because he had the hinterland most rock stars only pretended to have. He could go from referring to himself as 'a raspberry' (from the rhyming slang 'raspberry ripple – cripple') to unusual gentleness and lyricism in the way he expressed himself. On one famous occasion he reduced a journalist to tears of sympathy. Dury could do that.

As a boss he brooked no contradiction. He demanded that people involved with him drop everything to be at his beck and call. He had managers but he did the manipulation himself. He saw a group as a tableau as well as a collection of musicians. Every gesture he made, every item of clothing he wore, every shape he struck had been thought about beforehand. He missed no opportunity. He was a human billboard. When the record company paid for him to get his teeth fixed prior to a tour of America with Lou Reed he made sure they painted a Union Jack on the incisors at the front.

There was a strong streak of Little Englander in punk. The Clash had a song called 'I'm So Bored With The USA'. 'I don't like America,' said Dury in a TV interview. 'I think it's a pig sty.' Such statements didn't reflect anyone's true feelings. Like many Englishmen he found the place enthralling but wasn't going to give it the satisfaction of hearing him say so. Furthermore he resented having to leave a country where he was feted to go somewhere else where he had to start again at the bottom. When Dury and his band the Blockheads were supporting Lou Reed in Los Angeles in 1979 Rod Stewart and Ron Wood popped in to lend support to their compatriots, sabotaging Reed's guitars in a confused gesture of support. But no matter how much touring he did, Dury was never going to mean anything in America.

Many of the people in this book became rock stars because they had the special zeal that comes from only being good at one thing. Dury wasn't like that. Dury had a number of talents. He could draw, he could teach, he could act and he could write. But had he achieved top status in any of those fields it would still have been a poor substitute for the validating thrill he got from turning himself into a rock star. A rock star is what he most wanted to be. He burned with the longing. In his key song 'What A Waste' he recites, with pathos worthy of Buster Keaton, all the occupations he could have followed if he hadn't done what he did. He could have been the driver of an articulated lorry. He could have been a poet, he wouldn't have to worry. But he chose to play the fool in a six-piece band and face first-night nerves on every one-night stand. You know what? He was glad to have turned his back on all the other options. Call that a waste? Ian Dury didn't.

The success of *New Boots And Panties!!* transformed his life. In 1979 he moved out of his modest flat near the Oval cricket ground and went straight into the Montcalm, the five-star hotel favoured by the music business, then to the Dorchester, then to an enormous house out in the Kent countryside. The Christmas period of 1978 was his pinnacle. In November Ian Dury and the Blockheads released their single 'Hit Me With Your Rhythm Stick', which was their finest moment. It was a dance craze record but it was a dance craze record that had been to college, with words that were clever and worthy of rolling round the tongue; it was conveyed on a churning groove that was as breezy as a day out in Margate and as hard and clever as anything Nile Rodgers ever did. In the middle it had a sax break from Davey Payne that sounded as deranged as Davey looked and belatedly introduced the spirit of Rahsaan Roland Kirk to the final *Top of the Pops* editions of the year. This cult single from a cult act on a cult label sold over one million copies in the UK. Never again was he quite so in sync with an entire nation. The raspberry was on top. It was glorious while it lasted.

1978 PLAYLIST

Ian Dury and the Blockheads, 'Hit Me With Your Rhythm Stick'
Blondie, *Parallel Lines*
The Bee Gees, 'Night Fever'
Kate Bush, *The Kick Inside*
Bruce Springsteen, *Darkness On The Edge Of Town*
Talking Heads, *More Songs About Buildings And Food*
Devo, *Q: Are We Not Men? A: We Are Devo!*
Dire Straits, *Dire Straits*
Marvin Gaye, *Here, My Dear*
The Boomtown Rats, *A Tonic For The Troops*

4 AUGUST 1979
KNEBWORTH HOUSE, HERTFORDSHIRE

Twilight of the gods

I t says much about the lifestyles adopted by the handful of rock stars who had made fortunes in the seventies that after they scattered to enjoy the fruits of their labours they communicated in such unexpected ways. In 1978 Robert Plant of Led Zeppelin only knew his group were considering going back into action for the first time in over a year through the pages of *Farmers Weekly*.

Farmers Weekly was an obligatory read for anyone involved in British agriculture, among whom were suddenly a smattering of rock stars living out new lives as landed gentry. Plant had bought a significant spread near his home town of Kidderminster, as befitted a star of his magnitude. However, even jobbing troubadour and occasional Led Zeppelin opening act Roy Harper had somehow managed to acquire a smallholding in Herefordshire. Hence he gave an interview to *Farmers Weekly* in order to enthuse about his sheep. In the course of this interview he mentioned he had been writing the odd song with Jimmy Page.

This caused Plant to pick up the phone and for the first time in months make contact with the guitarist, the person with whom he had written such tunes as 'Whole Lotta Love', 'Trampled Under Foot' and 'Stairway To Heaven'. The idea that his songwriting partner might be cheating on him with another put Plant's nose slightly out of joint. Page reassured him that Harper had been talking up his part somewhat. The good news was that this was a sign the singer was finally interested in getting back into circulation for the first time since 1977.

In the middle of an American tour that year Plant had been given the shattering news that his five-year-old son Karac had contracted a stomach virus and died. He and drummer John Bonham, both of whom had been recruited into Led Zeppelin at the same time, flew directly home. The other two, the guitarist Page and bassist John Paul Jones, remained in the United States. When the boy's funeral took place they didn't attend.

This tour had already been blighted by an incident at a gig in Oakland, California. Their manager, the mountainous former wrestler Peter Grant, and one of his charmless semi-criminal associates had almost killed one of the promoter's staff after a misunderstanding over who was entitled to take away a sign from backstage. The Led Zeppelin operation had long been inclined to treat the outside world as the enemy. This tendency had recently been exacerbated by overindulgence in cocaine and access to the financial muscle it takes to settle even the ugliest debt.

Like most rock stars the members of Led Zeppelin didn't

know what to do with their time when they weren't working and were incapable of getting organized enough to do anything to fill that time. In the course of this enforced hiatus, which had no agreed ending, each slid off into his private world. Page resumed his hobbies, which were heroin and the occult. Bonham's main interest was drinking but he was also using heroin. John Paul Jones had his own farm in Sussex. Plant was rebuilding his family life, which had been shattered not only by the loss of his child but also by an article his wife had read in an American music magazine which suggested that once on the road her husband was not faithful.

In those days before the death of distance it was possible for even world-famous musicians to be accompanied on tour by a species of 'road wife' without their actual wives getting to hear about it. The tabloids weren't particularly interested in these people, the specialist press knew discretion was the price they paid for access, and the mobile phone and the internet were still the stuff of science fiction. Furthermore the dictionary of disapproval had not yet been developed. Drug users weren't said to have substance issues. Heavy drinkers weren't yet alcoholics. Rock stars who expected unfettered access to the bodies of any young women in their orbit weren't yet deemed to have a problem with male entitlement. The line 'no head, no backstage pass' wasn't a sexist outrage. It was just one of those many things that were only rock and roll and therefore to take it seriously would have been considered a drag.

This was also the peak of Led Zeppelin's dark imperium. Their followers had always loved them. Most other people shuddered at the mention of their name. The band's reputation went before them, darkening the perception of their music. Peter Grant was thought of as a real thug, his familiar John Bindon a violent criminal, their American lawyer

Steve Weiss did nothing to discourage the idea that he was a connected guy, the band's tour manager Richard Cole, who took even more drugs than the musicians, was unpolished in securing the payments in what was still overwhelmingly a cash business, John Bonham could always be kept amused by violence, and all of them sought to please Jimmy Page, who increasingly presented as a dissatisfied princeling at whose feet these various myrmidons would drop tribute. Whether Led Zeppelin actually directed the unpleasantness them-selves or whether it was merely power wielded by others on their behalf, they took no steps to correct the impression and therefore it seems probable that at some level the idea of being frightening rather appealed to them. Many rock stars pay others to perform unpleasant services on their behalf. Most of these people perform these services as pleasantly as they can. Led Zeppelin's people felt licensed not to bother.

The call Plant made to Page on the back of the *Farmers Weekly* item instigated a series of meetings and jams that would eventually lead to a 1979 album, *In Through The Out Door*. This was recorded in a very businesslike fashion at ABBA's Polar Studios in Stockholm. The band would fly out on Monday morning and, like executive commuters, return on Friday night. The record didn't have Page's full concentration since his main priority was heroin. The heavy lifting was done by Plant and Jones. Since Plant was the one who had suffered the appalling tragedy of losing a child the other three were simply relieved that he was back and weren't going to stand in the way when he arrived with material which was not in their traditional wheelhouse. When the record came out it went straight to number one in the USA but soon fell away. In the career of any recording artist there are a handful of classics and then there are the others that, despite the best efforts of all concerned, don't quite spark. *In Through The Out Door* was one of the latter.

But it didn't deserve the critical mauling it got. Like all people who say that the press doesn't matter, Led Zeppelin were inclined to overestimate how much the press did matter. Journalists spending time with them in the USA were given strict rules about how they were to behave in their presence, and one thing they could be assured of was that whatever they wrote would be read by the band. They were desperate for critical acclaim but the best they ever got in their lifetime was grudging respect. To make matters worse they were now stranded on the wrong side of what seemed like a cultural chasm. The paper I was working for at the time had published a disobliging review of *In Through The Out Door* that featured the word 'dinosaurs'.

It was four years since they had played in the UK. This was a lifetime in seventies terms. Any group with an appropriate sense of modesty would have been advised to break them-selves back in slowly by playing small theatre shows. Instead Grant, in whom cocaine had conspired with misplaced con-fidence to produce inevitable hubris, decided that they should make their comeback by playing a massive open-air show in the park of a stately home in Hertfordshire. Furthermore, because other acts like Pink Floyd and the Rolling Stones had already proved it was possible to sell a hundred thousand tickets to one Knebworth show, the penis-measuring con-test in which all major rock stars are involved demanded Led Zeppelin overshadow them by playing two consecutive Saturdays. The promoter, who was less confident that they would be able to sell that number of tickets, wanted to do the standard thing, which is announce one show and then add another later 'in response to unprecedented demand'.

Because Peter Grant had already assured the band that they would sell out two shows without any trouble he couldn't do this. Nothing could be seen to puncture either his prestige or the band's confidence.

As the band prepared for the show with rehearsals at Bray Studios, which were largely devoted to the solo showcase Page was slated to play from within a pyramid of lasers, and two anonymous shows in Denmark, they had worries. The one unarguable achievement of the punk rock generation was the way its rhetoric got under the skin of the slightly older generation of musicians, the ones being loudly written off as dinosaurs. Paul Simonon of the Clash said he didn't need to hear Led Zeppelin; he simply had to look at their album covers to feel like throwing up. In fact the one thing that was certain about the new breed of name callers, who wrote short songs, wore straight-legged jeans and had alarming haircuts, was that most of them were the kind of rock purists who knew every note of the music of the bands they were so gleefully writing off. Not since the 1950s, when Frank Sinatra described rock and roll as music 'played by cretinous goons', had one generation dismissed another in this way. Led Zeppelin claimed not to be bothered, but they were.

Much as was the case back in the fifties, this argument was less about music than style. A week before the August show Led Zeppelin turned up for a photocall in the grounds of Knebworth House. Aubrey Powell, who was in charge of visuals, had brought along a stripper to liven up the pictures a little. It was decided she wasn't needed. Significantly, Page and Plant were both wearing jackets and skinny ties. The skinny tie was the one concession to punk fashion that everybody felt comfortable making. On Led Zeppelin it never looked entirely right. It added to the feeling that 1979 might no longer be their moment. In an interview given to promote the shows Page said he had voted for Margaret Thatcher, who had just been elected the first woman Prime Minister. Here he was speaking as a wealthy man who had achieved the age of thirty-five, which seemed almost exotically ancient to the new generation of would-be stars who wore their age as a badge of moral superiority.

The following Saturday, in the same week that Michael Jackson's *Off The Wall*, the record that inaugurated the eighties, was being released, the members of Led Zeppelin were helicoptered into the grounds of Knebworth House. As they descended they could see the lines of old cars queueing to get off the A1, the ex-army tents that had been erected in the car parks and even the pale, shirtless figures of the Led Zeppelin faithful whiling away the day between sets by Todd Rundgren and Commander Cody by drinking warm Newcastle Brown Ale. This is what matters most to groups descending from the air: how it all looks. Did they still have the pull they'd had almost five years earlier? Had everything changed? They really weren't sure.

I was in the backstage area that day. Somebody from the record company told me 'they're sick with nerves'. They were certainly less than professional. Peter Grant was drinking Blue Nun directly from the bottle. Their tour manager Richard Cole confronted the promoter on the day and told him that he would be signing a waiver allowing the whole show to be filmed. In exchange for this he would be paid 5p. They were throwing their weight around to conceal the fact that the band were worried they weren't ready for such a big performance. Plant in particular was concerned that he might not be able to get through it. He was also the one who was most attuned to what was going on in the world outside Led Zeppelin's tent.

There had been such a change in manners around music in the two years Led Zeppelin had been away, there had been such a tilt towards brevity and harshness, such a move from the Cavalier to the Puritan, that when they took to the stage they couldn't help looking almost quaint. Page played the opening riffs of 'The Song Remains The Same' on, of all things, a twin-neck guitar, Plant had his shirt slashed to the waist, Bonham had the huge gong hung behind his kit. In the era of the Jam and the Stranglers this looked almost like historical re-enactment.

The show was intermittently impressive. It was over three hours, far too long to be able to hold the attention of more than half of any crowd that has been standing in a field all day. Nobody had yet got to grips with the requirements of playing to such a large group of people. The guys who played those shows had never known what it was like to be a member of the crowd and therefore their stage banter rang hollow. Something had happened in the latter part of the seventies. For a start we had heard the Ramones. There was no going back. Attention spans had got shorter. When Page embarked on his laser-bedecked party piece on the guitar Plant, who according to legend used to spend this part of the act back-stage being fellated by a willing helper, remained awkwardly on stage as if he was thinking, like the rest of us, that this sort of entertainment no longer had a reason to be. In later years Plant admitted, 'I wasn't as relaxed as I could have been. We maimed the beast for life, but we didn't kill it. It was good, but only because everybody made it good. There was that sense of event.'

There were ugly scenes in the week between the first gig and the second one. For a start Peter Grant believed the pro-moter had deceived him about the numbers of tickets sold.

He argued that while flying over the site he had been able to ascertain that there were forty thousand more people there than were reflected in the receipts. He further insisted on being paid in cash, which meant a meeting at the promoter's house with all the curtains drawn as £300,000 – an enormous amount of money now and an inconceivable amount of money then – was counted out. Disgruntled that the tickets for the second show were not selling – it was the middle of the holiday season in the UK – Grant also demanded the promoter turn over all the unsold tickets to him. It was chaos.

In a desperate attempt to increase the interest in the second show the New Barbarians, a band lashed together by Ron Wood to promote his solo record, was added to the bill. The New Barbarians' key element was Keith Richards, who was so chemically altered on the day that he had to be decanted out of his limo by hand. Discomfited by the idea of being down the bill to anyone, Wood and Richards refused to go on stage until they had been paid. The crowd, by now dead on their feet, were kept waiting until a member of the band's entourage had taken the £35,000 in cash back to the band's hotel in London, banked it in the hotel safe and had it fully receipted by the hotel manager. Led Zeppelin returned the compliment by not dropping in on their old friends at all during their time on the site. So much for the brotherhood of rock and roll. There were reckoned to be fifty thousand people there for the second show. This is a respectable number, unless they happen to be occupying a space big enough for twice as many. Led Zeppelin had overreached. In the process they had burned their brand. Neither Grant nor Page was in the land of the humans any longer. It was the last time Led Zeppelin appeared on British soil.

The two key figures in the Led Zeppelin tableau were Plant

and Page. Their poses were the ones young men essayed in front of their bedroom mirrors. There they stood, Plant with his cascade of curls, his shirt slashed to the navel, the microphone and its cord flexed across his chest like the foil of a chevalier, everything pointing in the direction of the apex of the hard rock singer's golden triangle, his crotch; off to one side was Page with his dark mane, his instrument dangled halfway down those impossibly thin legs, the acme of slovenly grandeur. Poses are vital in rock. They are not some optional extra. Poses are what send the pulses of young men racing. There was a splendour about Led Zeppelin's swagger. It was the apogee of a certain sort of rock dream. None of the hundreds of bands that came after them and tried to adopt the same shape were anything like as convincing. However, like everything else in show business, it was a trick based on confidence. Once Plant no longer believed he could get away with it, once the essential absurdity of it began to dawn on him, once he started to believe the things all those punks were whispering in his ear via the letters pages of the music papers, once he was no longer cocksure, the magic inevitably ebbed away. After all, he was an old man. He was thirty-one.

8 DECEMBER 1980
NEW YORK CITY

Death by fan

John Lennon had not returned to his homeland since leaving it in 1971. In the course of the last decade he and Yoko Ono had steadily adopted the lifestyle of what bankers call high-net-worth individuals. For somebody whose entire life had once been about music Lennon seemed to find it surprisingly easy to live without it. For five years he barely picked up a guitar. For somebody so bright Lennon could also remain remarkably incurious about aspects of the world. It was only when he saw the view of Central Park from the top floor of New York's famous old Dakota building that he realized such a view could be nourishing for the soul.

John and Yoko had to work hard on the Dakota's custodians to get permission to take up apartment 72, which was being vacated by the actor Robert Ryan in 1972, because the building had a rule that it didn't admit rock stars as residents. With the help of some well-placed sponsors they managed to persuade these worthies that there was nothing of the rock star about the life he and Yoko lived. This was even more the case after their son Sean was born in 1975. In his Lennon biography Philip Norman suggests that the sight of the Dakota may have awakened in Lennon memories of the equally impressive buildings of similar vintage which looked out over the Mersey in his home city. A historian of the building described the top floors as 'like some strange, gone-to-seed hotel in the British Midlands'.

Like most Englishmen abroad Lennon comforted himself with small pleasures from home. He was compensated for one interview with BBC television with the gift of some difficult-to-find English biscuits. He telephoned his beloved Aunt Mimi, now living on the Isle of Wight, every week. On Sunday evenings he liked to settle down in front of one of the British television dramas presented by Alistair Cooke under the title *Masterpiece Theatre*. In every respect it was a very comfortable life.

The couple built up their wealth thanks to Yoko's efforts. Her family came from banking stock and she had none of Lennon's middle-class squeamishness about accumulating money. The first thing they did was extend their holdings in the Dakota, until they had five apartments, some of which were used as offices for their organization, others to house their many possessions. On one visit Elton John was surprised that Yoko appeared to own more clothes than he did. The main rooms of the apartment they lived in were as sparsely furnished and minimally decorated as the rooms in Tittenhurst Park, their Georgian country house in Berkshire, through which they had floated in the video for 'Imagine' back in 1971. Such emptiness is doubly enviable because it hints that just off stage there are suites of rooms stacked to the ceiling with the impedimenta of millionaires. The couple had financial advisers whose words of wisdom they listened to far more than Lennon ever did in the days of the Beatles. They invested in paintings, ancient Egyptian artefacts and even the kind of prize dairy cattle that command six-figure prices.

John's relationships with the other former members of the Beatles were more cordial than they had been at any stage since the end of the sixties. There had even been a conversation about his taking part in George's Concert for Bangla Desh back in 1971 but nothing came of it. Paul McCartney would visit occasionally. One of these visits climaxed with an exhibition of slovenliness and grandeur that defines rockstar behaviour. John and Yoko and Paul and Linda finished the evening at Manhattan smart spot Elaine's where, finding nothing on the menu that they fancied, they sent out for pizza. The cordiality between the two lead Beatles did not in any way diminish their competitiveness. Lennon measured his fortune against McCartney, who had insured himself by buying up valuable music publishing copyrights. When he heard his erstwhile partner was worth $25 million he set Yoko the aim of matching that figure.

McCartney had stayed in the game of writing songs, releasing records and touring, whereas Lennon had stopped putting out anything new after 1974's *Walls And Bridges*. The Christmas number one at the end of 1979 was McCartney's 'Wonderful Christmastime', which might have been little more than a potboiler when set against his songs for the Beatles but would make more money than any single song he had written since those days. The record market was bigger in the late seventies, the profits to be made were greater, and John was no longer at the trough. He had the occasional taste, such as when he got a third of the writing credit on 'Fame',

David Bowie's first real hit in the United States in 1975, but he knew that he would at some stage have to jump back in to see if he could still do it.

In 1980 he came back from an extended vacation in Bermuda with Sean during which he had written some songs and made some modest demos. The songs were all about his new-found domestic contentment, his delight in spending time bringing up his second son (as opposed to his first son, who had to compete for attention with his career) and his embrace of a role in the family which would one day be widely recognized as that of the new man. When he returned to New York he went into the studio with producer Jack Douglas and some dependable session men to start recording. He put out the word that this would be a genuine collaboration between him and his wife with their lead vocals carefully alternating to prevent buyers leaving one side unplayed. David Geffen, reasoning that a new Lennon album, no matter its quality, would help establish his eponymous label in the marketplace, was the one who agreed.

It came out on 17 November to great anticipation and a reception that was no more than lukewarm. This wasn't purely because of its subject matter. John Lennon's recordings once he'd left the Beatles were if anything too often criticized for the overt messages in the lyrics – the shrill solipsism of the primal therapy years, the glib sloganeering of *Some Time In New York City* and now the somewhat cloying domesticity of *Double Fantasy*. What's more telling is the tone of all these records. The qualities they no longer had – humour, playfulness, that sense of the warm friction of equals – provide an idea of what a changed person he was. At the height of the Beatles he alchemized his misery into transcendentally happy-sounding songs like 'Help!'. The happiness he now genuinely felt resulted in records that were flat, mechanical, and sounded like the most rote products of the American studio system.

On the evening of 8 December 1980, David Geffen was in New York to meet up with John and Yoko. He was experienced enough to know that a few weeks after the album's release, when there had been enough industry reaction to make it plain that their record wasn't likely to take the world by storm, his job was to provide reassurance, to point to the fact that the single '(Just Like) Starting Over' was showing in the Top Forty and to make noises about the next tranche of reviews being more enthusiastic. Following the meeting John and Yoko got back in their limousine and drove back to the corner of Central Park West and West 72nd Street. They didn't drive into the courtyard of the building. Although Lennon had more than once remarked that if anybody killed him it would be a fan, he still expected to be able to get around one of the more violent cities on earth without needing a bodyguard. Hence he met his killer, twenty-five-year-old Mark Chapman, for the second time that day, out on the sidewalk. On the first occasion Chapman had got him to sign his copy of *Double Fantasy*. On the second occasion he fired five shots from a .38 Special revolver into Lennon's back. He died immediately. He was forty years old.

The news didn't reach London until the following day, Tuesday the 9th. We were woken up by the radio telling us that John Lennon, 'the former Beatle', had been killed in New York. There wasn't a lot more to add to that – the police said it had been done by 'a local screwball' – and in 1980 there were only a limited number of channels for news to travel along. That night there was a tribute on the BBC's rock programme *Whistle Test*. Annie Nightingale, the presenter, said something like 'a lot of us wouldn't be doing what we are doing now if it hadn't been for John Lennon'. I sat on the edge of the bath and blubbed, which is not my habit. Her words touched me off because they related to me, not to John Lennon. I haven't cried about the death of a famous person since. I have come to realize that if we do so what we're crying for is ourselves, our lost youth, the days of happiness we associate with the person who has died.

The Beatles created a great deal of happiness. The by-product of that process was fame. Fame on a mad, massive and eventually injurious scale. In killing a rock star, the ultimate somebody, Mark Chapman, the ultimate nobody, probably hoped he would cross over. He hoped he might obliterate the distance between his own puny life and the hero's life that he saw Lennon leading. His action foreshadowed in a uniquely terrible way our increasing desire to put ourselves at the centre of events, when our proper role should be as a spectator or appreciative listener. It underlined just how big rock stars had become and how much some people still expected those rock stars to be able to mend their own broken lives. It wasn't anything to do with what the rock stars said or did. It was to do with what people expected of them.

It's tempting to stop the clock in the second week of December 1980 and indulge in what historians call a counterfactual. What would have happened if John Lennon had got back into the Dakota unharmed and lived through the next day, which was slated to finish with seats for David Bowie in *The Elephant Man* on Broadway, the day after that, and all the days between then and now?

In the short term Kenny Rogers' 'Lady' might have remained at number one in the USA. The albums of the year would still have been Bruce Springsteen's *The River*, Talking

Heads' *Remain In Light* and Elvis Costello's *Get Happy!!*. The editors of *Rolling Stone, People, Time, Newsweek, Maclean's, New York, NME, Melody Maker* and hundreds of other titles would not have been engaged in a frantic scramble to remake their feature sections with copious reminiscences and place black borders around their front-cover tributes. A few prestigious publications might not have replaced their disobliging early reviews of *Double Fantasy* with appreciations more in keeping with the public mood of mourning.

In the medium term there may have been the tour he talked about, which would probably have included a return to the UK for the first time since 1971. The last time he had appeared on a stage, which was at Madison Square Garden in 1974 with Elton John, he had been literally sick with nerves. That was just a cameo. An appearance in his own right in an arena at a time when people's expectations of a live performance were beginning to be revised upwards would have been a lot more testing.

In the longer term there would almost certainly have been some kind of Beatles reunion, which probably wouldn't have amounted to much but would have been enough to remove some of the shine from the most powerful franchise in pop.

John Lennon might have led a long, happy and fulfilled life, which is the least owed to anyone who has brought so much pleasure to so many.

Rock and roll would of course have lost its key martyr figure, somebody whose untimely demise allowed us all to believe that the wages of rugged independence were at worst an assassin's bullet and at the very least some sort of Establishment stitch-up. Lennon's position as simultaneously the leader of the Beatles and also their most prominent detractor meant that he attracted support from anybody who saw themselves as being above the poison of popularity. Lennon is the rock star that would-be rock stars are keenest to be identified with. Everyone who picked up a guitar in the years after his death felt they weren't so much advancing their own personal agenda as signing up for John Lennon's army.

In the weeks between the murder and Christmas, as the airwaves were monopolized by Lennon's new record, 'Imagine', 'In My Life' and anything that seemed to strike the appropriate note of principled solemnity, as the current affairs programmes were inevitably turned over to discussions about John Lennon the peace campaigner and avant-garde artist, as the crowds gathered on both sides of the Atlantic, cupping votive candles, their voices raised in choruses of 'Give Peace A Chance', as every public figure from politicians to Churchmen came forward to make it clear that they personally felt the same wound everybody else felt, it seemed that something changed. In the wake of pop music's JFK moment it seemed only right to regard the rock star's trade as a very serious business.

Rock and roll arrived just a decade after the Second World War when life was still overwhelmingly a serious business. Rock and roll was a change, something for the kids to enjoy themselves with until the advent of responsibility meant they were forced to put away childish things. This gained force in the sixties, when the music and manners of the beat generation cast their influence over every corner of society and culture. The death of John Lennon and the period of mourning that followed it brought us face to face with the fact that we had taken this world of fun and escape with us as we got older and had not put it away with the things of childhood. This old music was imprinted on us and the characters who had made it were still part of our lives, whether they liked it or not.

The encomium of *Time* magazine demonstrated how the world of twisting and shouting now had to be redrawn as a long journey towards the light. Here Lennon, the anarchic figure who used to enjoy pretending to be what we used to call a spastic, who could never leave an acid retort unspoken, who thought that rock and roll had never improved on 'Tutti Frutti', became 'a figure of poetic political metaphor'. It added that 'his spiritual consciousness was directed inward'. It sympathized with an entire generation for whom, it said, 'a bright dream fades'. The final quote in that feature came from musician Steve Van Zandt. He seemed equally keen to elect Lennon to the triumphant company of latter-day saints. 'He beat the rock 'n' roll life. Beat the drugs, beat the fame, beat the damage. He was the only guy who beat it all.'

On the day the news broke Paul McCartney was caught by a TV crew leaving a recording studio. They asked him what his reaction was to the death of his partner. They clearly wanted something grave and fulsome to open the news with. They didn't get it. 'It's a drag, isn't it?' said McCartney with meaning in his eyes. Then he got in his car.

1980 PLAYLIST

John Lennon and Yoko Ono, *Double Fantasy*
The Cure, *Boys Don't Cry*
The Rolling Stones, *Emotional Rescue*
Dexys Midnight Runners, *Searching For The Young Soul Rebels*
David Bowie, *Scary Monsters (And Super Creeps)*
Bruce Springsteen, *The River*
The Jam, *Sound Affects*
Pink Floyd, 'Another Brick In The Wall'
Talking Heads, *Remain In Light*
Elvis Costello and the Attractions, *Get Happy!!*

13 AUGUST 1981
SHEPPERTON STUDIOS, ENGLAND

Sex, violence and television

The song was originally called 'Girls In Film'. A semi-pro musician called Andy Wickett came up with the idea for it while working on the night shift in a Birmingham chocolate factory. Andy Wickett left Duran Duran before they were successful. He signed a waiver which meant he was paid £600 in return for which he gave up all rights to the song that eventually became 'Girls On Film' and also their major hit 'Rio'. At the time he thought this was quite a good deal. He used the money to buy new keyboards. Later, as he watched his erstwhile bandmates disport themselves in Antony Price suits on board an ocean-going yacht on the blue Caribbean sea off the coast of Antigua, miming to what was no longer his song, he may have had cause to reconsider. The young men with whom he had so recently shared a cold rehearsal hall were now, via the newly ubiquitous medium of video, apparently translated to a land of dreams.

On 13 August 1981, just a couple of days after the world's

first fundraiser to combat the scourge of AIDS had raised a mere $6,000, the members of Duran Duran turned up at Shepperton Studios near London to make a video for their single 'Girls On Film'. The directors were Kevin Godley and Lol Creme, the two former members of 10cc who had transitioned smoothly into the nascent industry of shooting videos. Duran Duran had already had a couple of hits in the UK and had a growing teenage following. However, the band's managers wanted a video that would get them talked about by older people in the United States. In order to do this they agreed it had to be about sex. Creme and Godley had recently been on their travels, during which one of them had seen a fashion show and the other an exhibition of mud wrestling. They decided a conflation of the two might do the trick. There was no agonized discussion about whether this was a good idea on the grounds of either ideology or taste. They just did it. That's how the music business had traditionally worked. In the early eighties the video business was setting itself up as the more daring older brother of the sometimes prudish music business.

The footage they shot that day was subsequently re-cut a number of times in order to satisfy the sensibilities of different countries and broadcasters. At its fullest the video featured the band miming to their song from inside a boxing ring, two girls in baby-doll nighties trying to push each other off a greasy pole, a nurse in a short skirt, stockings and suspenders, a girl in the attire of a sumo wrestler throwing a real sumo wrestler over her shoulder, a naked girl whipping a naked male model, two girls wrestling in mud, and then, just in case there was anyone who hadn't got the point, naked girls being hosed down by an obliging technician. 'Girls On Film' saw the injection of girlie magazine aesthetics – lips parting in slow motion, crotch-bisecting thong, pouting pole worship, ice cube on the nipple, the full wardrobe of glamour stereotypes – into the mainstream of the music business. What they were up to that day seemed so naughty, even to the people doing it, that the band had to be kept away from the girls during the shoot. Nobody expected it to get shown beyond the Playboy channel and a few nightclubs that had recently taken to showing videos. However, as Kevin Godley was to recall, 'it had glamour, it had polish, it had sex, it had good-looking boys, it had girls sliding on poles. It was a dirty film. These were the ingredients that made it MTV-able.'

Obviously no network would show the full version. But they could do something better, which was ban it. It was the publicity surrounding TV's refusal to run their video that made Duran Duran a story in the United States. It was MTV's willingness to play a tame version that made them popular. When Duran Duran shot the video they had never heard of MTV. This new station had been launched only two weeks earlier in those parts of the United States where they had been able to sign up cable providers. The idea for the channel had come from a bunch of radio programmers who thought there could be something in showing music videos round the clock. The investors had difficulty believing there would ever be anything in music television. They had seen the increasing popularity of groups like Blondie, who were unquestionably telegenic and had gone so far as to shoot a clip for each track on their album *Eat To The Beat*, but they didn't believe there would be enough acceptable product to fill the screen time and they were worried about what it all might cost.

What they didn't realize is that the music business was not scientific. They underestimated how desperate it was for exposure. The music business paid for promotional clips if the act was popular in Europe because over there they had music shows and Saturday-morning kids shows that ran the clips and these were proven to sell records. Therefore it didn't have to cost MTV anything at all. Some record companies were happy to provide this material to MTV free of charge. Once they did that the other companies had to fall into line for fear that their artists wouldn't get the exposure. They placed enormous value on the all-important caption at the end of the video spelling out the track's full name and what album it came from, the absence of which was one of their main frustrations with radio. Once the backers realized that this was one cable network where the cost of the product being broadcast was virtually nil they scrambled on board.

It was an odd way to run a TV channel. The majority of MTV's output was provided for them by outside suppliers over whom they had no control. The videos were the products of the whims of artists, the ideas ones that directors wanted to try out in the hope that they could get a commercials deal, and the treatments a reflection of the limitations of their budgets. Only two minutes out of the average hour of programming actually came from the network. These two minutes were provided by a department called 'Programme Services'. The graphics, trails and stings that occupied this time were crucially important because it was here that the fledgling network could tell its viewers who they were, what they were providing and why they should want it. The key graphic was of an MTV flag being planted on the moon. The key message was 'I want my MTV'. They talked Mick Jagger into saying the words and soon they had everyone else parroting the same message. It was a marketing masterstroke in that it co-opted youthful idealism for the benefit of the business plans of Madison Avenue. At no cost.

The service launched at midnight on 1 August with 'Video Killed The Radio Star' by the Buggles. They figured it didn't matter that nobody in the USA knew the record because nobody would be watching. The second video to be aired was a more reliable clue to where MTV would soon head. This was 'You Better Run' by Pat Benatar. Pat had not sung anything that could be called rock until she was twenty-two but her time in stage musicals had equipped her with the ability to project herself. This was something the camera valued. She had only been in a rock band with her husband Neil Giraldo a short time but it was long enough for her to have inherited a few key pretensions and to make her suspicious of working with film people. During the shoot, she recalled, 'I got really angry. I kept thinking, "What do they think I am, a runway model?" As a musician, it was your whole life to be edgy and underground.' By the standards of subsequent videos, by her and a thousand others, Benatar is dressed quite demurely in a striped top, albeit with shiny leather trousers. Following the launch of MTV there would be a lot of leather trousers.

It's difficult to recall the excitement caused by the arrival of MTV. It took a while to establish itself thanks to the conservatism of cable operators. This was overcome by the fact that MTV was one product people couldn't take or leave. It was a revolution in its time as dramatic as the arrival of social media twenty years later. You emerged from your first exposure to it slack-jawed in the face of its effects, sated by the succession of newly familiar faces seen in close-up for the first time and dazzled by its plenty, which was its most important feature. Videos had once been as rare as truffles. Now here they were in stunning profusion, one after another. If you didn't care for what was showing you were bound to be beguiled by the next of its succession of racy images: Debbie

Harry's bare shoulders in Blondie's 'Rapture', Mick Jagger's oddly considered dance moves at the beginning of 'Start Me Up', Devo singing 'Whip It' in their black shorts and plant-pot hats, the boyish U2 doing 'Gloria' in the open air of Dublin docks, and even Foreigner dutifully miming to 'Waiting For A Girl Like You'.

MTV increased the visibility of both rock stars and would-be rock stars. It moved marginal acts with strong visuals quickly into the mainstream. People like the Stray Cats, who would previously have had to rely on college radio, suddenly found themselves drawing big crowds, some of whom were dressed up like them because they had seen the way they dressed. In the early days MTV had unusually high penetration in rural areas. Junior acts like Def Leppard noticed they were starting to show in retail charts in secondary markets, which could only be down to MTV. Whereas radio operated unspoken quotas of records by 'chick singers', MTV, knowing the early adopters of their service were young men, discriminated in favour of female acts, whether it was the Go-Go's, who initially had to be persuaded that there wasn't something essentially immoral about them being filmed driving around Hollywood in an open car while miming to 'Our Lips Are Sealed', or older acts like Olivia Newton-John, who happily cut her hair, toned her body and belatedly transformed herself into a sex symbol with 'Physical'.

Some musicians were remarkably conservative when it came to doing what video required them to do. At the time Miles Copeland was guiding the career of REM. Michael Stipe, who was twenty-one, recalled: 'He said, "I want you to make music videos and I want you to lip-sync." And I said, "No, I'm not going to do it." He said "OK" and that was the end of our meeting.' Stipe went on to lip-sync in scores of videos.

Some of the older acts were worried about what the close scrutiny of the camera would reveal of the shortcomings of their appearance. In 1981 Elton John's hair was at the end of the retreat from which it would triumphantly return. Thus his video offering had to be shot from one side only in a darkened room.

Making videos had previously been an optional extra for the rock star, a box to be ticked should he or she be so inclined. Once MTV was established as the gatekeeper to the hit parade, rock became a visual medium and making a video became part of the rock star's routine. Whole days of their lives were now spent sitting around on a draughty film lot or in a remote, inhospitable location while the really important people, the technicians, titivated the elements of the latest conceit, wondering whether they could get the thin model hired to play the adoring fan to come back to the hotel and staving off the boredom with the stimulants that had been laundered through the record company budget as 'fruit and flowers'.

In September 1981 Rod Stewart's organization took over the whole of Hollywood's Sunset Marquis, which at the time was promoting its reputation as the rockers' hotel of choice. His band set up on a stage by the shallow end of the swimming pool and he mimed to his new single 'Tonight I'm Yours' while all around him undulating young models advertised their availability from the balcony of every room and every recliner around the pool. Most TV can be quite adequately understood with the sound turned down. Hence it's a medium that sets great store by the power of dressing up. The MTV revolution flung open the world's biggest dressing-up box and invited the would-be rock stars to help themselves. They dragged themselves up as pirates, dandies, cowboys, gangsters, ghouls, city slickers, spacemen, soldiers and, inevitably, rock stars. As that Rod Stewart video proved, and numberless similar efforts in the years to come served to underline, this version of the rock-star life was about as faithful to reality as Adam Ant's version of the pirate life. It was, however, an idea of rock-star glamour that lots of people wanted to buy.

1981 PLAYLIST

Duran Duran, 'Girls On Film'
Phil Collins, 'In The Air Tonight'
Queen and David Bowie, 'Under Pressure'
Kraftwerk, *Computer World*
Kid Creole and the Coconuts, *Fresh Fruit In Foreign Places*
Foreigner, *4*
Bob Dylan, *Shot Of Love*
Pretenders, *Pretenders II*
Meat Loaf, *Dead Ringer*
The Police, *Ghost In The Machine*

19 MARCH 1982
LEESBURG, FLORIDA

Road fever

Ozzy Osbourne preferred to travel by bus. Apart from the saving on flights he found it was better to get in the bus and travel directly after a show than to have his hotel room used as the centre for drinking and drugging. He knew he would be too weak to resist joining in. Ozzy had been eased out of Black Sabbath two years earlier because the others, who had major substance issues of their own, found they simply couldn't deal with his as well. It had always been Ozzy's role in the band to be slightly further out of control than the rest. This was a role he took so seriously that eventually the other three asked him to leave.

Ozzy was fortunate at this time in having someone prepared to manage both his professional and personal life and keep his drinking under control. Sharon Arden was the daughter of Don Arden, a singer-turned-manager with a fearsome reputation within the business. Arden was the man seen trying to tempt Chuck Berry out of his dressing room during his 1964 tour by sliding dollar bills under the door. Sharon had grown up among people who settled their disputes with their fists rather than lawyers. She was learning the business by managing Ozzy's post-Sabbath group Blizzard of Ozz. The two weren't yet married but she was his partner and had already begun her journey from homely boss's daughter figure to sculpted Hollywood wife.

Ozzy's was a curious form of stardom. The majority of his fans were young men. They looked to him to play the traditional role of the member of the gang who always goes too far. Ozzy had quickly learned what was expected of him. He decided to enliven his show by hiring an actor who was 3ft 10in to dress as a monk and materialize through a trap-door on stage to hand him water and a towel. During the song 'Goodbye To Romance' the unfortunate man would to all intents and purposes be hanged on stage. On the same tour Ozzy appeared before a meeting of executives at his label in Los Angeles and appeared to bite the head off a dove he was supposed to be releasing. Actual witnesses to this surprising meeting are impossible to trace but what mattered is that the dove incident was appended to his growing legend. When he played Des Moines, Iowa in January 1982 teenager Mark Neal tossed a dead bat on to the stage. Ozzy naturally took a bite. Later he thought better of it and had a rabies shot. Although he played the wild man on stage, in the real world Ozzy was as helpless and needy as a small boy. Sharon found this side of him attractive. Without her he simply couldn't function. Together they flourished.

On 19 March 1982 the Blizzard of Ozz tour party had just driven all night following a show in Knoxville, Tennessee. Their bus driver, the thirty-three-year-old Andrew Aycock, took a detour to Leesburg, Florida. His plan was to go to the headquarters of the bus company and get a faulty air conditioner fixed. Ozzy and Sharon were asleep in their quarters at the back of the bus. Aycock, who was accompanied on this stage of the journey by his ex-wife, had been doing cocaine. There was a small commuter air strip adjacent to the property of the bus company. Aycock was a qualified pilot with a lapsed licence, and he decided to take a Beechcraft Bonanza up for a spin. He neglected to seek the owner's permission.

There was no other way to keep themselves amused so Aycock invited various members of the touring party to come up with him for quick joy rides. On the last of these circuits his passengers were Randy Rhoads, the elfin twenty-five-year-old Californian guitar player who was the star of Ozzy's new band, and Rachel Youngblood, the fifty-eight-year-old African-American woman who was subsequently described variously as make-up artist, hairdresser, wardrobe assistant and cook. She was the help, Sharon's live-in maid from back in California. She had joined the tour to help Sharon be Sharon while she was making it possible for Ozzy to be Ozzy. Neither Rhoads nor Youngblood were keen fliers but somehow on that sunny morning they were persuaded into boarding the Bonanza, a later version of the aircraft in which Buddy Holly had perished twenty-three years earlier.

In an attempt to either wake up Ozzy or tease his ex-wife, who was watching from below, Aycock repeatedly took the Beechcraft low enough to buzz the bus. On his third pass he miscalculated, clipped the bus with a wing, hit a tree and ploughed into a nearby mansion, where the plane immediately burst into flames. The initial impact with the bus woke Ozzy and Sharon who stumbled outside to be confronted by the sight of flaming wreckage. There were body parts strewn across the ground. All three who were on the plane died instantly. They had to be identified from their medical records.

After their deaths it was said that none of them had wanted to be on the tour in the first place, that what Randy had really wanted was to go to university and study classical composition, that Rachel had signed up for one last tour so that she could raise the money to buy an electric typewriter for her church, and that it was particularly surprising that they should perish together because she didn't like Randy and in fact had called him a little white bastard. Clearly the accident was the bus driver's fault but it seems the kind of grisly, pointless tragedy that could only have occurred in the course of a rock and roll tour. If the passengers had been members of a sporting team on their way to an away game or a touring theatre company en route to a festival it seems unlikely that reluctant fliers would have allowed themselves to be cajoled into getting into a small aircraft to go nowhere in particular with somebody they barely knew.

There is a disorientation in the atmosphere around a rock band on tour which brings about a certain detachment from the elementary laws of physics and chemistry governing normal life. Even if none of the protagonists are particularly unhinged or suffering from the need to test the limits of their own mortality there is a tendency to do the ill-advised which would only rarely arise in everyday life. This was particularly the case in 1982 when artists didn't yet employ people whose primary job was to protect them from themselves. The world in which these people lived and moved was attuned to extremes. Nobody was yet suggesting that exercise and abstinence might be the secret to surviving life on the road. They were all prone to thinking themselves indestructible. The touring life was sustained by drugs and drink. Very few didn't partake. All these people were moved to go beyond the red line, to hang themselves over the precipice, with predictable consequences.

1982 was a year rich in examples of similar recklessness. The day before the tragedy in Leesburg, Teddy Pendergrass, the black Elvis, was involved in an accident in his Rolls-Royce while speeding in Philadelphia. In June, James Honeyman-Scott, the guitarist with the Pretenders, was found dead of heart failure in a girlfriend's flat. 'Cocaine intolerance' was blamed. This was only days after he had agreed that bassist Pete Farndon should be fired from the same group because of his own addiction to heroin. Farndon would be found dead in his bath less than a year later.

Greater experience didn't bring with it any greater wisdom. In March the forty-year-old David Crosby was arrested after crashing into a guard rail on the San Diego Freeway while driving and simultaneously trying to roll a joint and take a hit from a pipe. The policeman at the scene noticed a pistol poking out of Crosby's bag and ran him in. A month later he was arrested again at a frowsy club in Dallas where he was playing a gig to get cash money for drugs. The police came upon him freebasing with his gun at his side. 'It gave him quick money to put in his pocket – and then in his pipe,' said a friend. 'It kept him going between royalty cheques that came in quarterly. Quarterly is a long time to a doper. Tomorrow is a long time for a doper.' Crosby had already mightily tried the patience of his fellow musicians – a star-studded intervention at his Marin County home the year before was rather spoiled by his being discovered halfway through in the bathroom sucking on a pipe – but Stills and Nash took him back on the road, albeit with his microphone turned down and his parts sung by another singer in the wings.

1982 seemed short on new rock stars but it was long on people who wanted to act like them. *Rolling Stone*'s cover stars for that year were mostly actors and TV people – David Letterman, Robin Williams, Mariel Hemingway, Matt Dillon, Timothy Hutton and Warren Beatty – all affecting the casual drag and 'we mean it' looks of rock stars. On 5 March the comedian and actor John Belushi was found dead in a bungalow at the Chateau Marmont, having ingested a speedball, a cocktail of heroin and cocaine. The woman who administered it to him, Cathy Smith, was a former associate of three members of the Band and Ron Wood of the Rolling Stones, a woman who had turned from using to dealing. In January of that year Belushi, who had made his name playing an amateur musician in *The Blues Brothers*, had appeared on the cover of *Rolling Stone* to accompany a feature saying that he had changed and was not the self-destructive hell-raiser of yore. In Hollywood the bigger the lie the higher it flies. An inscription on Belushi's tombstone, on Martha's Vineyard, read 'I may be gone but rock and roll lives on'. His widow subsequently arranged for him to be reburied in an unmarked grave to avoid attracting fans who wished to sit alongside this message and drink. In one of the interviews she gave she said, 'I wish somebody had ruined John's career by writing about his cocaine use.'

The death of Belushi confirmed a feeling that had been gaining ground, that in the entertainment business cocaine was a currency as well as a stimulant. Robin Williams, who at the time was holding down a drug habit as well as a prime-time role on *Mork and Mindy*, recalled, 'The Belushi tragedy was frightening. His death scared a whole group of show-business people. It caused a big exodus from drugs.' A BBC news report at the time by Robin Denselow confirmed that cocaine could be used to compensate poorly paid employees in a recording studio or to grease the wheels of a movie deal. It also made people who were prone to doubting themselves achieve the feeling of omnipotence with which they liked to go about their work. In October the *New York Times* published a major report on the rise of cocaine use in Hollywood. Lloyd's of London was apparently refusing to insure certain stars because their cocaine habits made them bad risks for movies trying to hit completion dates.

These weren't the only heirs to the throne of James Dean. Despite the actor having rolled his car several times in the middle of Beverly Hills, the agent of Richard Dreyfuss said, with affronted professional pride in his voice, that as far as he knew his client had never been a cocaine user. Dreyfuss, who dates his sobriety from that incident, later told the truth. 'By the time of the crash I had become a board member and probably chairman of admissions for the Assholes Center,' he said.

On 30 April Lester Bangs, the rock critic whose words were as impressive in print as their author was unimpressive in person, whose reviews were a plea for acceptance from musicians and hipsters who wouldn't spare him the time of day, who liked to say that rock and roll wasn't so much a music as a way of living your life, finished the final draft of a new book he called *Rock Gomorrah*. His idea of celebrating completion was to take a number of Valium pills together with a strong cold remedy. He never woke up. He was thirty-three.

Meanwhile, far away from Hollywood, far away from this gilded high society, something stirred. The most significant musical moment of 1982 was the release of 'The Message' by Grandmaster Flash and the Furious Five. This would prove to be as significant in its time as 'Tutti Frutti' was in 1955. Writing about it in *Rolling Stone* in September, Kurt Loder described it as 'the most detailed and devastating report from underclass America since Bob Dylan decried the lonesome death of Hattie Carroll – or, perhaps more to the point, since Marvin Gaye took a long look around and wondered what was going on.'

In the immediate wake of the Leesburg tragedy, Ozzy took to the bottle. He said he wanted to retire. Sharon knew there was no question of him doing that. How could they go back to normal life after this? What else were a pair of show folk to do?

Three weeks later they were auditioning replacement guitarists.

1982 PLAYLIST

Iron Maiden, *The Number Of The Beast*
Sonic Youth, *Sonic Youth*
The Clash, *Combat Rock*
Roxy Music, *Avalon*
Yazoo, *Upstairs At Eric's*
Grandmaster Flash and the Furious Five, 'The Message'
Kate Bush, *The Dreaming*
Peter Gabriel, *Peter Gabriel*
Bruce Springsteen, *Nebraska*
Prince, *1999*

31 SEPTEMBER 1983
THE CONTINENTAL HYATT HOUSE, HOLLYWOOD

The absurdity of rock stars

In 1983 Rob Reiner, who had made his name as an actor on the TV comedy *All In The Family*, got together with comic actors Christopher Guest, Michael McKean and Harry Shearer, begged a small amount of money from a film fund headed up by Lew Grade and began shooting a modest film. The film they made was to do for the anonymous rock band trying to make a living what *Dont Look Back* did for Bob Dylan. It had no script; they made it on the fly and improvised the dialogue. The notional band played their own music. Their repertoire featured such self-composed tunes as 'Big Bottom' and 'Tonight I'm Gonna Rock You Tonight'. Where possible they shot in real-world rock locations. They filmed at Elvis Presley's graveside. The end-of-tour wrap party was shot around the pool on the roof of the Continental Hyatt House in Hollywood. This was the rock and roll boarding house that had been known in the days when Keith Moon stayed there as the Continental Riot House.

The fictional subjects of the documentary *This Is Spinal Tap* were Spinal Tap, a band of prog rock plodders from the English provinces. In the film they were embarking on an American tour in support of their new album, *Smell The Glove*. The three members who mattered – a succession of drummers had all met with unfortunate ends – were David St Hubbins, Nigel Tufnel and Derek Smalls. All three looked like classically unmemorable members of rock's army of anonymous foot soldiers. Their faces were slightly too old for their haircuts. These were men with nothing notably wild and untamed about them, men who for the most part lived standard lower-middle-class lives of blameless tedium, interrupted only by the occasional call to go out on the road and play the rock star for the benefit of the concertgoers of Moose Droppings, Ohio. Once there they would be temporarily decanted into a pair of spandex trousers in order to perform an overheated number in praise of their amatory member or their girlfriend's bottom. Clearly, it was no job for a grown-up. Nonetheless it was the only job certain grown-ups could do.

Between them Spinal Tap had but three facial expressions: hubristic over-confidence when pronouncing what they were about to do, burning embarrassment when it became evident that the plan wasn't working out, and stammering anger as they thrashed around afterwards for somebody to blame. The performances of the three lead actors, Guest, Shearer and McKean, were such note-perfect depictions of passive aggressivness that ever since we have been unable to imagine rock bands trying to solve their differences in anything other than the same wounded suburban register. They dressed like

Reggae star turned rock star Bob Marley electrified London's Lyceum on 18 July 1975 with a show that would go down in history and put him in the charts.

It was the songs of Fleetwood Mac that made them popular. It was the charisma of Stevie Nicks, pictured here in 1976, that made them fascinating.

Above and left: When Elvis Presley died at Graceland in 1977, he was a has-been. The unexpected public outpouring of grief gave him a new dignity in death and turned him into a bigger star than ever.

Below: Punk rock introduced a rich new cast of characters to music. Ian Dury is pictured here in 1978, when his 'Hit Me With Your Rhythm Stick' made him for a while the UK's most popular, and most unlikely, rock star.

Above: Robert Plant and John Paul Jones of Led Zeppelin consult their manager Peter Grant backstage at Knebworth House on 4 August 1979. The singer, who was turning thirty-one, was starting to feel his age.

Right: The murder of John Lennon in December 1980 transformed his public image from sardonic rocker to martyred artist. The *Rolling Stone* cover picture, taken earlier on the day he died, featured Yoko Ono at his insistence.

Below: Duran Duran were unaware there was such a thing as MTV when they made their video for 'Girls On Film' in 1981. Getting the clip banned was far better for business than getting it shown.

Above: The elfin guitar hero Randy Rhoads was a key part of the act in Ozzy Osbourne's *Blizzard Of Ozz*. At the time of his death in an avoidable air crash in 1982, he was said to be planning to quit to study classical music.

Above: Actor Harry Shearer in 1983, playing Derek Smalls during the shooting of *This Is Spinal Tap*, the film that taught the world to see rock stars as essentially middle-aged men in preposterous trousers.

Above: After suffering third-degree burns to his scalp during the shooting of a Pepsi commercial in 1984 Michael Jackson, the self-christened King of Pop, began taking the painkillers that would eventually contribute to his death.

Above: 13 July 1985. Rock and royalty bask in a new level of acclaim at the Live Aid concert in Wembley Stadium, the show that won Bob Geldof a knighthood and launched the live-rock boom.

Left: Bob Dylan with Tom Petty at Madison Square Garden in 1986. Earlier that year Dylan had secretly married and was having such trouble writing new songs that he was seriously considering retirement.

Below: The members of Guns N' Roses surrounding Tom Zutaut and Teresa Ensenat, who signed them to Geffen Records because they looked like MTV's idea of what rock stars should look like.

Above: Elton John poses in the midst of just a fraction of the luxurious impedimenta he sold through the auction house Sotheby's in September 1988 as part of his short-lived back-to-basics campaign.

Below: Bonnie Raitt decided to get sober when a fan asked about her weight. The resulting album *Nick Of Time*, one of a number of records reflecting middle-aged preoccupations, was a huge hit in 1989.

Above: During her Blond Ambition tour of 1990, Madonna's writhing with her dancers was designed to generate the publicity that was her artistic currency.

Below: The walls of Freddie Mercury's Kensington home were turned into an improvised shrine following the Queen singer's death from an AIDS-related illness in November 1991.

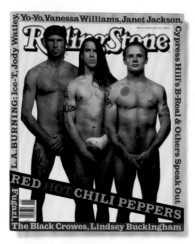

Above: Guitarist John Frusciante was unsentimentally cropped out of the Red Hot Chili Peppers line-up on the cover of *Rolling Stone* after he had a breakdown and left the group in the middle of a 1992 Japanese tour.

Above: In the midst of a dispute in 1993 Prince thought he could escape his own identity by disavowing his contracts, swapping his name for a glyph and, in some extreme cases, appearing in concert behind a mask.

Left and below: Worried he couldn't properly live up to what he expected a rock star to be, Kurt Cobain of Nirvana (*below*) killed himself in 1994. The band may be no more; the brand lives on (*left*).

rock stars. They sounded like three men trying to fix a lawn mower.

This Is Spinal Tap is not a film that improves the more you watch it. It was shot on 16mm and then blown up to twice the size, which adds to the feeling of a project on which the budget is about to be exhausted. It doesn't have many finer points to be appreciated on repeated viewings. All that matters is that first viewing when you recognize that you are watching how generic rock bands behave at a particular point in their career arc. It doesn't focus on how they might be at the moment they were just starting to happen, which is the traditional point at which you freeze the pop process and depict it. Instead what the notional director Marty Di Bergi – 'enough of my yackin', let's boogie!' – unwittingly captures is the moment at which a band that has been going for years realizes it's never going to be quite as good as it was ever again – a realization that was stealing up on many sixties and seventies bands in the early eighties.

No matter how their manager Ian Faith paints it – 'it's not that we're less popular, it's just that our appeal is becoming more selective' – Spinal Tap are on their way down. The bands they once looked down on are now playing venues they can only dream of playing, nobody turns up to their album signing, the budget for everything gets smaller, the limo turns into a van, nobody takes their calls and they are clearly hurtling back to the position where they started from, where the only people they can rely on are each other and their relatives and the only thing they can hope for is that it's a controlled descent and that the occasions on which they're brought face to face with how far they have fallen can be kept to a tolerable minimum.

Comedy and tragedy are often the same story told at

different speeds. Tom Waits says he cried the first time he saw *This Is Spinal Tap*. The film certainly captures many aspects of the rock and roll experience with a brutal candour not seen in more serious films. One of them is the group dynamic. Bands are like small political parties, presenting a united front to the outside world while a low-level internecine war is being perpetually waged within, a war in which nothing is forgiven or forgotten, nothing is openly discussed, and any person brave enough to propose a change of direction suffers the fate of being openly derided for doing what so clearly needs doing. *This Is Spinal Tap* captures the imperceptible heightening of tension and meaningful sidelong glances that greet any member apparently seeking the approval of anyone outside the group. It captures how the one pliable member, in this case bass player Derek Smalls, is caught in the crossfire between the would-be alpha males who write the songs and come up with the ideas. It captures the grenade-rolled-under-the-door effect of the arrival on tour of David St Hubbins' girlfriend who graduates from supportive onlooker in the wings to the person who's clearly operating one member remotely, who even takes over management of the band, at the exact point when nobody else in their right mind would take the job. She is last seen achieving her ultimate wish, which is to be on stage with the band, rattling a tambourine. She will clearly go on to sleep with the band's other leader. In time her memoirs will be privately published. She will eventually marry an arms dealer and run a yoga retreat.

This Is Spinal Tap also captures the absurdities of the rockumentary format, which was burgeoning at the time in step with the growth of music TV stations looking for rock content. It has all the elements: the individual interviews in which members advertise their special interests, the hardware sequence in which Nigel explains that his amplifier goes up to number eleven and therefore is clearly one louder, the camera that tracks the band through the labyrinth below the stage as the distant cheers of the audience begin audibly to flag, the dressing-room tantrum sparked by the fact that the slices of bread are slightly too small for the slices of ham. Everything that can fall apart falls apart. As it does so the camera refuses to avert its eyes. All the lines that seemed a good idea at the time, all the would-be profundities and witty retorts that the protagonists wished they could take back, are there on the soundtrack. 'What's wrong with being sexy?' 'I rise above it. I'm a professional.' 'There's such a fine line between stupid and clever.' See the finished film once and lines like that remain in your head to be reawakened at the slightest prompting.

Although the film makers stated that the misadventures of Spinal Tap were not based on any particular group, many real-life bands fell over themselves to claim that they inspired it. It was in 1983, when the film was being made, that Black Sabbath found that the Stonehenge set they had ordered was too big to fit on the stage. The British blues band Foghat were adamant that their management had once been taken over by a girlfriend of one of the members who insisted on planning their tour schedule according to numerology. They half-jokingly accused the film makers of having bugged their tour bus to get pointers. Every band wanted to own certain scenes. Everybody talked about the time they got lost going to the stage or when their amplifiers picked up the transmissions of a local car firm. Eddie Van Halen insisted on ordering an amp that went up to eleven. That was all part of their way of reassuring us that they were in on the joke. But the core joke of *This Is Spinal Tap*, that bands keep going long after they should stop because stopping is the very thing they don't dare do, is too bitter a pill to swallow.

Rock had been spoofed before but usually by people like Peter Sellers and Phil Silvers, who may have been geniuses but didn't really understand the thing they were spoofing. The difference this time was that Guest, McKean and Shearer knew whereof they spoke. They slid in the stiletto with loving tenderness. To them had been vouchsafed a glimpse of the overarching truth of what was now a rock industry: that it relies on the audience's willing suspension of disbelief. Once you're no longer swept along by the power of its grand illusion, once you begin to question the conventions to which it clings, once the wires along which it dances are plainly visible, once you actually glimpse the desperation in the musicians' eyes as they see some piece of on-stage business begin to unravel, once the amplification fails and you hear them barking at each other like any bunch of workmen in crisis, then you are seeing the world through the lens of Spinal Tap.

And once you have seen the world of rock through the lens of Spinal Tap nothing can ever be quite the same again. Once glimpsed through that glass the standard bunch of rock demi-gods are instantly revealed before you as middle-aged men in unsuitable trousers. Once daylight has flooded in on magic to that degree it takes a million dollars' worth of illusion to turn you back into a believer.

1983 PLAYLIST

David Bowie, *Let's Dance*
Culture Club, 'Karma Chameleon'
Michael Jackson, *Thriller*
Def Leppard, *Pyromania*
U2, *War*
Paul Young, *No Parlez*
Tom Waits, *Swordfishtrombones*
The Rolling Stones, *Undercover*
The Fall, *Perverted By Language*
Jackson Browne, *Lawyers In Love*

27 JANUARY 1984
THE SHRINE AUDITORIUM, LOS ANGELES, CALIFORNIA

A superstar on fire

Between 24 December 1983 and 14 April 1984 the number one album in the United States remained the same. It was Michael Jackson's *Thriller*. By the middle of February 1984 *Thriller* had already sold enough to be officially announced as the best-selling album of all time, surpassing earlier contenders such as the soundtrack of *The Sound of Music*. On 28 February the annual Grammy awards presentation in Los Angeles revolved around the twenty-five-year-old singer. On that night he picked up no fewer than eight awards, including the trophy for best single for 'Beat It', the award for album of 1983 and, together with Quincy Jones, the prize for best producer. It was the highest-rated televised Grammy awards in history. Almost fifty-two million Americans tuned in. Music had never been bigger.

At the time Michael Jackson seemed to be bigger than

the entire music business. The producers of the Grammy awards certainly appeared to think so. Jackson seemed to be permanently in shot throughout the entire ceremony as if the evening was being held in his honour. He sat in the front row, wearing mirror shades, his signature glove and what appeared to be the spangly regalia of the ambassador from the Republic of Fame. Seated next to him was the eighteen-year-old starlet Brooke Shields. His other companion for the evening was Emmanuel Lewis, the twelve-year-old star of the TV comedy *Webster*. Despite his age Lewis was only forty-two inches tall. Jackson picked him up and carried him around as though he was an exhausted toddler.

What Jackson shared with his guests was an upbringing in which normal life had played no part. All three had been managed by over bearing parents. All three had had difficulty negotiating the transition from child to adult star. At the age of just fifteen Shields had been featured in a provocative ad for Calvin Klein jeans. In this she'd fixed the camera with her sultry look and said, 'What comes between me and my Calvins? Nothing.' Lewis had been the junior spokesperson for the Burger King Whopper. Now, thanks to a deal that was far bigger than any of the agreements that had previously been reached between a music star and Madison Avenue, Michael Jackson had signed up to advertise Pepsi-Cola.

Under the terms of this agreement Michael would lend the singing and dancing skills that had made him the biggest star of MTV to a video that would adapt one of his songs to sing the praises of the drink that was allegedly the choice of a new generation of young people. It was at Michael's suggestion that they took the chorus of the song 'Billie Jean', a song inspired by a real-life case of his being on the receiving end of a paternity suit, and changed them to 'You're the

Pepsi generation / Guzzle down and taste the thrill of the day / And feel the Pepsi way'. His team had only settled on a deal with Pepsi after they had failed to get the sum of money they wanted out of Coca-Cola, for whom he would have been just as keen to shill. It was made clear to Pepsi that because of his strict diet Michael would not at any stage be seen actually imbibing their drink. His enthusiasm for the product was a matter of form, not substance, and even his form was strictly rationed: in the commercial he restricted the appearance of his face to just four seconds. He told the producers it would be perfectly possible to suggest his presence via close-ups of his shoes and the outline of his silhouette. He had designed himself as a brand. He expected to be similarly recognizable.

Like a major athlete using his muscle to renegotiate his contract, Jackson preferred to see people's affection and respect expressed in a way he could understand: in greater sums of money than had ever been paid to an entertainer before. He thereby hoped not only to continue to finance a lifestyle of unprecedented lavishness, but also to show his elder brothers, now reduced to minor players in his circus, his tyrant of a father, who insisted that he do one last tour for his brothers' sake, and all the other superstars such as Paul McCartney, Barbra Streisand and Stevie Wonder that he had achieved what they had never achieved and had done so on his own.

By January 1984 Michael Jackson had climbed as high as any star had climbed in the years since Elvis Presley. He was selling records in quantities nobody had ever sold them before. Furthermore, because he had negotiated higher royalty rates than anyone else, he was making more money out of them than anybody had ever made before. He had signed a million-dollar deal to do some kind of book which was to be edited by another national icon, Jackie Onassis. He was the acknowledged master of a new form of entertainment which brought together music and movement into a seamless whole. He was reaching beyond the usual base of a popular entertainer for the simple reason that he was black (although he had already had plastic surgery to accentuate his cheekbones and give him a Disney nose, he was still almost his original colour) and therefore he reached into communities in the United States and beyond that had never really been penetrated by the Beatles and Elvis Presley. This made him the presiding superstar of a world that seemed to be getting bigger all the time.

Several years later I was driving across Ethiopia in the company of an English-speaking Ethiopian who had travelled overseas. In the course of a long discussion about popular music I found myself having to explain who the Beatles and Elvis Presley were. This young man had literally never heard of them. Michael Jackson, of course, he knew. He was a citizen of Michael's world – a good indication of how the world was beginning to bend away from rock in the middle of the 1980s and move in the direction of dance music. At the time Michael Jackson was in his imperial phase. This is the most dangerous point in anyone's career. It's the time when things work in such a way as to make you think they will work that way for ever.

On 27 January 1984 Michael Jackson was in the Shrine Auditorium in Los Angeles to shoot the Pepsi commercial. The director was Bob Giraldi, a big name in TV commercials who had directed his clips for 'Beat It' and 'Billie Jean'. Giraldi was in a dressing room at the venue with Jermaine Jackson when they heard a piercing scream which was clearly emanating from Michael. Fearing that some potential Mark Chapman figure had somehow penetrated security, they dashed to the star's dressing room. They found Michael staring horrified at one of his signature white gloves. He had dropped it in the lavatory and was screaming for some minion to come and get it out. This delicate operation was eventually accomplished by a prop man with a wire coat hanger.

At 6.15 that evening he was on stage at the Shrine performing in front of a three-thousand-strong audience that had been bussed in to lend authenticity. Jackson's dance movements were often accentuated with special effects the better to emphasize the superhuman discipline of his dancing. On this occasion he was to emerge from a burst of flames and then sashay his way to join the band in his characteristic motion, which was a combination of combat soldier and pimp. People who were there that day still argue about where the responsibility lay. What's certain is that Jackson got too close to the flame effect. A spark landed on his head, which ignited his hair. With impressive professionalism Jackson continued to dance for a few seconds with his hair fully aflame until technicians and security men came to his aid with blankets to put out the fire and hurry him away. He was taken straight to the Cedars-Sinai Medical Center where it was noted that he had sustained 'a palm-sized area of 2nd and small area of 3rd degree burns'. He was prescribed Darvocet, a painkiller that was subsequently removed from sale of any kind in the United States. Here is where Jackson's long descent into addiction to prescription painkillers began.

At the time any kind of descent seemed impossible to imagine. Michael Jackson's domination of a market that was in the process of expanding dramatically was causing people to redefine what success meant. By 1984 *Thriller* had already sold a difficult-to-credit twenty-five million copies. Jackson was clearly amassing money in quantities that surely nobody would ever be able to spend. At the same time as he was breaking all sales records nobody pointed out that the leader of the last group to sell records in unprecedented numbers, Mick Fleetwood of Fleetwood Mac, was already filing for bankruptcy. Fleetwood had expanded beyond even his considerable means during the fat years and now he was paying the price. But it seemed inconceivable that anything similar could happen to Michael Jackson.

Jackson never claimed to be a rock star. After careful consideration of what category he thought he could boss he came up with the idea that he should be called the King of Pop. He instructed his PR handlers that he would only talk to organs of the media that were happy to refer to him as such. He did, of course, have an acute understanding of how he might reach out to the rock demographic. He wooed it by getting Eddie Van Halen to contribute a neuralgic guitar solo to 'Beat It'. His success certainly changed the expectations of rock stars. After *Thriller*, every record company wanted a record similarly full of crossover potential. They were prepared to cover any studio bills provided the artist was prepared to make sure the record included a country duet or something for the dance crowd. Michael Jackson changed the business for everyone. After *Thriller*, everyone had to be some kind of dancer as well as a singer. Even Bruce Springsteen, who had up to that point been all about the sweat and the grit, hauled the young actress Courteney Cox out of the audience and danced with her for the shoot for his 1984 breakthrough hit 'Dancing In The Dark'. He thus set in place a ritual that would be re-enacted with hundreds of different partners in hundreds of different locations all over the world as an ever-larger audience came along to see what they had already seen on the

TV but on a massive scale. Springsteen had written the song, with its mulish insistence that 'you can't start a fire without a spark', when his manager Jon Landau had told him that his new album *Born In The U.S.A.* needed a hit. Once he'd done the grunt work of the album he felt he could allow himself the indulgence of a disco-friendly party single. The next thing he knew he was up on stage dancing like Tom Cruise in *Risky Business*, twirling this gorgeous thin girl around like a pop star. Or at least a pop star's idea of a rock star.

There were just five number-one albums in the USA in 1984 – an indication of how deep the sales went. None of the people who put out those records ever did quite as well again. Michael Jackson never again sold as many records as he did in 1984. Nor did Bruce Springsteen. Nor Prince. Nor Huey Lewis and the News. In 1984 people were just crazy for records. In September, a new Sony plant in Terre Haute, Indiana opened for business with great fanfare. This was going to manufacture an exciting new product, the compact disc. The first CD to come off their production line was Springsteen's *Born In The U.S.A.*, which was manufactured in the USA, albeit for a Japanese-owned company. Although most people didn't have the kind of hi-fi set-up that enabled them to appreciate the improved dynamic range they did respond to the idea that these new sound carriers were as robust and easy to use as cassettes and bought them by the million.

At the same time there was also a strong singles market, particularly in the UK. In 1984 Frankie Goes to Hollywood became only the second act to have their first three singles go to number one in the UK – the first group to achieve this feat since another group from Liverpool. That group was Gerry and the Pacemakers, the mere mention of whose name should serve as a corrective for anyone entertaining delusions of grandeur. In Britain the year 1984 climaxed with the best-selling British single of all time. It was a record that over the subsequent year would do more than any other to change the perception of who rock stars were and what they could do.

1984 PLAYLIST

George Michael, 'Careless Whisper'
Cyndi Lauper, 'Girls Just Want To Have Fun'
Frankie Goes to Hollywood, 'Relax'
Bruce Springsteen, *Born In The U.S.A.*
Prince, *Purple Rain*
U2, *The Unforgettable Fire*
Talking Heads, *Stop Making Sense*
Frankie Goes to Hollywood, *Welcome To The Pleasuredome*
Madonna, 'Like A Virgin'
Van Halen, *1984*

13 JULY 1985
WEMBLEY STADIUM, LONDON

From dumper to sainthood

In the mid-eighties I was working in London on music magazines. Many of these tracked the comings and goings of the UK market for pop 45s. Among the professionals who worked on these magazines, who liked to affect the armour of the hard-bitten, it was common to refer to any pop star who had passed the point of being in peak demand for interviews and could no longer get played on the radio or featured on the weekly TV programme *Top of the Pops* as being 'in the dumper'. While observers of the pop scene might have differed on many things, the one they could all have agreed on as the autumn of the year 1984 slipped into winter was that the foremost inmate of said dumper was the lead singer of the Irish group the Boomtown Rats, Bob Geldof. Indeed had the citizens of the dumper been electing a mayor in late 1984 then Geldof would have been odds-on favourite. His group's string of hits had come to an end in 1980 and there was no indication of it being resumed, making Geldof's fabled garrulousness his one remaining claim on public attention.

Bob Geldof made a perfect target for that peculiarly British meanness that likes nothing more than to see last year's star reduced to the ranks. Geldof had opinions about everything and seemed incapable of keeping any of them to himself. He was the pop star every TV producer called on when he needed a talking head with a modern haircut. He had been a newspaper journalist for a while, which meant he was inclined to think he could do the job of the writers sent to interview him better than they could do it themselves. Plus he was married to Paula Yates, the flirty co-host of the music television programme *The Tube*. Together they had children they seemed to delight in giving provocatively cute names. His band was on the point of releasing their fifth album, and the fact that this release was being eagerly anticipated by absolutely nobody seemed only correct and proper. Geldof's place on the covers of magazines had been usurped by Boy George, Annie Lennox and George Michael. It all appeared to be over. The game was clearly up.

This changed on 24 October when Geldof saw a report on the BBC news by Michael Buerk, who was in Korem in the Tigray region of Ethiopia. In that vast area a combination of drought and civil war had forced tens of thousands of famished people from hundreds of miles around off their land and sent them to Korem's Red Cross feeding station – their only hope of saving their children from death by starvation. This was in the days before satellite and cable news when there were just four television channels in the United Kingdom and therefore any major news event galvanized the public in a way that was soon to become in conceivable. Moved by the suffering he saw in the report, as many people were, Geldof decided to do something. The only thing he could do was write, record and release a record. If it sold well enough and everything went in its favour, he reasoned, it might generate a five-figure sum which could be contributed towards famine relief.

He started with the musicians he knew, Midge Ure, Sting and Duran Duran, all of whom agreed to take part. Then he moved on to the ones he didn't such as Wham! and Culture Club. Wherever possible he contacted the artists directly. They all agreed they would be there to record their contribution if they could. Then he contacted the managers of the ones he couldn't get through to directly. Many of these people declined as decorously as they could. But by the time the recording sessions came around, Sunday, 25 November, he had that most valuable of political tools, a following wind. He was also perfectly prepared to accuse anyone who didn't come on board of colluding in the deaths of innocent children.

When I arrived at Sarm Studios in Basing Street, Notting Hill that Sunday morning to cover the session I was as surprised as anybody else to be confronted with Wham!, Paul Weller, Sting, Status Quo, George Michael, U2, Kool and the Gang and Paul Young. What was even more surprising was that this array of A-list talent had been marshalled by somebody whose star seemed in every other respect to have crashed to earth. Bob Geldof was a more effective politician than he was a rock star. Lyndon Johnson became one of the most effective Presidents of the United States not because he could charm but because he could cajole, torment and even bully. These were the same talents Geldof used to get everyone together to make the Band Aid single happen. When it was finished he played further hardball with the bosses at BBC to make sure that the video could be debuted in a special slot cleared from the schedules just before *Top of the Pops*, as if it were some kind of message from the sovereign. When the record came out it sold 320,000 copies a day. It sold so many that all the pressing plants in the UK had to be put into production. It went straight to number one and earned £3 million for famine relief.

As the enterprise gathered force, spawning a local version in the United States, performers, fans and media were suddenly energized by the tang of virtue in the air. Ordinary citizens doing their bit for charity equals ordinary compassion. Rock stars giving up their time to do the same somehow amounts to something heroic. As Band Aid turned into Live Aid in the spring of 1985 even the most mundane parts of the process were hailed as the workings of destiny. When Geldof attended the recording of 'We Are The World', the United States' answer to 'Do They Know It's Christmas?', in Hollywood in January 1985 he found the organizers unable to believe that a star of Bruce Springsteen's magnitude had actually driven himself to the session and was capable of getting from his car to the studio unaided.

The shows, which took place on 13 July 1985 at Wembley Stadium in London and at the JFK Stadium in Philadelphia, were carnivals of enlightened self-interest. All the musicians got the thing they wanted most, which was increased profile. The furious ones were those not invited. Geldof's memoirs are a good account of how he always used the threat of being outshone by a peer when the appeal to save lives failed to move the dial. For every act that immediately agreed to do it there was another that would do it but wanted to be more equal than others. Billy Joel wouldn't do it because his usual sax player was unavailable, the Stones wouldn't do it 'because Keith doesn't give a fuck' (although he scrambled on board as a member of Bob Dylan's folk combo as soon as he found out Mick was going to do it with Tina Turner), George Harrison wouldn't sing 'Let It Be' with Paul because 'he didn't ask me to sing on it ten years ago – why does he want me now?' Stevie Wonder said yes and then had his manager say no. Geldof ran into the inevitable flak for mounting a concert in Philadelphia with so few black acts. He argued that none of those he had attempted to contact – Michael Jackson, Prince, Diana Ross and Lionel Richie – had called back.

It was still a show in the most traditional sense. Everybody was determined to steal it. Older people probably thought it had been stolen by Queen, who unlike most of the veteran bands had gone to the trouble of putting together a tightly packed medley of their hits and had absorbed the key lesson of the open-air gig, which is to make the audience part of the show. Younger people decided it had been stolen by U2. They were on their third album and had a solid following but hadn't yet entered the mass consciousness. Jack Nicholson introduced U2 that afternoon as 'a band who have no trouble saying what they think'. It wasn't always easy to decipher the exact meaning of U2's statements but they certainly carried themselves like a group who had a lot to say. They did two songs that day. The first was 'Sunday Bloody Sunday'. During the second one, 'Bad', their singer Bono descended two levels from Wembley's high stage in order to draw girls out of the audience. Having extricated them he then enfolded them into a priestly embrace before returning them to the multitude. During this bizarre peregrination he was entirely invisible to the rest of the band. They had to keep churning away in the hope that their singer would eventually be returned in one piece. When he did so they left the stage, leaving one number undone, and departed the venue assuming it had been a career-ending disaster. But what Bono intuited was that at its heart Live Aid was a television show. 'I was looking for a TV moment,' he later confessed. He found one.

It is an extraordinary moment. It is arguably the most high-wire entertainment moment to be enacted in front of a worldwide TV audience. Many millions are watching on TV, tens of thousands are in the venue; all Bono's peers, all his elders and betters and all the people in the world who would most like to see him fail are watching closely; his fellow band members are playing with the singular fury of people who fear humiliation is at hand; and the only person who has got a ghost of a clue what he's going to do next is this twenty-five-year-old man with his motorcycle messenger's mullet, high-heeled boots, leather trousers and Principal Boy's jacket, this man who has set out in the middle of a song in search of he knows not what. Judging by the reaction of the crowd his TV moment was achieved when the girl reached him to be comforted, thus resulting in a gesture that was as unreadable as most of U2's songs but seemed at least to denote tenderness, a quality not to be found anywhere else that day. Live Aid made U2 stars.

In 1985 rock was only just beginning its embrace of the outdoors. The artists at Wembley that day were performing on a stage left behind by Bruce Springsteen. Before playing Slane Castle in Ireland on 1 June that year Springsteen had never played, or indeed attended, a large-scale outdoor show. He was always foremost among those who thought that as soon as you took the roof off the experience of live rock and roll then it changed from a unique, at best transcendental experience to one that was effectively about maximizing revenues. At the interval in the Slane show he raged at his manager for having put him in the position of facing a crowd that seemed to be a disaster in the making. His manager told him that he had better get used to it. He had spent his life dreaming of being a genuine sensation and now that he was one he didn't like it. Springsteen had successfully adjusted to the change in scale involved in moving from theatres to arenas – I stood at the side of the stage during one of those shows and watched how every detail of on-stage business was slowed down and slightly exaggerated to increase the chances of it communicating itself at the back of the venue – and now he had to do it again as he moved to the open air where you are inevitably competing for the audience's attention with the sky and their own gathering fatigue.

1985 was the year the scale of rock changed the nature of rock. The bigger the show is, the more it's about ritual rather than content. By the end of 1985 Springsteen had played forty-six shows in the open air in front of crowds of sixty thousand and more. Nobody would try harder than he did to bridge the gap between artist and crowd. He proved it was possible but it was still a stretch. People tend to enjoy their initial experiences of big stadium shows. After a while they begin to notice that their enjoyment is entirely conditional on the vantage point they've managed to get, their age and the degree of difficulty involved in getting home. This is even more pointed at festivals, which are tests of endurance where the performing musicians share none of the privations the crowd must put up with.

In 1985 it was all still fresh. The people who tuned in to Live Aid that day saw a rock spectacular taking place against a clear blue sky, a show that for the most part featured your favourite hits, a show that took place in the presence of royalty and the great and the good, a show from which you came away with the warm glow of self-congratulation that comes from having been part of something virtuous. If you attended, everyone else envied you. The crowd, as Dylan Jones pointed out in his book about Live Aid, seemed more like your neighbours than the drug-and-drink-inflamed super-fans who ruled the roost at most rock shows. The atmosphere in Wembley Stadium that day, where rock's gentry mingled with the MTV generation in front of the heir to the throne and his glamorous wife, was like a superior kind of village fete.

Live Aid mobilized a lot of money. It made a superstar and eventually a knight of the realm out of Bob Geldof. It set Elton John, Paul McCartney and Mick Jagger on the road to acceptance by the Establishment that would eventually result in their knighthoods. It made rock stars look like warriors who would take up noble causes on our behalf. In the public mind, large-scale rock and roll shows and displays of public virtue seemed to coalesce. Everybody at home looked at those sun-dappled arms being raised above suburban heads in rhythmic clapping along to Queen's 'Radio Ga Ga' and suddenly decided this live rock and roll might be for them after all.

The front page of the following day's *Mail on Sunday* called it 'Rock's Finest Hour'. The *New York Times* led with a picture of Geldof being hauled on to the shoulders of Pete Townshend and Paul McCartney. The *Daily Mirror* had a picture of Mick Jagger with Tina Turner above the headline 'Rocked With Love'. On the Monday *The Times* said there was an international campaign to award Geldof, formerly the mayor of the dumper, the Nobel Peace Prize. No rock star ever enjoyed more prestige than he did at that moment.

1985 PLAYLIST

Band Aid, 'Do They Know It's Christmas?'
USA for Africa, 'We Are The World'
Madonna, 'Material Girl'
The Smiths, *Meat Is Murder*
Tears for Fears, *Songs From The Big Chair*
Kate Bush, *Hounds Of Love*
Tom Waits, *Rain Dogs*
Fine Young Cannibals, *Fine Young Cannibals*
Run-DMC, *King Of Rock*
REM, *Fables Of The Reconstruction*

16 JULY 1986
MADISON SQUARE GARDEN, NEW YORK CITY

Rock royalty up close

The rock interview is an artificial interaction. It's primarily a business transaction, entered into by both parties for their mutual commercial benefit. At the same time form dictates that it must masquerade as a friendly, almost flirtatious exchange of ideas. It often takes months of negotiation to set up but then takes place as if it's a chance meeting. It demands a display of outward nonchalance from both interviewer and interviewee. The former is flushed and excited but pretends to be relaxed. The latter is suspicious and guarded but pretends to be relaxed.

When the interviewee is a superstar who is as familiar to you as Bob Dylan is, and has been familiar to you since you were a kid, the correct form is not to betray even a tenth of how excited you are. Therefore there's a marked contrast between your outer being, which has to compose itself into a pose indicative of faux relaxation, and your inner being, where a little demon is bouncing up and down, pointing and shouting, 'Look! Bob Dylan! Right next to me!' The rational part of you tilts your head to suggest rapt attention. All the while your animal senses are working overtime to absorb and retain as much information as possible about the clothes, hair, smell, smoking habits and body language of the person you're sitting alone with. This is made more intense by the fact that for my generation no star of films or literature or sport or politics could possibly outshine a star of rock. And no star of rock has more mystique and magnetism than Bob Dylan. He is the Everest of rock interviews.

We were in a dressing room at Madison Square Garden during a three-night stand in the summer of 1986. The interview was to go in the first issue of a new music magazine in the UK. He had been persuaded to do it by the woman who was in charge of international media relations at his record company, CBS. I was conducted into a dressing room and there he was. He didn't get up. At close quarters he looked reassuringly like Bob Dylan, almost spookily so. It was as if he was an actor emerging from wardrobe immediately prior to playing Bob Dylan. His penumbra of curls was at a position of maximum elevation. The bulk of what he was wearing seemed to be made of black leather. Black leather motorcycle boots, black leather waistcoat, black leather fingerless gloves. Like many over-photographed people he seemed to have a large head atop a slight frame (this is probably merely a reflection of the fact that we have spent hours searching their faces but have never met the original). He narrowed his eyes like cowboys do when a stranger presents himself in town. He offered a hand. His features were wreathed in the smoke from the Kool he had in his other hand. He was clearly thinking what artists are always thinking before an interview: let's get this over with. A large dog sat at his feet. What's the dog called? 'He has no name,' Dylan said, then, realizing he'd missed the opportunity for a witticism, added, 'No. He's called late for dinner.'

The humour of this only occurred to me afterwards. At the time I was too flustered by the need to survive each moment. When you meet a Bob Dylan, a Paul McCartney, a Mick Jagger or a Bruce Springsteen, the scales are so loaded in their favour that all the pressure is on the person who's supposed to be asking the questions. The more accommodating of these personalities see it as part of their job to make you feel at home. Bob Dylan is not one of that sort. One of his great strengths is that he gives the impression of genuinely not caring what you or anybody else thinks of him. This must be a natural reaction to having spent most of your life surrounded by people who are desperate to please you.

Our conversation, such as it was, took place over two meetings at Madison Square Garden. After the first one the woman from the record company asked him how it was going. 'I don't know,' he said. 'He keeps asking me questions.' Friends have laughed at this. What did he expect? Of course I was asking questions. It was an interview. There was a time I might have laughed too, but now I can entirely sympathize with him. The truth is I didn't really have any questions for Dylan. He's not a politician. He didn't solicit my vote and doesn't owe me an explanation for anything. When you interview somebody like Bob Dylan all you're really hoping for is that they will find it within themselves to just talk to you, to open up, to say what's on their mind, what they thought about the last show or even what they watched on TV last night. Sometimes they do. Sometimes even Bob Dylan gets loquacious. This was not one of those times.

I tried to get him to talk about Blind Willie McTell. He'd recorded a song named after him. It was the best thing he'd done in years, but in a characteristic act of cussedness he had refused to put it out. I tried and tried again but he clearly wasn't going to be led in the direction of that subject. Then he cut across me to ask, 'You heard the McPeake Family?' No, I said, I hadn't. I looked them up afterwards and found they were traditional musicians from Northern Ireland. Was he just trying to change the subject to something he did want to talk about or was he saying, you Brits come over here asking about long-dead blues singers while you have no knowledge of your own culture? That's the way I took it.

At the time of this interview Bob Dylan was forty-five, which in 1986 was Methuselah in rock music terms. His tour with Tom Petty and the Heartbreakers, which was being hailed in some quarters as the return of the *Blonde On Blonde* sound which he had shrewdly described as 'that thin wild mercury sound', was in reality a marriage cooked up by his management, who also handled Petty, to justify them being able to play large arenas. Dylan was still the older brother that everyone in rock wanted to impress and critics were always apt to claim every new record as some sort of 'return to form', even though it manifestly wasn't. Dylan with the Heartbreakers was one of those match-ups that did neither of them any favours, partly because Dylan was up to his usual tricks – refusing to play the songs the band wanted to play, changing keys without warning, seeming to wish to wrong-foot everyone who was sharing the stage with him.

The new album, *Knocked Out Loaded*, was clearly exactly that. It was thrashed out in two weeks of sessions immediately prior to rehearsals beginning for the American leg of his tour, and it sounded like it. Dylan had got to the point where he realized his records all sold round about the same number of copies and figured that it didn't matter much what those records were like. Therefore the best thing to do was just get on with recording one and putting it out. When I gave him a copy of the album to sign backstage at Madison Square Garden it was the first time he'd seen a finished copy. He wasn't madly interested in the record but he took a felt-tip, gripped it in his left hand (he's right-handed) and signed it for my friend.

He signed it on the inner bag where the names of the musicians were listed on a halftone picture of a woman. What nobody knew at the time was that this woman was Carolyn Dennis and Dylan had secretly married her just a few weeks before. In the same year that Madonna, Michael Jackson and Bruce Springsteen seemed to be buckling under the weight of scrutiny from a media establishment that grew more hydra-headed every day, Bob Dylan seemed to have found a way to hide in plain sight. Dennis had given birth to their child in January and he had set the two of them up in a house. His new daughter's name was listed among the people thanked on the cover of the album. She was his fifth child. And Dennis wasn't the only woman in Dylan's life at the time. He also maintained Carole Childs in another home. Whether or not they knew each other's precise status, they behaved as though they didn't. 'I could just disappear into a crowd,' he said to me. It's not impossible he was being mischievous.

By the mid-eighties the family structures of rock super-stars had come to resemble those of all-powerful sovereigns or landed aristocrats of years gone by. Their success meant that they, and they alone, sat at the top of a pyramid of wealth, status and power. As they looked down from the summit they could see the serried ranks of their heirs, their heirs' tow-headed dependents, the long-established courtiers who transacted their business for them, the vassals and liegemen who handled the tasks beneath their dignity or competence, the new mistresses and the old ones who always knew far more than they let on, even the fools and soothsayers whose job it was to calm their troubled mind, and all these people were thinking the same thought. What must I do to remain in the sunshine of the favour of my lord? For his part, my lord is thinking: if I don't work all these people don't eat.

Tom Petty was only thirty-five but he also had responsibilities. His marriage to his teenage sweetheart Jane, who had been at home having babies while he was enjoying his ride to fame, was coming apart. They had both found that far from solving all their problems, success and money would be only the beginning of them. Throughout their marriage she had battled mental illness and substance issues. These are the kind of problems an artist is half-expected to have. If they're happening to the artist's partner the machine has trouble coping. Even within such an apparently sane rock and roll band as the Heartbreakers painful issues were never far from the surface. There was always tension between Petty and the drummer Stan Lynch. The bass player Howie Epstein was already using heroin. Bands get more complicated as they get older. Secrets are built on secrets.

The other secret Dylan didn't share with anyone at the time was that he was going through his first bout of writer's block. The songs of *Knocked Out Loaded* were either retreads of old rhythm and blues tunes, tracks salvaged from older sessions or collaborations with writers who didn't even know they were in a collaboration. It was poor. He knew it was poor. Despite the fake enthusiasm of all the musicians at the sessions it was plain that it was poor. He was having a crisis of confidence as a performer. He could no longer find his voice.

Years later in his book *Chronicles* he described going missing at this time and taking himself off until he found a bunch of old jazz musicians playing in a bar. He was impressed by the way the singer was singing with power but the power wasn't coming from his voice. Next time he sang he found he could do the same thing, as long as he concentrated but didn't think, which is the athlete's knack.

He was actually planning to retire at the end of the tour. This was the year after he had closed out Live Aid with the most anti-climactic performance anyone had ever seen. He was still sore about the critical response. He didn't think he was getting any more popular. They were on the last leg of the tour, in Locarno in Switzerland, when, as he explained years later, he changed the way he sang. 'I just did it automatically out of thin air, cast my own spell to drive out the devil. Everything came back and it came back in multi-dimension.' When the tour finished 'I saw that instead of being stranded at the end of the story, I was actually in the prelude to the beginning of another one'. At the age of forty-five Bob Dylan was getting a second wind.

He couldn't have picked a better time to think about his comeback. In the middle of November 1986 CBS released the Bruce Springsteen live album the market had been awaiting since his record-breaking tour the previous year. Within a day public demand was so great that the stores were having to reorder it on vinyl, on cassette and also, most profitably, on the brand-new CD format which was clearly going to take off. As it did so it would render the old mathematics of the music business null and void and make the rock stars of the future richer than any who had come before. Yes, no better time for Bob Dylan to start again.

1986 PLAYLIST

Pet Shop Boys, 'West End Girls'
Berlin, 'Take My Breath Away'
The Rolling Stones, *Dirty Work*
Hüsker Dü, *Candy Apple Grey*
Queen, *A Kind Of Magic*
Crowded House, *Crowded House*
Bob Dylan, *Knocked Out Loaded*
Paul Simon, *Graceland*
Bruce Springsteen and the E Street Band, *Live/1975–85*
Beastie Boys, *Licensed To Ill*

1 AUGUST 1987
GREYHOUND BUS STATION, HOLLYWOOD

Looking the part

xl Rose had first come to Hollywood in 1982, when he was just twenty years old. After five years of hustling he was given the rare privilege of being able to turn his life into myth when Nigel Dick, the director of the first Guns N' Roses video 'Welcome To The Jungle', took him back to the bus station at the intersection of Hollywood and Vine to film him making his arrival all over again. To drive home the point that Axl had landed in Gomorrah from the land of *Parks and Recreation*, he actually had him chewing a straw as he alighted from the bus. Following two brief encounters on the street, one with a drug dealer and the other with a hooker, he catches sight of himself on a screen in a TV store window playing with his band. Now his hair is the full pompadour, his T-shirt is slashed to reveal his tattoos, he's wearing leather pants and he's winding his hips in the direction of the admiring girls in the audience. When Axl came to Hollywood his dream was to cross over from the ordinary, everyday life he had been condemned to back in Indiana and live the dream life of a rock star in the city of dreams. Now here he was, starring in a little film about that very transition, a film that was destined to excite the next generation of fourteen-year-old dreamers.

The most impressionable group in society are teenage boys. They have a touching readiness to believe that somewhere nearby a bunch of young men only slightly older than they are and certainly no more exceptional are living a life larger, louder and more licentious than any in human history and are getting paid a fortune for doing so. Ever since heavy metal unilaterally declared its independence from the mainstream of popular music in the early eighties, round about the time of the launch of the British magazine *Kerrang!*, the first publication to define its area of operations in terms of sheer volume, hard rock has been a world in which each new generation has hoped to exceed the excess and double down on the debauchery of the one before.

In the early eighties the centre of this world was a small area of Hollywood's Sunset Boulevard where Tower Records sat close to the Whisky, the Roxy, the Troubadour and the Rainbow Bar and Grill. Here on a Saturday night a succession of big-haired men wearing tight leathers accompanied by their equally big-haired girlfriends would alight from limos to disport themselves in front of enthralled young onlookers. These men might be the members of Mötley Crüe, Ratt, WASP, Stryper, Quiet Riot or any of the other Los Angeles-based bands who played the combination of hard rock and pop that was known disrespectfully as 'hair metal'. The enthralled onlookers might be kids drawn from the San

Fernando Valley by the prospect of proximity to this new star system. They might be showbiz kids like Saul 'Slash' Hudson who were handing out fliers to get people to come see their hopefully up-and-coming band. They might be from further afield, like Bill Bailey, who had come from Lafayette, Indiana, adopted the name Axl Rose, and was spending his time star-spotting on the Strip in between dealing drugs in the parking lots behind the clubs.

The two of them, plus Izzy Stradlin (a friend of Rose's from home), Steven Adler and Duff McKagan, who had been in a failed band with Slash, came together in 1986. The talent scout who spotted them told David Geffen that they could sell as many records as the Rolling Stones and Led Zeppelin and that they were the greatest rock and roll band in the world. This was stretching it a little because they didn't have a sound of their own and the drummer couldn't play. What they did have was a look. The golden rule in music is that the more people protest that it's all about the music, the more certain it is that it's all about something else entirely. The thing that mattered most in hard rock was not the rock or the hardness thereof; it was looking the part. And Guns N' Roses did. They combined glamour and danger in just the right proportions. This is the quality that was impossible to contrive. This had been evident when they first turned twenty-one and could finally enter the clubs rather than rubberneck on the sidewalk. Rose and Stradlin went in one night with such mad aplomb that the members of Mötley Crüe, who were in the VIP section, leaned over to see who they were. They must be rock stars because they looked like rock stars.

As individuals, Guns N' Roses were authentically impossible. All five members of the band came from homes where the parents split up when they were young. They were all in trouble with the authorities as teen agers, and it wasn't the authorities' fault. Their primary interests were drugs, alcohol and fornication. They were interested in rock stardom too because it promised to increase their opportunities for those three things. When Geffen signed them the company had the greatest difficulty getting anyone to manage them, so bad was their reputation. It was a reputation built on their record of substance abuse and the ethical shortcuts they had been prepared to make to pursue that substance abuse. At the time three of them were enthusiastic users of the Iranian heroin that had come into the USA in the wake of the Islamic Revolution, and the bass player was an alcoholic. Axl Rose was the most sober member of the band. He made up for this by being psychologically unstable.

When Frank Zappa, speaking of the Mothers of Invention back in the sixties, had said 'we're the kind of band that if we moved in next door to you your lawn will die', the statement was in the nature of a rueful apology for the necessarily sloppy standards of musicians when it came to matters of grooming. When Guns N' Roses talked about how they were creatures of their appetites it was a flat-out boast. There was nothing about Guns N' Roses that was not calculated to offend right-thinking people and thereby attract the support of fifteen-year-old boys. Before they adopted their name they actually toyed with calling themselves AIDS. Rose was arrested by police for throwing a fifteen-year-old girl out of their rehearsal space and into the street without her clothes. Their first proper interview with an LA music magazine resulted in them destroying the reporter's tape recorder and then insisting the magazine run the piece with a rambling letter from Rose in which both his lack of formal education and his staggering arrogance became clear. 'We are our own political party within a government just as any small business,' he said. Guns N' Roses didn't feel their first album *Appetite For Destruction* was complete until they'd added the sounds of one of their camp followers having sexual intercourse with Rose in a sound booth at New York's Mediasound Studios. They were rock stars such as might have been invented by an over-excited movie producer, with all the elements brought to the surface, where they really counted.

While their music celebrated the liberation of doing actual things with actual girls in actual places, the new hard rock acts owed their popularity to television just as much as Mary Tyler Moore. Whereas the progenitors of these bands, acts like Led Zeppelin, Black Sabbath and Aerosmith, had been invisible to anyone except those who bothered to buy a ticket to see them, this new regiment of overstated hell-raisers were beamed into living rooms by MTV. Therefore their clips had to be not simply a visual depiction of their new song; they had to be advertisements for the lifestyles those songs were supposed to celebrate. Because this new, younger audience had grown up with multi-channel TV and didn't regard music as anything particularly special in itself, the bands that ministered to them realized that they needed to organize their stage acts so that the impact was as much visual as musical. In the wake of Tipper Gore's successful efforts to get the record business to sticker its potentially controversial products with Parental Advisory notices, the arrival of Guns N' Roses was a calculated affront to all that was decent. Their rise signalled the end of the Hollywood scene they had spent so much time trying to elbow their way into.

It didn't happen immediately because MTV took time to come on board. In 1987, as their reputation grew and their album started to chart, Guns N' Roses were booked as support on tours headlined by senior bands, the kind of bands they could easily show up, the kind of bands that relied on special effects to make up for their own charisma deficit. One of them was Mötley Crüe. In 1987 Mötley Crüe were touring the United States. Their show began with lights playing on crimson curtains, which then dropped to reveal a bare stage on to which three levels of amplifiers were raised by pneumatic lifts, then drummer Tommy Lee would appear already playing in a forklifted cage. In a rare fit of modesty they had abandoned the plan to make their entrance from between a woman's legs, but their opening song 'All In The Name Of . . .' reassuringly concerned a girl who was only fifteen and assured the listeners that 'for sex and sex I'd sell my soul'. It made 'Midnight Rambler' seem like Schubert.

The Crüe act was the perfect example of what was starting to happen to live performance as the technology involved grew more capable and audiences increasingly assessed value for money on the basis of spectacle and sensation rather than anything else. The high point came when the cage containing Lee did two complete revolutions as the drummer continued to thrash away at his kit. Earth, Wind & Fire's act had a similar trick at the time but their drummer didn't introduce it by announcing 'I had a fucking dream. I wanted to play the fucking drums upside down.' This in itself was an instructive example of Crüe's modus operandi. It obeyed two iron rules: the first was that the f-word had to be included in every sentence spoken from the stage, and the second that there shouldn't be the minutest departure from the agreed script, every word of which was written in Magic Marker and attached to monitors prior to the performance. The impression of mayhem, like the impression of sincerity, was something clearly too important not to be faked.

By 1987 the rock tent was big enough to accommodate very different visions of what rock stars were supposed to be about, some of which were in direct opposition to others. If you sided with Peter Gabriel, U2 or Tracy Chapman, who were all enjoying career high points that year, the point of being a rock star was to nudge mankind in the direction of virtue. If, on the other hand, you sided with Mötley Crüe, Twisted Sister, WASP or Poison, the point was to sleep with strippers. The interesting thing about this wave of bands, who favoured big hair and wore their guitars around their crotches, was their apparent determination to be so much like each other. The visual shorthand of MTV demanded that hip hop acts look a certain way, country acts another and hard rock acts another again. Within their niches the only differentiation they accepted was that of competitive sport, whereby you achieve prominence by kicking the asses of all the competitors, either by playing louder than them, selling more records than them, carrying off their womenfolk or outstripping them in matters of excess.

The need of these men to live up to the rock-star image they so energetically promoted rebounded on them. As the Mötley Crüe/Guns N' Roses tour wound down in December, Nikki Sixx of Mötley Crüe decided he would pay tribute to Slash, the member of Guns N' Roses he had befriended during the tour, by turning up at his hotel in a limo with presents of a gallon jug of Jack Daniel's, an antique beaver-fur top hat and a few bags of heroin he had picked up earlier that evening. He then did too much of the latter himself, turned blue, and his life was only saved by the timely intervention of an ambulance crew.

In the sixties and seventies bands had argued that they weren't anything like as bad as they might look. Bands like

Guns N' Roses, on the other hand, were determined to prove that they were every bit as bad as they looked. And the way they looked was every bit as important as the music. It remains the case that when fashion editors think of a rock star they think of Axl Rose in 1987. Nobody has ever looked more the part.

1987 PLAYLIST

U2, *The Joshua Tree*
Prince, *Sign O' The Times*
Public Enemy, *Yo! Bum Rush The Show*
Guns N' Roses, *Appetite For Destruction*
Def Leppard, *Hysteria*
Twisted Sister, *Love Is For Suckers*
George Michael, *Faith*
Pet Shop Boys, 'It's A Sin'
Madonna, *Who's That Girl*
Pink Floyd, *A Momentary Lapse Of Reason*

overcome what he sees as his physical limitations – his stature, his weight and, most notably, his hairline. He is capable of conducting himself in a cultivated enough way to walk with kings but is equally capable of displays of surprising vulgarity and aggression. He has made massive contributions to charity but sometimes has an unkind tongue which he finds impossible to keep on the leash. A succession of duets with pop sensations du jour suggests he worries about being seen as what he is, a seventy-year-old rock star. All the most painful episodes of his private life – his addictions, his squabbles with those closest to him, his search for a partner – have been acted out in public for all to see. Elton John's life is the classic journey beloved of the producers of contemporary television.

He grew up in an age of austerity, an era of cleaning your plate, doing your homework and keeping whatever problems you had bottled up inside; he has, by accident or design, become the symbol of a new age of therapy, where you avoid doing anything that makes you unhappy, share your innermost feelings at the drop of a hat and design your own life as a succession of new beginnings. The year 1988, which is roughly halfway between the beginning of his career and the present day, was the occasion of one of those new beginnings. The year before he had turned forty. This event had been celebrated with a party at his manager John Reid's mansion. Three hundred and fifty guests attended. Renate Blauel, the recording engineer he had puzzled the world by marrying four years earlier, was not among them, despite this being the event at which they were supposed to appear together and put paid to the stories that their marriage was a sham. Elton rose above her non-appearance to entertain his guests that day, who included two Beatles, Bob Geldof and the Duke and Duchess of York. The day after the party a statement from

Reid's office announced that Elton and Renate would continue living apart but there were no plans for a divorce.

We who live ordinary lives often dream of living the larger life of rock superstars. Those same rock superstars often fantasize about living ordinary lives. In both cases it seldom turns out happily. We like our domestic routine too much to wish it to be disturbed by sudden upheavals. They are too fond of their sudden upheavals to be able to tolerate domestic routine. The touring musician phones home from the road, pining to hear the sound of his children's voices. Once he's been home from tour a few days he finds the company of those same children palls and longs to set off again.

Elton John's marriage to Renate Blauel was based partly on his genuine affection for her but mainly on his mistaken belief that she could provide him with a home and hearth to return to at the end of his working day. This was never going to work, if only because he felt, as rock stars are wont to feel, that domestication could enhance his existing life without his having to give up any of the key elements of that life. When everyone in his immediate circle was an employee it was possible to insist on silence at breakfast. When the person over the breakfast table was his wife this was less easy. For her part Renate was as lost in his house in Windsor as any heroine of a nineteenth-century novel who wakes to find she has married one of those men who insists things should remain as they were before the marriage.

In 1988 there was no open discussion of the sexuality of rock stars. Even Boy George, who had been the most famous musical figure in the world for a year in 1982, had been able to deflect any enquiries by saying he preferred a cup of tea. Early in 1988 George Michael was at the top of the charts on both sides of the Atlantic with 'Faith'. It would be another ten years before he came out as gay and that followed his arrest in Los Angeles for 'engaging in a lewd act'. But by the mid-eighties the climate was already beginning to change. The death of movie star Rock Hudson in 1985 from AIDS made the epidemic into a front-page story and had allowed some sections of the British press to conceal malicious gossip behind a mask of public concern. Elton John had spent much of 1987 involved in legal fights with the *Sun* and the *News of the World* over stories about his cocaine use, alleged participation in gay orgies and a fantastical claim that the dogs patrolling the grounds of his house in Windsor had had their voice boxes cut to ensure that they could fall upon any intruders without warning.

In the summer of 1988 he released his first new album since having surgery on his own voice box in Australia. The title of the record, *Reg Strikes Back*, was a reference to the name he was known by when he first began singing in public at the Northwood Hills Hotel back in Pinner. The cover was given over to a display of the various hats he had worn in concert over the years. Here were boaters, baseball caps, beanies, berets and boas; here were Stetsons, orange fright wigs, Uncle Sam stovepipes and even the peaked hat of an admiral in a Ruritanian navy; here, he seemed to be saying, are all the selves I have been and will no longer be. He began a tour in October. The American leg included five nights at Madison Square Garden, a record for an artist at the time. Interviewed backstage by *Rolling Stone*, he said, 'I want to run with the George Michaels, the U2s and Bon Jovis. To do that you have to keep yourself mentally fresh. I've stopped drinking. The costumes had to go. I found being Elton John suffocating.' But being Elton John had made him rich. His contract meant he made very little from his first few albums, but from *Goodbye Yellow Brick Road* on he was one of the biggest earners in an expanding market. That market had grown once again in the mid-eighties when CDs meant it was suddenly possible to sell people the records they already owned and charge them double for the privilege.

At Madison Square Garden a New York property developer who was in the business of making himself famous visited Elton backstage and had his picture taken with him. Donald Trump and his wife Ivana had not previously been noted for their interest in music. Suddenly, in the new equality of celebrity, the most unlikely people were clustering around rock stars. Elton's celebrity even extended to his possessions. When Renate had first arrived in Old Windsor she had been intimidated by the fact that his house felt like a cross between a five-star hotel and a museum for those of a shorter attention span. Elton had kept every outlandish artefact that attached to his career, from the high-rise boots he wore in Ken Russell's *Tommy* to the glasses that spelled out his first name, and had then impulse-bought a staggering array of real art, including a Rembrandt self-portrait, pre-loved tat such as the plastic guitar that played 'Love Me Tender' as it revolved, showbiz souvenirs such as the camisole worn by Judy Garland in *Meet Me in St Louis*, all manner of art nouveau and art deco plus enough expensive trinkets to turn heads at an Essex wedding. He had a pair of Cartier silver baskets. He used them as soap dishes.

And now he was going to sell it all through the venerable auction house Sotheby's. Just as the Yorks felt there was something to be gained by showing up at the fortieth birthday bash of this former pub singer and a vulgar millionaire like Trump thought it was worth some grip-and-grin time backstage at Madison Square Garden, so the formerly snooty denizens of St James's and the guardians of classical culture were now only too keen to profit by the idea that a bunch of stuff that happened to be owned by a mayfly rock star was in fact a good deal more than a bunch of stuff. Rock stars are their own certificate of provenance. The artefacts of Andy Warhol and Liberace had been sold off recently by smart auction houses but both men had had to die to qualify for the accolade. Elton wasn't going to wait. He followed the four days of the sale closely from Miami, where he was on tour. He used his new toy, a mobile phone costing around £2,000, to keep in touch with Sotheby's chairman Lord Gowrie. Gowrie was the aristocrat who had resigned from the Cabinet claiming it was impossible to live in London on a minister's salary.

Future sales of Elton John's possessions would be to benefit his AIDS charity. This one was meant not just to shake off the accumulated baggage of the past and prepare himself for a new streamlined future. Elton was also the beneficiary. Reviewing the collection, the *Daily Telegraph* made the observation that Elton's taste in jewellery 'oddly mixes the tastes of a conservative duchess and a mid-Thirties flapper'. Nonetheless, the *New York Times* reported that the sale realized over $8 million. This was three million more than they had been expecting. One Magritte painting went for over $100,000.

There is a time to build up and a time to break down. For Elton this had been a year of breaking things down. He had relinquished some of the responsibilities he had recklessly built up in the first flush of his success, including the chairmanship of Watford Football Club and the artist roster at his label, Rocket Records. There was one more thing to let go. Two months later, on 18 November, a statement from John Reid's office announced that Elton and Renate were going to divorce. There was something about mutual respect; nobody was at fault; their schedules simply didn't allow them to spend enough time together. It was the familiar litany of excuses the special ones use to explain that their lives are not like ours.

Then he went back to work. Since turning pro as a member of Bluesology in 1965 Elton has been on some kind of road, first as an anonymous sideman, then as a modest emergent singer-songwriter, crowningly as a pop sensation and finally as a national and international treasure. That same combination of status anxiety, need for the approval of a crowd and showman's addiction to a steady income stream that put him on the road in the United States in the late sixties keeps him on a far more de luxe road today. It appears to be the only thing that inoculates him against his greatest fear, which is inactivity.

He also resumed his shopping habit. He spent lavishly on a new set of treasures to replace the ones he had sold. But the form of shopping that meant most to him, the one through which he satisfied the small boy inside, was the one that took place regularly at music megastores all over the world. Elton John would turn up in shops like Tower or Virgin, depending on where he was in the world, holding a long list of new releases and chart entries. He would be accompanied by a chauffeur whose job it was to carry away his acquisitions. He would comb the racks and then buy multiple copies of everything, one for each of his houses. These shopping trips were a record fan's dream come true. Elton was the only rock star who cared enough about records to behave this way. To be like that you have to be still in touch with your inner child. Sir Elton John's undiminished passion for the love that got him started may be the thing we like most about him.

1988 PLAYLIST

Elton John, *Reg Strikes Back*
The Pogues, *If I Should Fall From Grace With God*
Leonard Cohen, *I'm Your Man*
Morrissey, *Viva Hate*
NWA, *Straight Outta Compton*
U2, *Rattle And Hum*
REM, *Green*
Pet Shop Boys, 'Always On My Mind'
Metallica, . . . *And Justice For All*
Pat Benatar, *Wide Awake In Dreamland*

21 MARCH 1989
UNITED STATES OF AMERICA

Clean and sober

Rock was feeling its age. The stars who had been born during the Second World War were now in their forties. The men were learning they were no more immortal than the hair that had been the crowning glory of flaming youth. The vestigial pony tail, that puny sprig of often greying hair widely sported by the formerly hirsute in 1989, was suddenly the harbinger of rock's looming mid-life crisis. At the time Elton John had one, as did Pete Townshend and Ringo Starr.

Since the Beatles finished in the late sixties Ringo had compensated for his periods of enforced inactivity by filling his days with drink. Drinking was his primary occupation. He even turned down invitations that might involve a forty-minute drive because that was forty minutes when he couldn't drink brandy. His wife Barbara Bach was no more in demand as a former Bond girl than he was as a former Beatle, so there was a lot of idleness to contend with. The drinking came to a head in late 1988. Following a drunken brawl with his wife in a Jamaican hotel, an incident that found its way into the British papers, the two of them checked into the Sierra Tucson Center in Arizona to dry out.

They weren't the only entertainers seeking medical help for a condition that had traditionally been put down to character flaws. It had gone past the point of being acceptable to laugh alcoholism off, as Townshend had done in 1980 when he publicly thanked Rémy Martin for 'saving my life by making the stuff so expensive'. In 1987 Eric Clapton had once again checked himself into the Hazelden clinic in Minnesota to deal with his problem. At the time he was continuing to function in his normal way. A two-hour show in the evening fits quite neatly into the drinker's day. None of his admirers would have known anything was wrong. The playing didn't really suffer. The mother of the singer James Taylor, who had watched this process at close quarters, sagely observed that where musicians are concerned 'The work is always the last thing that goes because it's the thing that holds their life together.'

Their counsellors had to deal with the toxic combination of arrogance and self-abasement that is often the lot of the rock star. Performing provided its own high, both in terms of the sheer satisfaction it brought with it and also the transformational effect it had on their status. When not performing they were prone to feeling that others had detected their inner worthlessness. All entertainers think they're getting away with something they shouldn't be getting away with and fear that at any moment their bluff will be called. Drinking is one way to blot out that feeling. It helped that drinking was also socially acceptable. It could begin in polite society. It might finish in sordid seclusion. People like Clapton and Ringo had more than a need to soften the edges of the day. They had to drink until they passed out.

While booze had a dated image, cocaine was chic. It was still expensive enough to seem enviably upmarket and its association with the world of deadlines, workload and pressure made many musicians perceive it as a servant rather than a master. Linda Ronstadt was one of the first to give it up when a doctor pointed out how cocaine can cause the hair cells in the ear canal to lie down. This may explain why so many of the solo albums made in the eighties sounded brilliant to the people who made them but unlovely to the listeners. Nevertheless cocaine still seemed an attractive part of the crackle around rock stardom. Stevie Nicks initially resisted going into rehab in 1987 even after her friends and family intervened because she felt sure that it would be bad for her image if it got out that she was trying to quit coke. She also knew that submitting to the doctors would mean she couldn't play the star card, which was the way she dealt with everything else in her life. As part of her treatment at the Betty Ford Center, where she was an in-patient with Tammy Wynette, Nicks had to write the words 'I am not special: I am dying' on a piece of paper. 'That's a serious thing to swallow,' she reflected.

Ringo and Clapton were among the first wave of rock stars to change their ways with professional help. In time they would be joined by hundreds of others until it seemed that whenever you interviewed a musician over the age of forty they would volunteer their stories of how they'd stopped using drugs or alcohol. People who in the past were reluctant talkers would now hold forth at length with the practised ease of those accustomed to giving a detached account of their strengths and weaknesses. The confessional press interview became almost an extension of the process of therapy. Major retrospective features increasingly followed a standard arc: I flew high, I went too far, I crashed, I put myself back together with the help of a good woman/man/manager/therapist, and now what I want most of all from my public is forgiveness. Therapy saved the lives of a lot of rock stars, which is a blessing. It also diminished their mystique, which isn't.

On 21 March 1989 Bonnie Raitt released her tenth album. This was a watershed for the thirty-nine-year-old singer/ guitarist because after her ninth album her record company Warner Brothers had decided to let her go. They'd sent her a letter explaining that they wouldn't be renewing. At that stage Raitt was an admired artist who had yet to break through. The admired recording artist, like the admired novelist, feels that all those good notices should entitle them to some form of tenure. The people at the label, on the other hand, think they can take the money it would cost to roll the dice on them one more time and spend it on somebody new. This is not unreasonable in itself but is an unpopular move within the music business, which can be surprisingly sentimental. When this happened to her, Raitt was looking at the prospect of turning forty with no label. She had also recently broken up with the man in her life.

The daughter of a successful singer in film and stage musicals, Raitt had rejected all family advice in her teens and gone to live with an older man. Dick Waterman handled the careers of bluesmen who had been rediscovered in the great folk sweep of the sixties. Young Bonnie, who admired their craft and identified as much as she was able with the terrible disadvantages they had had to contend with throughout their lives, watched and learned. The learning wasn't just in the technique of the slide guitar or the right way to sell a barrelhouse blues. She was also, like many of the wide-eyed white kids who got into folk music in the sixties, tempted to believe that these people were great artists because of the lives they had led, and that if she could bring herself to suffer similarly she might be almost as good. She carried the booze for these intimidating men, many of whom were alcoholics who played for drink rather than anything else. She got to know how it worked. She knew that Son House, who taught Robert Johnson how to play, was allowed a bottle of vodka an hour before he went on. Any more than that he would forget the words. Any less than that he would forget the words. Like thousands of other touring musicians she accepted without question that you needed a few drinks to reach the appropriate level of looseness to be able to entertain an audience. She had also come to know that at the very time that audience is taking its clothes off and climbing into its bed the musician is still fizzing with the undischarged electricity that is the residue of every live performance. That raging storm is traditionally quelled in the bar. Furthermore she found that cocaine made her more capable of staying up in the bar with the boys from her band, drinking for longer.

There was another factor, one never far from anyone's thoughts in a business where what you look like is profoundly important. At around the time Raitt was being dropped by her record company she was playing a show in Louisiana. Somebody in the audience, motivated by the combination of concern and rank effrontery which is the mark of the true fan, passed up a note. It asked how come she had got so fat. It suggested she should maybe think about working out. Then somebody else asked her when the baby was due. The final straw was the call from Prince suggesting that the two of them might like to work together. 'It's one thing to go on stage if you're a little chunky – it's another to make a video with a guy who's known for looking foxy,' says Raitt. The record with Prince never happened – she had no more wish to be manipulated by a maverick genius than by a standard corporation – but the prospect of shooting a video with him drove her to her first AA meeting. She knew there were two sorts of musician who become addicts. There are the unsuccessful ones who drink and drug to deal with their feelings of rejection and, like her contemporaries Paul Butterfield and Richard Manuel, end up dead. Then there are the successful ones who drink and drug to deal with their fear of no longer being successful and who can generally afford to get help in expensive clinics. Bonnie Raitt simply bought a bike and planned her next record.

She had no thoughts of great commercial success when she started making that record with producer Don Was. She had a new deal with Capitol and her only ambition was to sell enough to be allowed to make another one after that. She didn't realize how different the album would be until she'd finished it. The engineer Ed Cherney remembers, 'We were coming out of an era of big hair and big noises on records. When we were listening to the playback on the first song Don said, "Why don't you take some of that echo off the snare drum?"' Cherney took the advice, which made for a drier, more modest-sounding record, something more suited to the living room than the rock concert hall. They thought it was going quite well but they had no particular commercial expectations of it until the A&R man visited the sessions and, before he left, said, 'You'd better get a tuxedo because you're going to the Grammys.'

The song that had made him think that was written by Bonnie and was called 'Nick Of Time'. The preoccupations of pop lyrics tend to be quite narrow. This opened with lines that went somewhere no pop song had gone before. Bonnie Raitt sang about a friend of hers who called her on the phone at night and cried about the fact that all her friends but her were having babies. This sharply painful rumination on the passing of time became the album's title track. 'Nick Of Time' sold a million copies.

The A&R man was right about the Grammys. The following year Raitt went up on stage five times to pick up awards in various categories. Sitting next to her was her father, the Broadway star who had never known the same honour his daughter was finally tasting in her forties. They both wept buckets. 'The whole building saw him lose it. And I started crying, and we held each other for a good minute and a half until they told us to sit down,' she remembered. 'Nick Of Time' won Best Female Performance for both pop and rock categories. It was a rock song about middle age.

Eric Clapton and Ringo Starr might have been newly sober too at the time but the sponsors of their tours were alcohol advertisers. Eric's sponsor was Michelob. The Michelob campaign was aimed at yuppies. Yuppie was a term that had come into use in 1984 to describe people who had the careers of professionals but carried with them the stylistic hinterland of the hippies they once were. They drank Michelob. They went to see Eric Clapton. Being baby boomers they were prone to believe that whatever stage they were going through – raising children, setting up home, getting a promotion, buying a car – had never been gone through by anyone else in the past or if it had it had never been gone through quite as soulfully and stylishly. There was even a television programme that celebrated them. *Thirtysomething* was about a pair of writers who get married and raise a family in the suburbs while still trying to hang on to what they see as their wild, untamed rock and roll past. In 1989 this option was available for the first time. The concerns of yuppies were different from those of earlier generations because widely available contraception had provided them with the option of timing the planning of a family until it suited them.

There were many musical careers that were prospering in 1989 by ministering to the yuppie condition. Phil Collins' ... *But Seriously* had a song about relating to his son. Eurythmics' *We Too Are One* had one about a woman who is not so much angry about her partner's infidelity as she is disappointed by it. Bette Midler had one of the biggest hits of the year with 'Wind Beneath My Wings'. All of these songs are identifiably set within marriage. They portray the ups and downs of love and family as noble and heroic. This goes down well with those who have found this is their lot. In the fifties and sixties the people who bought pop records were overwhelmingly in their teens and twenties. As we headed into the nineties this was no longer the case. The majority of people listening to it were not kids anymore. In fact they were middle-aged.

1989 PLAYLIST

Bonnie Raitt, 'Nick Of Time'
The B-52s, 'Love Shack'
Grateful Dead, *Built To Last*
The Jesus and Mary Chain, *Automatic*
Tracy Chapman, *Crossroads*
Bob Dylan, *Oh Mercy*
Nirvana, *Bleach*
Tom Petty, *Full Moon Fever*
Soul II Soul, *Club Classics Vol. One*
New Order, *Technique*

29 MAY 1990
TORONTO SKYDOME, CANADA

Rock star as celeb

Madonna was preparing to play the last of three shows at Toronto's SkyDome. Twenty thousand tickets had been sold, as they had for every night of her Blond Ambition world tour. This was Madonna getting back to what she did best after her most recent attempt to establish herself as an above-the-title actress, in the movie *Shanghai Surprise*. That film featured her then husband Sean Penn. The new one, *Dick Tracy*, was due to be released in the summer. This starred her latest boyfriend Warren Beatty. Beatty was fifty-three, which was twenty-two years older than Madonna.

He needed her more than she needed him. Warren had once been a big movie star but in 1990 he had very little chance of being allowed to make a big-budget movie like this without using a music star like Madonna. And in 1990 there was no music star quite like Madonna. Her presence on a project meant a $10 million saving on the marketing budget because Madonna was publicity. Publicity was not a by-product of what Madonna did, it was the product itself. Her profile owed as much to her ability to generate yards of press coverage as it did to the quality of her records. It was impossible to know whether this was by accident or design, just as it was impossible to know whether there was any distinction between her private and public lives. Certainly she seemed to delight in being the centre of attention, and she didn't much care whether the attention was admiring or not.

In Toronto the local police force had received complaints about Madonna's rendition of 'Like A Virgin' from people who had attended the previous night's show. She performed this number wearing a Jean-Paul Gaultier bustier while undulating on a bed and pawing her crotch with unmistakable intent. On the afternoon of 29 May a senior police officer turned up at the SkyDome with a Crown attorney. He told the promoter that something had to be done about the lewd and indecent display involved in this number. The threat was that if no adjustments were made then the show would not be able to go ahead. There were negotiations. The promoter and Madonna's manager proposed starting the show with the announcement that what followed contained adult themes and therefore anyone likely to be offended should leave. Madonna was having none of this because, as she loudly declared for the benefit of the movie cameras that were tailing her to make the tour documentary, she was an artist and nobody could censor her show.

The sequence of events that took place backstage, which made up part of the film *In Bed With Madonna*, is in one sense the real Madonna show. Madonna is a drama queen who achieves her full height only when bristling with indignation. She makes sure everyone around her shares her feelings. Her dancers are all of a twitter, some at the prospect of being carried from the stage by Mounties. Everyone is fairly secure in the knowledge that nothing bad is actually going to happen.

Madonna's was not the kind of civil disobedience that leads to the busting of heads. By 1990 her travelling show was operating behind a ring of steel made up of security, management, catering, functionaries, limos, blacked-out people carriers and the rest of the services that made the modern touring environment feel as secure and as detached from normal life as a Presidential motorcade. Madonna and her dancers gathered into a gospel huddle. She announced that they were in 'the fascist state of Toronto' and would soon be back in the United States where freedom of expression was respected. On their way to the stage they sang the old spiritual of resistance 'We Shall Overcome'.

It was all a lark. When they got in front of the audience Madonna made much of the police presence during her show. She asked the crowd if they wanted her to be bad. Of course they wanted her to be bad. Bad was what they had paid for. She did 'Like A Virgin'. She undulated. She pawed. Nothing interrupted the show. Nobody stepped up to arrest her. The parameters of outrage had clearly been moved in a big way since Jim Morrison in Florida twenty years earlier. Madonna was denied her Rosa Parks moment, but she got a scene for her film and added another coat of lustre to her brand. Next time round she would have to bring religion into the argument to get some kind of reaction out of an establishment that didn't seem to be up for the fight any longer. Madonna's show was no longer the racy alternative to the mainstream. Her show was the new mainstream.

The Blond Ambition tour was the progenitor of the modern multi-media spectacle. It was what a generation raised on MTV had come to expect of a live show, which was that it should take the form of a very big, very loud TV show. It should involve regular changes of costume. It should have stunts and special effects. The performers should wear headsets and earpieces which hinted that they were performing completely live courtesy of some new miracle of sound reproduction. It was an experience so beholden to click tracks, autocue machines and technological whizz-bangs that nothing could stand in its way or alter one step or one word from night to night. The performers were elements in a production rather than autonomous individuals who might at any stage stop what they were doing and change their mind. It was a Broadway show taken on the road and magnified many times over.

Popular music was testing the limits of its scalability. In the summer of 1990 even the Stone Roses, who just a year earlier had barely been able to fill a bath outside the north-west of England, played Spike Island in front of thirty thousand young adults all apparently wearing the same clothes and taking the same drugs.

The world for touring artists was starting to get flatter. The fall of the Berlin Wall in 1989 was seen in some quarters as an episode in the forty-year struggle between seriousness and triviality. P. J. O'Rourke wrote in *Rolling Stone*, 'The best thing about our victory is we did it with Levi 501s. Seventy-two years of Communist propaganda got drowned out with the three-ounce Walkman. A totalitarian system has been brought down because nobody wants to wear Bulgarian shoes.'

As the big leisure and fashion brands rushed to export to this new world they found that the stars of music were their best ambassadors. Paul McGuinness, the manager of U2, chided the big names of the sixties for taking the money of these advertisers. Paul McCartney, who was rumoured to have been paid over $8 million by the credit card company Visa for having their name on his first major tour of the United States, said McGuinness should grow up. The older generation, however, had older-generation worries that could only be relieved by the windfalls that came from touring. There was a dawning realization on the part of acts like McCartney and the Who that the market didn't want their new songs but was happy to hear them play the old ones. The latest US tour would eventually net Townshend £4 million, which would set him and his family up for the future. But he knew that he owed his first loyalty to his fellow band members. The real motivation for the tour was bassist John Entwistle's need to pay his back taxes. After almost thirty years as a rock star Entwistle was primarily surviving by selling his guitars. In this, the rock acts of the sixties and seventies still belonged in a tradition that stretched back to the classical players of the past, who would sell their best violin at the end of their career to buy a pension.

The Madonna show made all this look rather quaint. The central performing unit of a Madonna show was the dance troupe. She led and they followed. Every move she made was shadowed by them and echoed by a movement of their own. In a device imported wholesale from the shiny floor shows of television, the star was twirled, lifted, swung, ground up against and adoringly pawed by lightly oiled muscular young men dressed as firemen or farmhands in a ceremony of adoration that seemed designed to boost the ravenous self-esteem of the star and to relegate the audience to mere onlookers of an orgy of self-congratulation.

Madonna had come to New York when she was only

eighteen to try and make it as a dancer. The music came later. Her first reviews pointed out the music was always ancillary. She was a dancer first and foremost. She made records to give herself something to dance to. Many of the young women who came after her were cut from similar cloth. Most of the biggest stars of the pop music world we live in today are women. Madonna is the person who proved that was possible, who opened up a new world for them to grow into. As radio fragmented and rock was directed into its own morose silo, country was pushed thataway and indie was given its own playground in which to polish its illusions, the mainstream became largely about dancing.

1990 was the year of Demi Moore and Patrick Swayze doing half-naked pottery in the middle of the night in the movie *Ghost*, of Julia Roberts almost making prostitution seem attractive in *Pretty Woman*, of Victoria Abril healing Antonio Banderas's cuts and bruises with her kisses in *Tie Me Up! Tie Me Down!*, and Sherilyn Fenn getting a job in a brothel because she could tie a cherry stem with her tongue in *Twin Peaks*. The plot of the opening episode of NBC's new comedy show *Seinfeld* hinged on whether the girl in the hero's apartment was just a friend or intended to sleep with him. Suddenly it seemed there was no distinction between what had been known as adult entertainment and the mainstream. The issues once confined to the TV in the bedroom were now in everybody's living rooms. One of the things that had put them there was MTV. And while the sex objects in most videos had tended to be women, like the one being drenched with a firehose by the members of Warrant in 'Cherry Pie', now they were just as likely to be male models with six-packs wandering the halls of luxury hotels ready to gratify the womanly needs of Janet Jackson, Whitney Houston or

En Vogue. It was also the year of one of the most overt hits about masturbation, the Divinyls' 'I Touch Myself'. In no mood to cede ground in this new erotic arms race, Madonna released 'Justify My Love', the most controversial video of the year. In this she dressed and conducted herself like a character from the *Penthouse* letters page.

(The song was also characteristic of the new ways records were being made in a digital era. It started life as a poem by Ingrid Chavez. Lenny Kravitz worked it up into a song and presented it to Madonna, who changed one line. By the time the record came out it only had Madonna's and Kravitz's credits on it; Chavez eventually got hers, and a substantial out-of-court settlement. Another collaborator claimed he didn't get paid for developing the rhythm track, which owed something to Public Enemy's 'Security Of The First World', which in turn was made at least in part from components of James Brown's 'Funky Drummer', which actually owed everything to the eponymous Clyde Stubblefield. This was the new hip hop way. New hits could be made from re-conditioned parts of old ones. Putting together the records would be the producer's job. The role of the artist was to get them noticed.)

What fascinated Madonna most was her own stardom. 'People talk about how stardom changes you but they never talk about how stardom changes the people around you,' she says at one point in the *In Bed With Madonna* film. One by one the people close to her float through the action, looking on in various degrees of shock and awe at what their daughter/sister/girlfriend has achieved through the force of her own singular drive. Her father, presumably not thrilled at sharing the spectacle of his daughter rogering herself in front of a few thousand fellow Detroit natives, thinks there are a couple of numbers he could have done without. An old friend appears to ask if she would be godmother to her child and gets a brush-off. She takes the film crew to cover her visiting the grave of her mother. One member of her entourage is filmed talking about her experience of being sexually assaulted. Near the end of the film Madonna is asked to say who is the love of her life and she replies 'Sean', the husband she's recently divorced.

She didn't seem to have any problem with bringing those people into her own personal drama. Warren Beatty is the sharpest operator in the film because he's already sated himself on all the attention anyone could have and therefore he's capable of hanging back from the camera's ravenous eye. Everybody else just tumbles helplessly towards it. Beatty, who is trying to avoid the camera when Madonna drags him and the crew in to witness her consultation with a throat specialist in New York, asks her where this desperate need to over-share stops. Warren, who was born before the Second World War, tries to get the camera on his side by pleading that 'She doesn't want to live off-camera, much less talk. There's nothing to say off-camera. Why would you say something if it's off-camera? What point is there existing?'

It was too late to win that argument. After Madonna, stars had no secrets. What's more, the technology that would eventually enable us all to be the stars of our own lives was already on its way.

1990 PLAYLIST

Madonna, 'Vogue'
Sinéad O'Connor, 'Nothing Compares 2 U'
MC Hammer, 'U Can't Touch This'
Garth Brooks, *No Fences*
George Michael, *Listen Without Prejudice Vol. 1*
Angelo Badalamenti, *Twin Peaks* soundtrack
Depeche Mode, *Violator*
The Who, *Join Together*
Happy Mondays, *Pills 'N' Thrills And Bellyaches*
Megadeth, *Rust In Peace*

24 NOVEMBER 1991
KENSINGTON, LONDON

The party's over

In January 1991, at a lavish launch party on board the *Queen Mary* in Long Beach, California – a party that was paid for by Disney, the owners of Queen's new record company in the United States – guitarist Brian May was asked by a member of the American press whether it was true that Freddie Mercury had AIDS. He responded, as is traditional among British stars who happen to be in America, with an attack on the British tabloid press – 'a low form of life' – and a hearty assurance that the band's singer was in good health.

It was certainly the case that the British press had been trying to stand up the story of Mercury's illness ever since he had appeared in public looking gaunt and unwell. Indeed, as May spoke a number of them were stationed outside Mercury's home, the Garden Lodge in Logan Place in one of London's more prosperous boroughs, awaiting his end. Brian May and Roger Taylor, the only two members of Queen who attended the launch, knew that when they said Freddie didn't feel like touring at the moment they were telling less than the truth. They had a party line to uphold. The British press pretended they had a sacred duty to shed light on the news-worthy secrets of prominent entertainers. Freddie had plenty of those.

For the bulk of the twenty years of his fame there was a wall between the gay and the straight world, even within show business. Gay people in the world of rock, which likes to congratulate itself on being an outrider for new ways of living, were no quicker to announce their sexuality than their counterparts in Parliament, business, sport or the movies. The nearest they traditionally got was to declare themselves bisexual, as if this were no more than another manifest-ation of their all-round liberal-mindedness. This never quite seemed convincing.

For twenty years Freddie Mercury had met any questions about his sexuality with camp jokes and sentences that ended with the word 'darling'. There was no coming out, no tell-all autobiography, no going to the sofas. In the gay clubs of Munich and the discreet hotels of Brazil he behaved like one of the less savoury Roman emperors. In the straight world he kept himself on a very tight leash. The life he lived outside Queen was a closed book even to the members of Queen. The band had only known how bad his health was for the pre-vious two years. Before that it had remained a secret shared between Freddie, his doctors, the close friends who tended to him and the band's manager.

Once he'd finally told the band that he didn't have much time left they had busied themselves in the studio in Montreux, Switzerland. This had the double benefit of giving him something to do while also stockpiling material the band could release after his death. Although he had lost weight, was on painkillers and had to have the lesions on his face covered by make-up, he continued to chain-smoke Silk Cut and chug Stolichnaya even in the studio. This was Freddie's way. When the AIDS epidemic had hit in the mid-eighties and he had been asked whether he intended to let this in any way inhibit his sex life he'd snorted at the very idea and said that he would continue to do 'everything with everybody'. History doesn't record whether he added the word 'darling'.

There was a time, not so long ago, when forms of behaviour now taken as a formal announcement of certain forms of sexuality were simply accepted as amusing displays. When just a boy, Freddie, then known as Farrokh Bulsara, would go into raptures about things his schoolmates scarcely saw fit to comment on. His friends, while intuiting there was something about Farrokh that was different, didn't discuss the possibility of his being gay. This was not merely because the use of that adjective to describe sexual orientation was not much known in the sixties beyond the more bohemian quarters of London. It was also because baby boomers growing up at that time, whether in London or in Bombay, did not connect what they knew about homosexuality with the life they themselves lived. Not only did they not discuss him being gay, neither did they entertain the idea in their own minds. It's entirely possible that young Farrokh didn't either.

He was born in Zanzibar in 1946 to the young wife of a government clerk. They were Parsis, which, according to the elaborate taxonomy of Empire, meant they were descended from Persian stock and followed the prophet Zoroaster. When the blood-letting that accompanied the partition of the Indian subcontinent was over, Farrokh was sent to a boarding school in India run along lines familiar to readers of English school stories. Here he won the school's prize for Best All Rounder, junior section. Noting that four extra teeth at the back of his mouth had given him a pronounced overbite, his classmates called him 'Bucky'. When his teachers, possibly wishing to head off this unkindness, began to call him Freddie he seized on this more palatable alternative. Although he was shy in class he grasped any opportunity to perform. It was at school that Freddie formed his first band, the Hectics, who did their versions of hits by Elvis Presley and Little Richard.

In 1964, when a rising against the Arab-dominated government made life hazardous for anyone in Zanzibar whose skin colour was lighter than black, the Bulsaras decided to get out. Because Freddie's father had worked for the Raj he had a British passport and therefore they decided to escape to England rather than India. They settled in Feltham, directly under the Heathrow flight path. This was certainly a life less privileged than the one they had known in Zanzibar. For eighteen-year-old Freddie it was all he had ever wanted.

When he arrived he was immediately aware the Beatles' 'A Hard Day's Night' was about to be released. He was presumably less aware that legislation was being prepared in Parliament that would lead in the next three years to the legalization of homosexual acts between consenting adults in private. He was probably not aware of his own sexuality. He was certainly not aware that on the day of his death his sexuality would vie with his celebrity for prominence on the front pages and the news bulletins.

In 1966 Freddie was supposed to be studying Fashion Design at Ealing College of Art. His main interest was rock stardom. After seeing Jimi Hendrix on TV he went to watch the guitarist nine nights in a row, studying how he was able to galvanize a room by the simple act of wandering on and playing. Although he played some piano, Freddie's entry into music was via the gestural arts. When he first befriended the three members of a group who called themselves Smile he confined his input to suggestions about how they might put themselves over more winningly. The members of Smile, like most young men trying to get a start in 1969, didn't even realize they were in show business. In fact they were so myopic they failed to realize that Freddie was aching to be asked to join the band but was too shy to put himself forward. It wasn't until they saw him sing in front of another band that they appreciated how good he was at it. Because bands spend so much of their energies on their equipment they are inclined to overlook the person who brings the least equipment with him – the singer. They think that singing is something you can do in addition to other duties. For the audience, however, the singer is the human link between them and the musicians on stage.

All performers suffer from nerves, but to stand up in front of a rock band and sing takes special qualities. Laurence Olivier said that if you aren't sick with nerves you aren't trying. But Olivier, even at his lowliest rung on the ladder, had the support system provided by a company of actors, a script, scenery, lights, and the agreement between the audience and the people on the stage that underpins theatre. Singers in rock bands have none of this. Instead they need the belief that if they act like they have the right to be the frontman then they have won the right to be that frontman. Freddie had a further challenge. He knew that he looked odd. In fact he looked more like Dame Edith Evans than Elvis Presley. To stand up in front of an unknown rock band and behave like a star when you know that you don't look like one requires belief in the transfiguring power of performance.

People in rock bands can't afford to allow themselves to glimpse the preposterousness of what they do. While Brian

May, Roger Taylor and John Deacon were all positioned behind their instruments with a protective wall of equipment between the audience and their genitalia, the traditional seat of all feelings of insecurity in the male, Freddie was out there, often with shirt slashed down to the navel, often arrayed in an all-white outfit that had been designed purely to catch the eye, and as such he was utterly exposed. But Freddie didn't mind. That was his strength, to be able to do something that no other member of the band could imagine themselves doing. On stage, Freddie was fearless. While most musicians avoid catching the audience's eye, for fear of how that gaze might be returned, Freddie's eyes sought them out as he worked to consume the space between him and the crowd. That was his area of operation, his workspace. His job, every night, was simple: to reach across that gulf to the people out there and win them over. It's what he loved doing.

He could never have been a star in any other field. Success in theatre or film would have depended on him being picked out from the crowd. That was never going to happen. Only in a field as untouched by professionalism as rock, only in a moment as low-budget as glam rock, only within the context of a group that was young, ambitious and didn't have a better idea could Freddie Bulsara have turned himself into Freddie Mercury and Smile have turned themselves into a band with the preposterous name Queen and in one mad holding-hands moment jump off the cliff and take flight. One day in 1975 Farrokh Bulsara woke up to find he was the star he had always dreamed of being.

When Queen became successful, Freddie had a girlfriend. He was as devoted to her as he was to anyone in his life. They lived together as a standard young couple. When Queen went big time and started coming up against big-time temptations and Freddie didn't come home quite so regularly she worried there might be another woman, which is a measure of how unworldly even the young sophisticates of the seventies could be. Freddie didn't come out partly because he feared it might affect the group's popularity, but also because he wasn't sure he wished to be categorical about the matter.

When Freddie finally went all-out full-time gay he more than made up for it. In the eighties he adopted the moustachioed gym bunny look favoured by clones all over the world. That look didn't mean the same to the people watching him on TV as it did to the people in the gay clubs where he spent much of his spare time. Marc Almond, an eighties pop star every bit as slight, unlikely and gay as Freddie had been when he came along ten years earlier, was effusively hailed as 'Marcia' in a London club and whisked on to the dance floor and was taken aback by how G-A-Y Freddie was. Furthermore, even by the standards of famous rock stars, Freddie was promiscuous. 'He was the good time who was being had by all,' said Almond.

A few months after Queen's appearance at Live Aid the Hollywood actor Rock Hudson died. Hudson's celebrity meant his was the first case of an AIDS-related death making its way into the public arena. All sexually active gay men suddenly had something very specific to be concerned about. Freddie had more to be concerned about than most. He had cut a vodka-fuelled and cocaine-laced swathe through the gay nightlife of Munich for much of the last decade and knew full well what that was likely to mean. When he was eventually diagnosed as HIV positive in the spring of 1987 it came as no surprise.

He made his last public appearance at the 1990 BRIT Awards in London where Queen were given an Outstanding

Contribution award. All four of them came on stage to receive the prize. Freddie stood at the back while Brian May made the speech, which seemed unusual. As they left the stage he couldn't resist being the last to go. He leaned into the microphone and said, 'Thank you, good night.' It must have broken his heart.

Twenty-one months later, on 23 November 1991, he made the most uncharacteristic move of putting out a press release. It confirmed that he had AIDS. He wished his friends and fans to know this from him rather than from some tabloid. The following day he died in his home in Kensington. Tottenham's Dave Clark, who had been a big pop star ten years earlier than Freddie, was with the son of Zanzibar when he breathed his last.

His parents, who knew he was ill but not why, were the first to be informed. The woman who told them was the woman who had been his girlfriend back in the days before fame. His parents still lived in the same house in Feltham they had moved into in 1964. They never knew he was gay.

1991 PLAYLIST

Queen, *Innuendo*
REM, 'Losing My Religion'
Bryan Adams, '(Everything I Do) I Do It For You'
Sting, *The Soul Cages*
De La Soul, *De La Soul Is Dead*
Ice-T, *O.G. Original Gangster*
Crowded House, *Woodface*
Massive Attack, *Blue Lines*
Red Hot Chili Peppers, *Blood Sugar Sex Magik*
Nirvana, *Nevermind*

7 MAY 1992
TOKYO, JAPAN

Man overboard

Before leaving Los Angeles to tour Japan, Australia and New Zealand in April 1992, the four members of the LA group Red Hot Chili Peppers had gathered at the studio of *Rolling Stone*'s chief photographer Mark Seliger to have their picture taken for the cover of the magazine. It was the first time for them and they were very excited. *Blood Sugar Sex Magik*, their first album for their new record company Warner Brothers, had already sold over a million copies, thanks to the radio popularity of its uncharacteristic ballad 'Under The Bridge'. Now it finally looked as though this hyperactive, heavily tattooed quartet, whose look reflected Los Angeles' skating sub-culture and whose sound owed as much to Funkadelic as it did to the Clash, were finally breaking through.

The early nineties were a golden time for the music magazines. Bands relied on them to reflect and magnify their prestige and to confirm that they merited their place in the hierarchy. Magazine covers were a key index of success. There was politics involved at every stage. Once an act had got over the excitement of being featured in print the next thing they demanded was the cover. Being considered big enough to 'get the cover' was a powerful indicator that you had made it, a handy lever when it came to raising your asking price and a reminder to your rivals that your tanks were on their lawn. (Rock stars are not interested in sharing the limelight. Rock bands are only interested in domination. Rock bands don't just want to win, they want to be assured that their rivals lose as a consequence of them winning. When Q magazine moved from a multi-image to a single-image cover, the bands were suddenly very keen to get on it. When they'd had to share it they were not so bothered.)

In 1992 the stakes were being raised in the visuals department. The emergent rock bands who were shot for the cover of *Rolling Stone* that year – Def Leppard, Nirvana and REM – were suddenly in danger of appearing slightly dull and prosaic when set alongside Ice-T in the uniform of an officer of the LAPD, Sharon Stone in a ripped bathing costume and the pert, pretty cast of *Beverly Hills 90210*. Rock's rebel glamour no longer punched through on its own. The youth had choices.

What made the Red Hot Chili Peppers popular was their music. What made them famous was the sock stunt. This had its origin in an incident when singer Anthony Kiedis had sought to turn down the overtures of a young woman by greeting her at his door stark naked except for a tube sock enveloping his penis. This coup de théâtre had grown and developed until it became an occasional and much-anticipated feature of the band's set. All four members

– Kiedis, bassist Flea, drummer Chad Smith and guitarist John Frusciante – would resume the stage for an encore wearing nothing but four socks over their four members. They first tried this at a Hollywood strip bar called the Kit Kat Club. Although the stunt had been cleared in advance the club's manager was nonetheless somewhat exercised by the magnificent brazenness of the reality, rushing backstage protesting, 'No pubes! I told you no pubes!' Local police, alerted to the possibility that the Red Hot Chili Peppers might repeat the trick while playing in their jurisdiction, were reassured that the socks were held in place by wires. This was not true. The only things keeping those socks in place were friction and the venue's central heating.

It was clear that the *Rolling Stone* cover would have to make reference to the stunt that had made them famous. The Red Hot Chili Peppers weren't the kind of band to shrink from the obvious. However, a straight repeat of the sock trick might have been too much for *Rolling Stone*'s distributors. Instead, Seliger shot them with their hands clasped over their privates.

The band approved the pictures and set off on their tour of Japan. They played five gigs and were in Tokyo on 7 May preparing to play their sixth. Kiedis was on the phone to a journalist in New Zealand, prior to their upcoming dates in that country, when Flea appeared in his room to tell him that John Frusciante had decided he was leaving the band. He wasn't handing in his notice prior to leaving at the end of the tour; he needed to get out immediately. That night's show would have to be cancelled and the rest of the tour was off until they could find a replacement. Kiedis went to see his guitarist. One look in his eyes was enough to convince him that John had made up his mind. There was no attempt to remonstrate with him or draw attention to the terms of his employment. What Kiedis was facing was one of those situations which happens in a rock band and doesn't happen in any other professional unit.

Frusciante was just twenty-two years old, which placed him in a different generation from the rest. He had been a fan of the band since the age of fifteen and had joined them following the death of their previous guitarist. His need to leave the tour immediately and the other three's willingness to accommodate him underlined what a curious bunch of individuals the Red Hot Chili Peppers were. This wasn't just because, like so many bands breaking through at the time, they thought of themselves as having derived from punk rock and therefore their one non-negotiable was independence. They were also Hollywood kids, which made them naturally inclined to look down on everywhere else. However, like most Hollywood kids they hadn't begun there.

During Anthony Kiedis's upbringing he was shuttled between his mother in Michigan and his father in Hollywood. The most generous thing to be said about his father is that he hung out on the scene. He also supplied drugs to Led Zeppelin, Keith Moon and other patrons of the Rainbow Bar and Grill. He liked to dress his son up in scaled-down versions of the clothes he favoured himself and would take him out on the town with him. The pair would make a bizarre couple, turning up together at X-certificate Hollywood parties, the father looking too old for the scene and the boy looking too young. Like a French parent giving his children watered-down wine at the family meal, he would allow his boy 'a little bit of acid'. Like a Victorian aristocrat he felt the need to supervise his son's introduction to sex, arranging for the hospitable Kimberly from the Rainbow Bar and Grill to relieve him of the burden of his virginity while still under the age of consent. He had a simple policy about parenthood: 'I would let him do anything he wanted to.'

The notion that a little liberality early on avoids a grand crisis later was dented somewhat by the way things turned out for young Anthony. He lived in Hollywood full-time as a teenager. His father was so all over the place that the boy eventually found some stability in the unlikely form of Sonny Bono, who was a friend of one of his father's girlfriends. He befriended Bono's daughter Chastity. Tensions with his father meant he moved out while still a teenager and lived on friends' couches and even in unoccupied buildings. During this time he developed a heroin addiction for which he didn't seek help until his friend and fellow band member Hillel Slovak died of an overdose in 1988. The members of the band had originally bonded over music and drugs but, as is customary in bands, they avoided getting to know how serious each other's drug use was. Being traditional units of male bonding, bands prefer not to probe too deep. As the members of Joy Division had said after Ian Curtis's suicide, 'We didn't realize he meant it.' The drug use within the Red Hot Chili Peppers was the secret they kept from each other. Before his death, Slovak and Kiedis had last seen each other at the airport in LA after returning from a European tour. They'd embraced and promised each other they would be good. 'Then we both made a bee-line for our individual dealers,' remembered Kiedis later.

The bass player Flea was born in Australia. One emigration and a family breakdown later he too was in Hollywood with a stepfather who was a jazz musician nobody wished to employ. He fixed cars in the backyard, did drugs, and sometimes his frustrations with the hand he'd been dealt by fate boiled over into violent outbursts and the young boy would be afraid to go to sleep in the house. There were probably a lot of kids who had similar feelings at Fairfax High, where a huge proportion of the student body had parents who were either in show business or were hanging on by their fingernails to the pretence that they were.

Unlike the rock stars of earlier decades these were kids who'd grown up on a very long leash. They were allowed to grow their hair at high school and do everything that went with it. John Frusciante, who had been born in 1970, was one of the foremost bedroom guitar players in southern California. The parents of kids like Frusciante didn't mind if they were in their room smoking weed and painstakingly copying the licks of Steve Vai because at least they knew where they were. Essentially a very shy man who was younger and less gregarious than the rest of the band, he had developed his skills as a guitar player in seclusion. Hence he had woken up to find himself a professional musician and entertainer without being socialized into the smell, chaos and hurly-burly that are part of the life. When the band weren't actually playing, Frusciante lived what he fancied was a Captain Beefheart kind of life: smoking weed, drinking wine, playing his guitar and filling in colouring books. It was a world far removed from the brutal imperatives of life on the road where the show must go on. Now that the band had a big hit album and a tour schedule to match, Frusciante started to feel anxious. The problem began when they were recording *Blood Sugar Sex Magik*. During the sessions for the album Frusciante started to hear voices in his head. They told him that if he went on tour with the band he wouldn't see the experience through. He saw through the American and European legs in 1991 but by Japan it had all got too much.

A band is such an unmanaged operation that it is perfectly

possible for a problem like Frusciante's to bubble up without anyone else either noticing it or talking about it. He'd joined the band when he was still young and impressionable enough to notice that Flea appeared to get deliberately stoned before going on stage, and to assume that this would be good behaviour to emulate. He had then started dabbling in heroin. After he left the band, he later said, 'I decided to become a drug addict. I believe I made the right choice. It was what I needed then. I needed to completely isolate myself from the frenetic rhythm of the world.' Later that year he turned up for an audition with the Meat Puppets in Arizona. He was barefoot and his guitar was not in its case. The band went through with the audition for the sake of form but it was clear to them that he was not of sound mind.

In other areas of the arts, such as the theatre or classical music, it's unusual for one of the performers suddenly to make themselves unavailable with such burdensome consequences for their colleagues. There is no understudy system in rock. There are no stunt men, no stand-ins. It is assumed that each player has a particular unique fingerprint which it would be quite impossible and very disrespectful to try to replicate. It's also assumed that the players have to be thoroughly invested in the enterprise, and therefore if their heart is no longer in it to ask them to carry on even for a few nights would be cruel and unusual punishment.

The Red Hot Chili Peppers tried first one replacement guitarist and then another. They resumed the tour in June. Luckily Frusciante's abrupt departure happened before *Rolling Stone* had gone to press with the cover picture featuring all four members of the band. Thanks to the arrival of digital reproduction technology the art director was able to remove the guitarist's naked picture from the line-up on the cover, and they were temporarily down to a three-piece. A naked three-piece. Frusciante was excised from the picture and from this particular bit of history. The Red Hot Chili Peppers were temporarily one member down. Given the nature of the photograph, that wasn't the only member they were missing.

1992 PLAYLIST

Tori Amos, *Little Earthquakes*
Spiritualized, *Lazer Guided Melodies*
Take That, *Take That & Party*
REM, *Automatic For The People*
Leonard Cohen, *The Future*
Manic Street Preachers, *Generation Terrorists*
k.d. lang, *Ingénue*
Pavement, *Slanted And Enchanted*
The Lemonheads, *It's A Shame About Ray*
Eric Clapton, *Unplugged*

7 JUNE 1993
MINNEAPOLIS, MINNESOTA

Career suicide

Prince Rogers Nelson turned thirty-five on 7 June 1993. The following day his publicist in Minneapolis announced that henceforth he wished to be referred to not by his name but by a symbol. This symbol, which resembled a cross between the symbols for male and female, had been introduced on the cover of his last album, which had come out late in 1992. The publicist couldn't help MTV or anyone else with advice on how to articulate this new title. His record company Warner Brothers, with whom he had a contract said to be worth $100 million, said they had no more idea than anyone else. They had to issue all media outlets with a piece of type so that the symbol could appear in print. If the artist's intention had been to confound the music business this latest move had succeeded. An English journalist called him the Artist Formerly Known as Prince, which was the nearest thing to a name that stuck.

Prince could do anything. In terms of all-round ability he

was probably the most accomplished rock star of them all. He could play most instruments, he had written huge hit songs like 'Purple Rain' and 'Little Red Corvette', he could sing in a variety of styles, he produced himself, he had his own studio base up in Minneapolis far away from the power centres of the music business, and he had teams of backing musicians he could call on. He could even dance, which was not a talent to be overlooked.

In an area of operation where it's perfectly possible to reach a position of eminence with a narrow range of abilities providing you use those abilities wisely, as Bono has done, Prince had an embarrassment of talent. Unlike so many musicians, he didn't have a problem making up his mind. If anything he was over-productive. Once he had written a song and recorded it, he wanted it out. Like so many musicians, he had never got over the thrill of hearing his new tune on the radio for the first time. He just wanted to have that thrill more often. Oddly enough, the people standing in his way were the people at his record company, Warner Brothers.

The functions of a traditional record company like Warner Brothers were threefold. They would provide finance to the artist in exchange for an agreed number of records over an agreed period of time. They had the factories and specialist skills that meant they knew how to manufacture those records. And they had the distribution network, the trucks and the salesmen and the clerks, that meant they could get them to the public; they also had the relationships within radio that enabled them to get the records aired. Neither they nor the radio particularly wanted the new record from Prince quite as often as he did. It lessened the novelty. Over time it was bound to reduce the value of the name they had helped Prince build up.

Prince's argument was cute. He claimed that since Warner Brothers had their contract with the guy called Prince they had no choice but to release the material the guy called Prince had done. The symbol, meanwhile, was free to start again somewhere else. This was the contractual equivalent of faking his own disappearance. Warners, who had him under exclusive contract as a recording artist, were naturally reluctant to let him start again somewhere else. In return, he said they were treating him like a slave. He took to appearing in public, mainly to pick up awards, with the word 'slave' written on his cheek.

Prince had no problem with self-belief and here he was at the high point of the period where he thought he could do anything. The work didn't have to come out under his famous name because it would be popular on the basis of its obvious quality. This theory was tested. He tried working remotely through his hired hands. He put his protégée Carmen Electra in a multi-media reworking of Homer's *Odyssey* called *Glam Slam Ulysses*. The *LA Times* said the musical production was 'simply silly'. It closed in no time. He gave moviemaker James Brooks four songs for his new film. This tested so badly that all the songs were removed from the soundtrack. Very few of the acts he had signed to his Paisley Park label fulfilled their promise and Warner Brothers wondered why they were having to pay for it all. Meanwhile they were doing quite well out of selling copies of a compilation of his hits and B-sides, which they had priced at an unprecedented $49.99.

At the same time as Prince was getting involved in this game of bluff and counter-bluff with Warner Brothers in the United States the singer George Michael began an action against his record company, Sony, in the High Court in London. He was arguing that his contract with them was unfair and that they had not properly promoted his most recent album because they didn't agree with the artistic direction he had chosen to take. In starting this sort of action George Michael certainly didn't lack courage. There must have been times during the seventeen days he spent in court listening to the technical arguments of lawyers for both sides when he feared that no good could come of it. During the three days he spent giving evidence he must have suspected that nobody was less likely to qualify for the sympathy of the general public than a pop star who hadn't been able to bring himself to say in open court how much money he was worth. Instead he'd handed the judge a piece of paper on which was written the figure: £100 million.

The nub of the case was that while George Michael's first solo album after leaving the pop duo Wham! had sold twenty-five million copies worldwide, the follow-up had managed a mere eight million. George's argument was that this disparity was down to Sony's failure to promote it properly. It is a truth universally acknowledged that when a record does well the artist deserves all the praise and when a record does poorly the record company deserves all the blame. At the same time, only in the record business, which at least makes a show of following the artist's wishes, would someone be permitted to follow up a record as light and ingratiating as George Michael's first one with one as dark and introspective as his second. Only in the music business would the artist be given complete unfettered control of the packaging of these records. Only in the record business would he be allowed to follow a package with a colour picture of the artist on the cover with another one where the cover was taken up by a vintage black-and-white picture of the crowd at Coney Island in 1940.

Only in the music business would a person be allowed to call this record *Listen Without Prejudice Vol. 1.* George Michael was so desperate to shake off what he thought of as the frivolous image of the party songs that had made his name that he gave his album what would go down as the neediest title in history. Both Prince and George Michael thought that if people could listen to their records without knowing who had made them they would be even more favourably inclined towards them. In fact, as the people at the record company knew, the very opposite was the case. Indeed prejudice was the attitude upon which the music business operated, the muscle upon which the whole rock-star system turned. Prejudice is just as likely to be favourable as negative: thanks to prejudice fans are likely to interpret the actions of their favourites in a good light. It's prejudice that makes those same fans go out and buy records they already have for just one extra track. It's prejudice that makes them spend money they do not have to come to see an artist in concert, from ever greater distances. Fans are prejudiced. That's what makes them fans. The people most likely to buy your new record are the people who bought the last one. Prejudice in the form of name recognition and brand loyalty was the basis upon which record companies handed out million-pound advances. Until you were known, the record companies needed to hear your songs. Once you had a name they were buying that name because they knew lots of people were prejudiced in favour of it. The last thing they wanted was people listening *without* prejudice. Without prejudice they might not get round to listening to your record for years. They might go and listen to something else.

Neither Prince nor George Michael would have got involved in confrontations with their record companies if they had been in groups. Groups generally have one member who fears the consequences of doing anything that doesn't have to be done and therefore they tend to be less reckless. If in 1993 Michael Jackson had still been a member of the Jacksons rather than a solo performer, it's possible that somebody in their circle would have told him that sharing his bed with thirteen-year-old Jordan Chandler was likely to be interpreted unsympathetically. But there was a booming entertainment business, then there was Michael Jackson, who seemed like another business altogether. Jackson had more power and money than any one individual in the history of the game. People in that position don't get much advice. If they do, they don't listen.

On 21 August 1993 the police obtained a search warrant to gain access to 5225 Figueroa Mountain Road, Los Olivos, Santa Barbara. This was the address of the Neverland Ranch. In the two thousand acres surrounding Jackson's twenty-five-room mansion was an amusement park as lavish as anything open to the public elsewhere in southern California. There were creatures like lions and elephants selected for their capacity to inspire awe as well as miniature creatures such as might appeal to children. Disney music played from a hundred speakers disguised as rocks throughout the grounds. There was a Ferris wheel, a steam train and thirty full-time gardeners. The running costs of Neverland were over a million dollars a month. When the police arrived at the ranch, and at other Jackson properties, to gather evidence as part of an investigation begun by the Los Angeles Police Department's Sexually Exploited Child Unit, it was as though they had breached the diplomatic immunity of the sovereign state of stardom.

Jackson cancelled the rest of his Dangerous tour and fled with Elizabeth Taylor by private jet to London where he sought help from the fashionable therapist of the time, Beechy Colclough. He was taking the painkillers Percodan and Demerol – a legacy of the treatment he'd been prescribed after the 1984 fire. One of the people who persuaded him that he should seek help was Lisa Marie Presley, who had become his new phone girlfriend. She also counselled paying off his accusers just to make the charges go away. The authorities let it be known that Jordan had described Michael's penis, and when he returned they would need to photograph it. The humiliation was made worse by the fact that the media of 1993 didn't shrink from describing any detail. There had been scandals before. This was going to be something different. This was heading for shame on a massive scale.

It was the year that Bill Clinton was invested as the 42nd President of the United States. It was the year that Janet Jackson appeared on the cover of *Rolling Stone* with somebody else's hands cupping her naked breasts. It was the year the thirteen-year-old Ryan Gosling was relocated from Canada to Florida to become a member of the cast of *The All-New Mickey Mouse Club* alongside the equally unknown Justin Timberlake, Britney Spears and Christina Aguilera.

The biggest album of 1993 was the soundtrack to *The Bodyguard*. This starred Whitney Houston as a diva with a dark secret. The extent of Houston's real-life dark secret would not emerge until after her death, but her marriage to Bobby Brown was already the stuff of supermarket magazines and twenty-four-hour rolling news. The ups and downs of the private lives of the people who made records were now in the public domain in a way they had never previously been. It was good for business. The soundtrack of *The Bodyguard* was the first and last album to sell a million copies in just one week.

George Michael didn't win his case. Prince moved away from Warner Brothers, releasing his music on a variety of labels. Stung by a Warner Brothers executive who'd allegedly said he'd 'lost it', he sat down and wrote a song called 'The Most Beautiful Girl In The World'. It took him just a day. The song was a huge hit all over the world in 1994. It was the last time he had the whole world's attention.

1993 PLAYLIST

Radiohead, *Pablo Honey*
Suede, *Suede*
David Bowie, *Black Tie White Noise*
P. J. Harvey, *Rid Of Me*
The Roots, *Organix*
Liz Phair, *Exile In Guyville*
The Smashing Pumpkins, *Siamese Dream*
Kate Bush, *The Red Shoes*
Wu-Tang Clan, *Enter The Wu-Tang (36 Chambers)*
Bob Dylan, *World Gone Wrong*

5 APRIL 1994
SEATTLE, WASHINGTON

The last rock star

It wasn't until Friday, 8 April, when an electrician working on Kurt Cobain's house looked through the window of one of the out buildings and saw a man's body with a shotgun and a pool of blood beside it, that anyone knew he was dead. The leader of Nirvana had been lying there for three days. Although Cobain had clearly been under great stress, having recently checked himself out of an upmarket rehab facility in Los Angeles and broken off relations with his wife Courtney Love, who was making her own attempt to quit heroin, the process was deliberate. He had taken his own life after writing a series of notes and smoking a number of cigarettes. He'd also thoughtfully provided a towel for whoever might have to swab up the blood.

The news got out just as quickly as the news of Buddy Holly's death in 1959, and largely by the same route, the radio. It immediately struck a similar chord with a very different generation. Nirvana's second album, *Nevermind*, which had been released in 1991, did something more for Generation X than other, better-known albums had done for their parents. The lyrics of *Nevermind* were opaque but you could read the band's intentions in the sound. The people who mourned felt it said something that needed saying on their behalf. Following Cobain's death it seemed to mean something more. Seattle's record stores ran out of stock of Nirvana's records. Some people wanted to become fans in order to join in the feeling of loss. At the gathering that took place in Seattle on the Sunday somebody was already wearing a T-shirt saying 'Kurt died for your sins'.

Kurt Cobain was a genuine rock star, possibly the last one. If there was anything manufactured about him, he did the manufacturing himself. He had a powerful personality and that personality was always very near the surface. He believed in his music. He also believed in the world from which it had come. He believed in the indie rock ideal of an invisible republic of cool people from all walks of life, people who rejected the siren call of earthly riches, people above the shabby, grabby routine of daily life, people magically united by their ability to detect the precious sincerity buried under the distorted guitars, slackened-off drums and impassioned vocals of a few records on tiny labels, records that they treasured, talked about and passed between them like sweet secrets. He believed nothing was more important than that.

He had no great interest in the trappings his rock stardom brought him. He just wanted to make some mark in the small world of punk rock in the Pacific North-West. That was taken out of his hands. It just so happened that Nirvana's moment of success coincided with the apogee in the business of recorded sound, which was waxing fat at the time on sales of compact discs priced far higher than any previous sound carrier had dared. That didn't just mean that record companies were looking at revenues they'd never seen before. It also meant that the margins on these records provided fortunes that could be spent on videos, on print advertising, and on flying journalists business class halfway around the world in order to celebrate and venerate the latest signing. It meant that if you were big in the early nineties you felt, with some justification, like the biggest thing there had ever been.

When the third Nirvana album, *In Utero*, was released in September 1993 it sold 180,000 copies in the United States in the first week alone. Cobain's manager estimated that in 1993 the singer would earn $1,400,000 from just the songwriting royalties. Their management company was called Gold Mountain. Money in this kind of quantity produces unfamiliar tensions within bands, particularly those who until that point have thought of themselves as noble conspiracies against Mammon. It also guarantees that the member of the band with the most will become the target of every false friend and low-life capable of crawling on their bellies towards the glow of the campfire. If you have a serious drug habit, as Cobain did, it will be impossible to tell real friends from the other kind. In Cobain's case matters were complicated by the fact that he was married to Courtney Love, who loved the money and fame every bit as much as they made him uncomfortable.

They had a small child. Although like most rock stars he was not above adopting the pose that implies nobody has had a baby before – 'holding her in my arms is the only drug I need,' he lied – there were signs they might find it tough to hold the family unit together. His own parents had split up when he was nine, and the strongest relationship he'd had in his family was with an aunt. Courtney's family background was flakier. In her adolescence she was passed between members of her family like a fizzing cartoon bomb. Kurt had no illusions about the stock his daughter was descended from. In a will made out after her birth he stipulated that even if every trusted person in their circle were deceased she could not be handed over either to his father or anybody in Courtney's family. Looking after a small baby is simultaneously the most demanding and the simplest thing anybody can be called upon to do. All it requires is to put yourself in second place. Rock stars can find this aspect a challenge.

Kurt and Courtney had domestic confrontations on an epic scale. If the characters in *Who's Afraid of Virginia Woolf?* had had heroin to add to their alcohol problems they might have experienced something like the rows that took place at their expensive home in Seattle's millionaires enclave (their next-door neighbour was the boss of Starbucks). They prowled the three floors, numerous reception rooms and five bedrooms of their lakeside property, a house that had been decorated lavishly if not lovingly, where the platinum discs, that epitome of uncherishable swag, were stacked against the walls and the only people allowed to turn up unannounced were those who supplied the drugs. They wandered until they were out of earshot of their eighteen-month-old child and her nannies and then loudly vented their frustration with the fact that he could no longer face going out to work and she could no longer face settling down.

Cobain was never sure how to respond to fame's awkward embrace. When his band finally appeared on the cover of *Rolling Stone*, which they had prayed for and planned for over the years, Kurt wore a T-shirt bearing the slogan 'Corporate magazines still suck' – a strangely eloquent illustration of the indie rock paradox. Like Bruce Springsteen, Cobain retained a very strong sense of what fans expected of their heroes. They expected them never to change, never to grow up. They expected them to keep it real – whatever keeping it real means to a multi-millionaire. They wanted everybody else to share in their special relationship with the artist but didn't want that relationship to become any less special.

The note he wrote immediately before shooting himself, poignantly addressed to an imaginary friend of his childhood, is in some respects like a reader's letter to a music paper. There's the same tendency to confuse music with life. In it he said he didn't feel the same about playing music as he used to feel. This made him feel guilty 'beyond words'. He felt bad about the fact that he was unable to enjoy the audience's appreciation like Freddie Mercury did. 'The worst crime I can think of would be to rip people off by faking it and pretending as if I'm having 100% fun.' He asks himself 'Why don't you enjoy it?' and answers, 'I don't know.' He finishes with a line from Neil Young: 'It's better to burn out than to fade away.'

These aren't just the words of somebody who has fallen out of love with playing. Nor are they just the words of somebody with a serious heroin habit. Nor are they just the words of somebody battling depression who possibly senses he's married the wrong woman. These are the words of a man who has grown up with all his hopes and dreams invested in the sole aim of becoming a rock star, and more than that a rock star in the mould of his heroes, and has found that he simply can't live up to the demands of the role in which he has cast himself. He is twenty-seven years old. He has a wife and child and all the material comforts anyone twice his age could ever dream of, yet he feels hollow and used up. It's like reading a letter from a priest who fears he has lost his vocation.

Cobain had invested so much belief in his own heroes that he couldn't face the idea that people were expecting as much of him as he'd expected of them. For a start he couldn't deal with the attention. The reality of being famous is frightening. People who dream of being rock stars dream of the fame without having the slightest idea what it means. Fame deprives us of the civil liberty we enjoy but never value; the freedom to pass unnoticed. As soon as Kurt Cobain was famous he became the centre of attention in every room he entered. He wasn't the kind of person who could just surf that attention. He felt that when people were looking at him they were looking to him. They expected things from him. They might be looking at him and finding him wanting. They might be expecting the same things from him that he had expected from the musicians he had looked up to when he was a teenager back in the small Washington town of Aberdeen.

The group that first inspired Kurt Cobain were the Melvins. He saw them play in a parking lot in 1983 not long after they had formed. They played loud, fast, intemperate rock and roll which was clearly more for their own pleasure than anyone else's. Cobain was sixteen. 'This was what I'd been looking for,' he wrote in his journal. The Melvins never troubled the charts, despite having a short period on a major label in the wake of Nirvana's success when those labels were signing up anyone who could be called 'grunge'. In an interview to promote their nineteenth album in 2013 their leader Buzz Osborne said he had no time for people who asked him if he was jealous of Kurt Cobain's money and fame. 'You think I would trade places with a dead guy? No. I win. He loses. I'm very happy with who I am and exactly what I'm doing, and it's way more than I ever expected. When I started this band thirty years ago my ambition was just to play a real show. And I surpassed that within six months. The rest is just gravy.'

When Cobain followed what he thought was the logic of Neil Young's observation about burning out and fading away, Osborne's band had already been together ten years, which was longer than the Beatles had managed. At the time of writing they're still going. The market for rock bands has, in the words of the economists, matured. All over the world there are hundreds of bands like the Melvins who have somehow managed to keep going. They've done that through careful housekeeping, cultivating their small fanbase and putting out of their minds any notion of being rock stars. Some are eaten up by the idea of what might have been. Others are as content with their lot as Buzz Osborne. The Melvins make another album in the hope that they can make another one after that. They play tonight's show in the hope that there will be another one tomorrow. When the time comes, they won't burn out. They will fade away. By refusing to play the game they may win in the end.

1994 PLAYLIST

Bruce Springsteen, 'Streets Of Philadelphia'
Beck, *Mellow Gold*
Morrissey, *Vauxhall And I*
Pink Floyd, *The Division Bell*
Spin Doctors, *Turn It Upside Down*
The Rolling Stones, *Voodoo Lounge*
The Melvins, *Prick*
Portishead, *Dummy*
Nirvana, *Unplugged in New York*
Oasis, *Definitely Maybe*

9 AUGUST 1995
MOUNTAIN VIEW, CALIFORNIA
Revenge of the nerds

In 1995 only the most adventurous 15 per cent of Americans had ever used the internet. Email was starting to be available to those working in more advanced businesses but it wasn't for everybody. The internet still looked like a technical undertaking rather than an artistic or commercial one. In 1995 computers took a long time to get started and made a lot of noise doing it. Once you had got on the internet it was a challenge to tell the difference between the content and the code that delivered it. The user-friendly skins which had been promised were yet to arrive.

Similarly, in 1995 only 7 per cent of the population of the UK had a mobile phone. Not one single person in the worldwide entertainment business was thinking about them. Not even the phone companies thought this technology would be used for anything other than work. The speed at which everybody was proved wrong was breathtaking. Only four years later a mobile phone was being sold in the UK every four seconds. Even then very few people were predicting that within less than twenty years these devices would supplant the personal stereo, the home CD player, the radio, the diary, the address book and the camera, or that they would reshape the whole space in which human interaction takes place, or that the consequences would be felt everywhere from the bedroom of a twelve-year-old to the Oval Office.

Even the people paid to know what was going to happen in the future had no idea how quickly that future was bearing down on them. In the spring of 1995 an executive of the electronics giant Philips blandly assured the German developer of a new sound compression technology that there would never be a commercial MP3 player. The new Pentium chips had only just become capable of playing a whole MP3 file without stalling; as computer hard drives were getting bigger and cheaper, it was conceivable that some of them might one day be able to accommodate an entire album of music. On 26 May 1995 Bill Gates sent a memo to everybody who worked for Microsoft telling them that the future was the internet and warning them that it could change their way of doing things. In 1995, Steve Jobs was still working for NeXT and was assuring the world that his former employer Apple didn't have much of a future.

In periods of great change it's less important to have a vision of the future in which you believe than it is to have a vision of the future in which you can persuade people to invest. Jim Clark had such a vision. In 1995 he was briefly employing his talent for making money as the CEO of a company called Netscape. The key employee at Netscape was a twenty-two-year-old nerd called Marc Andreessen. When Andreessen was at university he had played a part in developing the browser known as Mosaic, which promised to turn the experience of looking at pages on the internet from something that appeared to be a page of specifications into something that felt more like a magazine. Clark's plan was to launch Netscape on the stock market before any of his competitors. He hired an experienced corporate PR person and instructed her to 'promote Marc like a rock star'.

At the beginning of August 1995 the British press was getting more excited about a pair of British rock bands, more than at any stage since the Beatles-versus-Stones contests of the mid-sixties. On one side there was the clever, arty Blur. On the other was the plodding but charismatic Oasis. Both paid excessive tribute to the greats of the sixties, as if they could never hope to equal their elders and betters. The first was southern, the second northern. The first was middle class, the second working class. They both had singles coming out on the same day. Who would win? Who would win the nation's heart? They billed it as the battle of Britpop. It kept Britain thoroughly absorbed for a year. The rest of the world had other concerns.

The big story was taking place on Wall Street, although nobody in show business realized it. On 9 August shares in Netscape were offered for sale on the stock market. Demand was so great that trading had to be suspended after two hours. The efforts to position Marc Andreessen as a rock star had clearly excited the market.

In 1995 the first port of call for information about business, or anything else, was tomorrow's newspaper. The front page of *USA Today* on 10 August announced that shares in Netscape had risen from the offer price of $18 to a high of $171. This news was the starting pistol that began the great internet gold rush. This massively destabilized the world-wide communications and entertainment industry. It made a handful of people very rich indeed. It swept away many of the old certainties.

As had been the case in the original gold rush, the people who got rich were the ones who sold the shovels. By the end of the day of the stock launch, Jim Clark's share of the company was worth $633 million. He bought a plane and had the number 633 painted on its tail. The last issue of *Wired* magazine for the year announced 'the new Hollywood: silicon replaces superstars'. At the beginning of 1996 Marc Andreessen was on the cover of *Time* magazine. He didn't look like the traditional millionaire. He was wearing a black sweater, Levi's, his feet were bare, and he was sitting on a golden throne. The headline was 'The Golden Geeks'. All over the world smart young people looked on and dreamed about being tech stars in the way the previous generation had dreamed of being rock stars.

Andreessen didn't have long in the spotlight. The following year Microsoft responded by bundling their Internet Explorer browser with their Windows system. That year Netscape lost $132 million. In time the company was sold to AOL. In 1996 Steve Jobs was rehired to save Apple. His first big product was the candy-coloured iMac, which looked more like a pleasure machine than a work tool. People started realizing they could rip their CDs into MP3 files and play them from the computer. By 2001, when the pipes down which these noughts and ones travelled had grown wider and the parcels of data neater and more easily manipulated, the time was right for the iPod, the very mass-market MP3 player the man from Philips had solemnly promised would never arrive.

The phenomenal success of that product made Jobs not only the most powerful man in tech but also the most powerful man in leisure, and the most powerful man in the music business, for a while more famous, admired and envied than all the rock stars in the world put together. In the new world he had ushered into being there was no product release, no new album from Beyoncé or Jay Z or Adele, that could be quite as exciting or could touch quite as many people as the release of a new piece of free software. They promised content would be king. It wasn't. Distribution was king, as it always had been.

This was echoed in the world of dance music, which was what all pop music turned out to be. Here it was less about star names and devoted followers and more about one-off singles often released under mysterious names. Here the important thing was the tribal gathering. Here the new high priests were the DJs who could be paid huge sums of money for their ability to raise a room to a pitch of euphoria. The same digital technology that made it simple to distribute and copy music also put into the hands of young people all over the world music-making tools previously beyond the reach of all but the most successful professionals. A punk rock record made in the garage used to sound like a record made in the garage. Now that we all had access to the same tools there was no audible distinction between professional and amateur.

EPILOGUE

The business still needs stars. But many of today's stars have been developed in the hatcheries of Disney or the stage schools that have sprung up all over the world to cater for the fact that entertainment is a business people will now pay to get into. Because there are fewer places to play and the audience now has too many options to be prepared to put up with an evening's entertainment from somebody who is only just learning their trade, it's harder now for people to establish the balance between entertainment and invention that we see in the stories of some of the people in the pages of this book. It's never been easy to make it and it still isn't. You no longer need a record company to make a record, but you might need their money to make you a star. It's never been easier to play; it's never been harder to win.

Then there is hip hop, which was just hitting its golden age in 1995. Just as children brought up in the decades after the Second World War, with unhindered access to toy guns and a steady diet of 'take that, Fritz' war movies on the TV, grew up to lace daisies into each other's hair, so the generations raised in the eighties, who were deprived of war toys and encouraged to embrace their sensitive side, grew up not only to embrace music that was every bit as viscerally exciting as 'Tutti Frutti' had been half a century earlier, but also to express sentiments far more upsetting to conventional opinion. To ears raised on hip hop the sound of a rock band can seem as quaint as the sound of a Dixieland jazz band was to the Stones fans of the early sixties.

Concurrent with this has been the growth of social media, which has changed all our lives. It's inconceivable that any young musician coming along today could keep his background in the shadows as young Bob Dylan managed to do. It's unimaginable that a band of today would be able to behave as Led Zeppelin and David Bowie did during their early seventies tours. All their misbehaviour would be webcast live. They would be regularly required to do the one thing the stars of yesteryear never did – apologize. Rock fans like to feel that their heroes misbehave but wouldn't really wish to see the evidence. As Walter Bagehot said of the monarchy, you should never let daylight in on magic. The stars of the sixties and seventies had a long run in the spotlight because in their early days access to them was strictly limited. It's difficult to imagine the stars of today still being stars in twenty years' time because we already know everything there is to know about them.

At the age of seventeen, in 1967, I was fortunate enough to see Louis Armstrong play. He was in his mid-sixties by then and not in the best of health. Nevertheless it was a privilege to see an artist who had been there when the tradition he represented was first established. In the same spirit, I'd encourage any young person to see Bruce Springsteen or the Rolling Stones or Paul McCartney in concert, even though they might be having to sing their songs in the only key they can still reach and their knees might not be quite as forgiving as they once were. I would encourage young people to see them because they are the last of a breed. Once they've gone, nobody will be doing what they do. When they go, the art will go with them. I don't see any sign of the acts who came afterwards, who were born in the late eighties and nineties, accumulating successive generations of fans or acquiring the patina of legend in quite the same way. But that may just be the prejudice that comes from the perspective of my particular generation. It could be that Muse and Laura Marling will be headlining the main stage at Glastonbury in their seventies. All history is subjective. This book is no exception.

As I started out saying at the beginning, the age of the rock star, like the age of the cowboy, has gone. We now have a new set of different stereotypes: the soul-baring diva, the minted mogul of hip hop, the stars of social media, diarizing themselves for our amusement, the mayfly stars of TV talent shows. Then there are the score of ghettoes stretching to the horizon in which dwell indie bands, heavy rockers, dance acts, the svengalis of robo-pop, new country stars and more singer-songwriters than even the most melancholy society could ever have need of.

The widespread sense of bereavement many felt when David Bowie died in 2016 was puzzling in the sense that many of the people who missed him so badly had been quite content to miss much of the music he had made for the last twenty years of his life. However, after his passing there was a final recognition that his death represented the vanishing of a breed: smart, independent, wilful, funny, self-invented, slightly vain and rarely dull. What made Bowie a rock star was the fact that, even at the furthest reaches of his journey from Brixton to Manhattan, from genteel poverty to great wealth, through the time of his immoderation to the age of his unsought respectability, from the odiferous dressing rooms of the Marquee to the marbled halls of the Victoria and Albert Museum, he seemed to remain one of us.

David Bowie was always an evangelist for new ways of doing things. But he made his name in the vanished world of records you could hold in your hand. He wasn't available at all hours of the day and night except via a black vinyl disc, twelve inches in circumference, which we had secured by using all our available cash in one particular week – a record that would, for a while at least, be the most precious thing we owned.

Our favourite rock stars weren't mere consumer preferences. They were markers of our identity, like football teams or political affiliations. We followed them through thick and thin. Once a pop star stops making good records, people stop buying them. Rock stars, on the other hand, can go on making weak records for years and we will still stick our hands in our pockets.

Now we live in a world of unlimited supply and exhausted demand. Music can be every bit as good now as it used to be, but it can never be as precious as it used to be. It doesn't have our undivided attention any longer. We are no longer invested in it in quite the same way. Now that we have easy access to everything, the individual atoms that make up that 'everything' are less significant in themselves. The same applies to the people associated with those atoms. That's why we don't have rock stars any more. The business of entertainment has seen this kind of change before and will see it again.

In the 1950 movie *Sunset Boulevard*, William Holden says to Gloria Swanson, the old star of the silents, 'You used to be big.'

Her eyes widen. Her nostrils flare. 'I *am* big,' she assures him. 'It's the pictures that got small.'

BIBLIOGRAPHY

Altschuler, Glenn C., *All Shook Up: How Rock 'n' Roll Changed America* (Oxford University Press, 2003)

Anka, Paul, *My Way* (St Martin's Press, 2013)

Bego, Mark, *Bonnie Raitt: Just in the Nick of Time* (Birch Lane, 1995)

Berry, Chuck, *The Autobiography* (Faber and Faber, 1987)

Booth, Stanley, *The True Adventures of the Rolling Stones* (Canongate, 2012)

Boykin, Keith, *One More River to Cross: Black & Gay in America* (Random House, 1996)

Brown, Peter, and Steven Gaines, *The Love You Make: An Insider's Story of the Beatles* (Pan, 1982)

Burdon, Eric, *I Used to be an Animal But I'm All Right Now* (Faber and Faber, 1986)

Cann, Kevin, *David Bowie: Any Day Now* (Adelita, 2010)

Carlin, Peter Ames, *Bruce* (Simon & Schuster, 2012)

—*Catch a Wave: The Rise, Fall and Redemption of the Beach Boys' Brian Wilson* (Rodale, 2006)

Carroll, Cath, *Never Break the Chain: Fleetwood Mac and the Making of Rumours* (MQ Publications, 2004)

Coleman, Rick, *Blue Monday: Fats Domino and the Lost Dawn of Rock 'n' Roll* (Da Capo Press, 2007)

Costello, Elvis, *Unfaithful Music & Disappearing Ink* (Viking, 2015)

Cross, Charles R., *Backstreets: Springsteen: The Man and His Music* (Sidgwick & Jackson, 1989)

—*Heavier Than Heaven: The Biography of Kurt Cobain* (Hodder & Stoughton, 2001)

—*Room Full of Mirrors: A Biography of Jimi Hendrix* (Sceptre, 2005)

Doggett, Peter, *Electric Shock: From the Gramophone to the iPhone – 125 Years of Pop Music* (Bodley Head, 2015)

Dundy, Elaine, *Elvis and Gladys* (Macmillan, 1985)

Dylan, Bob, *Chronicles Volume One* (Simon & Schuster, 2004)

Echols, Alice, *Scars of Sweet Paradise: The Life and Times of Janis Joplin* (Metropolitan Books, 1999)

Egan, Sean, *Fleetwood Mac on Fleetwood Mac: Interviews and Encounters* (Omnibus, 2016)

Fleetwood, Mick, *Play On: The Autobiography* (Hodder & Stoughton, 2014)

Fletcher, Tony, *Dear Boy: The Life of Keith Moon* (Omnibus, 1998)

Frame, Pete, *The Restless Generation: How Rock Music Changed the Face of 1950s Britain* (Rogan House, 2007)

Geldof, Bob, *Is That It?* (Macmillan, 1986)

Goldman, Albert, *Elvis* (Allen Lane, 1981)

Goldrosen, John J., *Buddy Holly: His Life and Music* (Spice Box, 1975)

Greenfield, Robert, *Stones Touring Party: A Journey Through America with the Rolling Stones* (Michael Joseph, 1974)

Guralnick, Peter, *Careless Love: The Unmaking of Elvis Presley* (Back Bay, 2000)

— *Last Train to Memphis: The Rise of Elvis Presley* (Little, Brown, 1994)

—*Sam Phillips: The Man Who Invented Rock 'n' Roll* (Weidenfeld & Nicolson, 2015)

Hajdu, David, *Positively 4th Street: The Lives and Times of Joan Baez, Bob Dylan, Mimi Baez Fariña and Richard Fariña* (Bloomsbury, 2001)

Halberstam, David, *The Fifties* (Ballantine, 1993)

Harkins, Anthony, *Hillbilly: A Cultural History of an American Icon* (Oxford University Press, 2004)

Hennessy, Peter, *Having It So Good: Britain in the Fifties* (Penguin, 2006)

Hoggart, Richard, *The Uses of Literacy* (Penguin Classics, 1957)

Hopkins, Jerry, *No One Here Gets Out Alive* (Plexus, 1980)

Hoskyns, Barney, *Trampled Under Foot: The Power and Excess of Led Zeppelin* (Faber and Faber, 2012)

Howe, Zoë, *Stevie Nicks: Visions, Dreams & Rumours* (Omnibus, 2014)

Hynde, Chrissie, *Reckless* (Ebury Press, 2016)

Iommi, Tony, *Iron Man* (Simon & Schuster, 2012)

Jackson, John A., *Big Beat Heat: Alan Freed and the Early Years of Rock & Roll* (Schirmer Books, 1991)

Jones, Dylan, *The Eighties: One Day, One Decade* (Preface Publishing, 2013)

Kelly, Martin, Terry Foster and Paul Kelly, *Fender: The Golden Age 1946–1970* (Cassell, 2010)

Kennealy, Patricia, *Strange Days: My Life With and Without Jim Morrison* (HarperCollins, 1992)

Kirby, David, *Little Richard: The Birth of Rock 'n' Roll* (Bloomsbury, 2009)

Kynaston, David, *Modernity Britain: 1957–62* (Bloomsbury, 2013)

Laing, Dave, *Buddy Holly* (Littlehampton Book Services, 1971)

Bibliography

Lauterbach, Preston, *The Chitlin' Circuit and the Road to Rock 'n' Roll* (W. W. Norton & Company, 2011)

Lehmer, Larry, *The Day the Music Died* (Omnibus, 2004)

Lewis, Dave, *Led Zeppelin: The Concert File* (Omnibus, 2005)

Lewis, Michael, *The New New Thing* (Hodder & Stoughton, 1999)

Lewis, Myra, *Great Balls of Fire* (St Martin's Press, 1989)

Lewisohn, Mark, *The Beatles – All These Years, Volume 1: Tune In* (Little, Brown, 2015)

Love, Mike, *Good Vibrations: My Life as a Beach Boy* (Faber and Faber, 2016)

Matos, Michaelangelo, *All Roads Lead to 'Apache'*, (Experience Music Project, 2007)

Mitchell, Mitch, *The Hendrix Experience* (Pyramid, 1990)

Muir, John Kenneth, *Best in Show: The Films of Christopher Guest and Company* (Applause Theatre Books, 2004)

Nash, Alanna, *Baby, Let's Play House: The Life of Elvis Presley Through the Women Who Loved Him* (Aurum, 2010)

— *Elvis Aaron Presley: Revelations from the Memphis Mafia* (HarperCollins, 1996)

Norman, Philip, *Buddy: The Definitive Biography of Buddy Holly* (Macmillan, 2009)

— *Elton* (Hutchinson, 1991)

— *John Lennon: The Life* (HarperCollins, 2007)

Oldham, Andrew Loog, *Rolling Stoned* (Gegensatz Press, 2011)

Osbourne, Sharon, *Extreme: My Autobiography* (Sphere, 2005)

Pegg, Bruce, *Brown Eyed Handsome Man: The Life and Hard Times of Chuck Berry* (Routledge, 2002)

Richards, Matt and Mark Langthorne, *Somebody to Love: The Life, Death and Legacy of Freddie Mercury* (Blink, 2016)

Roxon, Lillian, *Rock Encyclopaedia* (Universal Library, 1969)

Bibliography

Sander, Ellen, *Trips: Rock Life in the Sixties* (Scribner, 1973)

Shapiro, Harry, and Caesar Glebbeek, *Jimi Hendrix: Electric Gypsy* (St Martin's, 1990)

Sounes, Howard, *Down the Highway: The Life of Bob Dylan* (Doubleday, 2011)

—*Notes from the Velvet Underground: The Life of Lou Reed* (Doubleday, 2015)

Springsteen, Bruce, *Born to Run* (Simon & Schuster, 2016)

Tannenbaum, Rob, *I Want My MTV: The Uncensored Story of the Music Video Revolution* (Plume, 2012)

Taraborrelli, J. Randy, *Michael Jackson: The Magic, The Madness, The Whole Story* (Pan, 2010)

Thomson, Graeme, *George Harrison: Behind the Locked Door* (Omnibus, 2013)

Tosches, Nick, *Hellfire: The Jerry Lee Lewis Story* (Plexus, 1982)

Townshend, Pete, *Who I Am* (HarperCollins, 2012)

Waksman, Steve, *Instruments of Desire* (Harvard University Press, 2000)

Wall, Mick, *Led Zeppelin: When Giants Walked the Earth* (Orion, 2008)

Wertheimer, Alfred A., *Elvis '56: In the Beginning* (Macmillan, 1979)

White, Charles, *The Life and Times of Little Richard* (Pan, 1984)

White, Timothy, *Catch a Fire: The Life of Bob Marley* (Corgi, 1983)

— *James Taylor, His Life and Music* (Omnibus, 2001)

Wilkinson, Paul, *Rat Salad: Black Sabbath, The Classic Years* (Pimlico, 2007)

Williamson, Joel, *Elvis Presley: A Southern Life* (OUP, 2015)

Wilson, Brian, and Ben Greenman, *I Am Brian Wilson* (Coronet, 2016)

Witt, Stephen, *How Music Got Free* (Bodley Head, 2015)

Bibliography

Woodward, Bob, *Wired: The Short Life and Fast Times of John Belushi* (Faber and Faber, 1984)

Zanes, Warren, *Petty: The Biography* (Henry Holt, 2015)

ACKNOWLEDGEMENTS

Thanks to Bill Scott-Kerr, Darcy Nicholson, Richard Shailer and Sally Wray at Transworld Publishers, Gillian Blake at Henry Holt and my agent Charlie Viney.

PICTURE ACKNOWLEDGEMENTS

Although every effort has been made to trace copyright holders and clear permission for the photographs in this book, the provenance of a number of them is uncertain. The author and publisher would welcome the opportunity to correct any mistakes.

First section

Page 1: Little Richard: © Michael Ochs Archive/Stringer/Getty; Elvis with his parents: © Rolf Adlercreutz/Alamy Stock Photo; Elvis at Tupelo State Fair: © LFI/Photoshot.

Pages 2–3: John Lennon and the Quarrymen: © Geoff Rhind; Jerry Lee Lewis in the newspaper: © UPPA/Photoshot; Surf Poster: © Zuma Press Inc./Alamy Stock Photo; Hank Marvin and the Shadows: © Dezo Hoffmann/REX/Shutterstock; Folk City Poster: © Blank Archives/Contributor/Getty; Bob Dylan: © Michael Ochs Archive/Stringer/Getty.

Pages 4–5: The Beatles: © V & A Images/Contributor/Getty; Rolling Stones: © Archive Photos/Stringer/Getty; Brian Wilson: © Getty; Keith Moon and Roger Daltrey: © Pictorial Press Ltd/Alamy Stock Photo; Jimi Hendrix and Eric Clapton: © REX/Shutterstock.

Pages 6–7: Janis Joplin: © Ted Streshinsky Photographic Archive/Getty; Lennon and McCartney: © Elliott Landy/Getty; Black Sabbath: © Michael Ochs Archive/Stringer/Getty; Lou Reed: © Michael Putland/Getty; Mick Jagger live: © New York Daily News/Getty.

INDEX

403

Index

Beastie Boys 313
Beatles, the 118, 291
  break up of 145–6
  Decca turns them down 61
  formation 108
  'A Hard Day's Night' 98, 106, 352
  'Help!' 110, 116, 256
  'Hey Jude' 147
  'I Feel Fine' 98, 106
  'I Want To Hold Your Hand'
    106
  influence of Buddy Holly on 52
  influence on Bruce Springsteen
    194, 199
  John Lennon's death 259
  John Lennon's relationship with
    255
  'Love Me Do' 83, 84, 86
  Magical Mystery Tour 141
  Michael Braun review 233
  myths xvi
  name 152
  'Paperback Writer' 126
  'Please Please Me' 91
  receive MBEs 113, 138
  and Ringo Starr 79–85, 94
  Rubber Soul 116
  Sgt Pepper's Lonely Hearts Club
    Band 131, 136, 144, 212
  'She Loves You' 96
  songwriting 98–9
  success 98, 137–46
  touring 65, 142, 151
  TV appearances 97, 119
Beatty, Warren 277, 340, 347
Beck, Jeff 62
Beck, Julian 161
Beck 383
Bee Gees, the 241
Belushi, John 277
Benatar, Pat 267, 330
Bendix, William 93
Benny, Jack 41
Berlin 313
Bernstein, Leonard 177

Berry, Chuck 8, 98, 272
  'Johnny B. Goode' 43, 190–1
  Mann Act charges 65
  'Maybellene' 4, 10
  'Rock and Roll Music' 33
  Rockin' At The Hops 88
  'Roll Over Beethoven' 22
  song themes 8
  'The Biggest Show of Stars' 26
Best, Pete 80, 81, 84–5
Beyoncé 388
Bieber, Justin xiv
Big Brother and the Holding
    Company 127, 129, 132, 133
'The Biggest Show of Stars' (1957)
    26, 46
Bill Evans Trio 77
Bill Haley and the Comets 10
Bindon, John 244
Bingenheimer, Rodney 187
Birch, Will 237
Björk xiv
Black, Bill 18
Black Dyke Mills Band 143
Black Sabbath 148–55, 193, 318
  Black Sabbath 153–4, 156
  Ozzy Osbourne 272
  Stonehenge set 285
Blackboard Jungle 27
Blackwell, Bumps 4, 5–6, 7
Blackwell, Chris 205–8
Blauel, Renate 324, 325, 327, 328
Blizzard of Ozz 273
Blockheads, the 236
Blodwyn Pig 153
Blondie 241, 252, 265, 268
Bloomfield, Mike 120
Bluesology 329
Blur 386–7
Bob Marley and the Wailers
    204–8, 210, 232
Bobby Fuller Four 126
Bolan, Marc 170
Bon Jovi 326
Bonds, Gary U.S. 77

Index

Index

Index

Janis Joplin 132
grunge 381
Guest, Christopher 281, 282, 286
Guns N' Roses 314–21
   Appetite For Destruction 317,
     318, 322
Guthrie, Woody 29, 60, 68–9, 76

Hair soundtrack 147
Hajdu, David 71
Haley, Bill 8, 37
Hammersmith Odeon, London
   188–9
Hammond, John 71, 73
Happy Mondays 348
Harper, Roy 242–3
Harris, Terence 'Jet' 56
Harrison, George 85, 215
   All Things Must Pass 165
   Concert for Bangla Desh 172,
     255
   Live Aid 301
   'My Sweet Lord' 173
   and Ringo Starr 79, 80, 81, 85
   Wonderwall 142
Harrison, Wilbert 54
Harry, Debbie 234, 267–8
Harvey, P. J. 375
Hawkins, Jay 150
Haley, Bill 10
Hearn, Barbara 14–15, 19, 21
heavy metal 315
Hectics, the 352
Hemingway, Mariel 277
Hendrix, Jimi 117–25
   'All Along The Watchtower' 147
   Are You Experienced 136
   death 163, 169
   and Eric Clapton 121, 122–5
   'Hey Joe' 123, 126
   influence of Bob Dylan on
     120–1
   influence on Freddie Mercury
     352
   relationships 121

   tour of Britain 132, 177
   US Army 119–20
Henley, Don 220
Henry, Clarence 'Frogman' 22
Hester, Carolyn 71
High Fidelity xvii
High Numbers 107
Hoggart, Richard 27
Holden, William 392
Hollies, the 140
Holly, Buddy 44–53, 61, 71, 228
   appearance 44, 54
   'The Biggest Show of Stars' 26,
     46
   death 49–50, 66, 274, 376
   early life 44–5
   'Everyday' 33
   as influence on others 51, 55, 57,
     66, 68
   'It Doesn't Matter Anymore' 54
   'Rave On' 43, 44
   Winter Dance Party 47–50
Holly, María Elena 46
Holzman, Jac 70
Honey 183
Honeyman-Scott, James 276
Hope, Bob 41
Hopkin, Mary 142
Hopper, Judy 18
House, Son 335
Houston, Whitney 345, 373
Hudmon, Clara (Georgia Peach) 3
Hudson, Rock 326, 355
Hudson, Saul 'Slash' 316–17, 320
Hunter, Ian 186
Hüsker Dü 313
Hutton, Timothy 277

Ian Dury and the Blockheads 239
   'Hit Me With Your Rhythm
     Stick' 239, 241
   New Boots And Panties!! 236,
     239
Ice-T 357, 359
Iggy Pop 172

Index

Index

Index

Index

Index

Index

Index

ABOUT THE AUTHOR

David Hepworth has been writing, broadcasting and speaking about music and media since the seventies. He was involved in the launch and editing of magazines such as *Smash Hits*, *Q*, *Mojo* and *The Word*, among many others.

He was one of the presenters of the BBC rock music programme *The Old Grey Whistle Test* and one of the anchors of the corporation's coverage of Live Aid in 1985. He has won the Editor of the Year and Writer of the Year awards from the Professional Publishers Association and the Mark Boxer Award from the British Society of Magazine Editors.

He lives in London, dividing his time between writing for a variety of newspapers and magazines, speaking at events, broadcasting work, podcasting at www.wordpodcast.co.uk and blogging at www.whatsheonaboutnow.blogspot.co.uk.

He says Chuck Berry's 'You Never Can Tell' is the best record ever made. 'This is not an opinion,' he says. 'It's a matter of fact.'

For more information on David Hepworth, see his website at www.davidhepworth.com

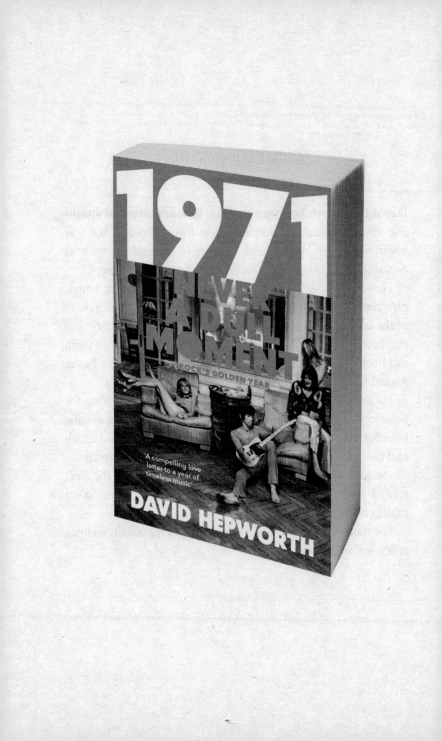

The Sixties ended a year late – on New Year's Eve 1970, when Paul McCartney initiated proceedings to wind up The Beatles. Music would never be the same again.

The next day began a new era. 1971 saw the release of more monumental albums than any year before or since and the establishment of a pantheon of stars to dominate the next forty years – Led Zeppelin, David Bowie, the Rolling Stones, Pink Floyd, Marvin Gaye, Carole King, Joni Mitchell, Rod Stewart, the solo Beatles and more.

January that year fired the gun on an unrepeatable surge of creativity, technological innovation, blissful ignorance, naked ambition and outrageous good fortune. By December rock had exploded into the mainstream.

How did it happen? This book tells you. It's the story of 1971, rock's golden year.

'Thoroughly absorbing and appropriately rollicking,
expertly guiding us through one miraculous year
in all its breathless tumble of creation'
DANNY BAKER

'A dry-eyed but deeply felt love note to the
date when rock was still busy inventing itself'
MAIL ON SUNDAY

'A good mix of entertainment, insight and odd facts'
MOJO

'A clever and entertaining book . . . Hepworth
proves a refreshingly independent thinker'
DAILY TELEGRAPH

The Beatles were Underrated

AND OTHER BEDTIME STORIES FOR ROCK FANS

Coming soon